Mike Ault's Oracle Internals Monitoring & Tuning Scripts

Advanced Internals & OCP Certification Insights for the Master DBA

Includes Oracle10g

D0746787

Mike Ault

RAMPANT TECHPRESS

I dedicate this book to my loving wife Susan Ault, whose love and support made this book possible. I also dedicate this book to my Father and his new wife Paulette, a welcome addition to our family.

--- Mike Ault

_____

Mike Ault's Oracle Internals Monitoring & Tuning Scripts

Advanced Internals & OCP Certification Insights for the Master DBA

By Mike Ault

Copyright © 2003 by Rampant TechPress. All rights reserved.

Printed in the United States of America.

Published by Rampant TechPress, Kittrell, North Carolina, USA

Oracle In-Focus Series: Book #9

Series Editor: Donald K. Burleson

Editors: Robert Strickland and John Lavender

Production Editor: Teri Wade

Cover Design: Bryan Hoff

Printing History:

October 2003 for First Edition

Oracle, Oracle7, Oracle8, Oracle8i, Oracle9i, Oracle Database 10*g*, Oracle 10*g*, and Oracle10*g* are trademarks of Oracle Corporation.

Many of the designations used by computer vendors to distinguish their products are claimed as Trademarks. All names known to Rampant TechPress to be trademark names appear in this text as initial caps.

The information provided by the authors of this work is believed to be accurate and reliable, but because of the possibility of human error by our authors and staff, Rampant TechPress cannot guarantee the accuracy or completeness of any information included in this work and is not responsible for any errors, omissions, or inaccurate results obtained from the use of information or scripts in this work.

ISBN: 0-9727513-8-6

Library of Congress Control Number: 2003112378

Table of Contents

Using the Online Code Depot

Your purchase of this book provides you with complete access to the online code depot that contains the sample code scripts.

All of the code depot scripts in this book are located at the following URL:

rampant.cc/internals.htm

All of the code scripts in this book are available for download in zip format, ready to load and use on your database.

If you need technical assistance in downloading or accessing the scripts, please contact Rampant TechPress at info@rampant.cc.

Conventions Used in this Book

It is critical for any technical publication to follow rigorous standards and employ consistent punctuation conventions to make the text easy to read.

However, this is not an easy task. Within Oracle there are many types of notation that can confuse a reader. Some Oracle utilities such as STATSPACK and TKPROF are always spelled in CAPITAL letters, while Oracle parameters and procedures have varying naming conventions in the Oracle documentation. It is also important to remember that many Oracle commands are case sensitive, and are always left in their original executable form, and never altered with italics or capitalization.

Hence, all Rampant TechPress books follow these conventions:

Parameters - All Oracle parameters will be *lowercase italics*. Exceptions to this rule are parameter arguments that are commonly capitalized (KEEP pool, TKPROF), these will be left in ALL CAPS.

Variables – All PL/SQL program variables and arguments will also remain in lowercase italics (*dbms_job, dbms_utility*).

Tables & dictionary objects – All data dictionary objects are referenced in lowercase italics (*dba_indexes, v$sql*). This includes all v$ and x$ views (*x$kcbcbh, v$parameter*) and dictionary views (*dba_tables, user_indexes*).

SQL – All SQL is formatted for easy use in the code depot, and all SQL is displayed in lowercase. The main SQL terms (select, from, where, group by, order by, having) will always appear on a separate line.

Programs & Products – All products and programs that are known to the author are capitalized according to the vendor specifications (IBM, DBXray, etc). All names known by Rampant TechPress to be trademark names appear in this text as initial caps. References to UNIX are always made in uppercase.

Preface

Since back in the days when the choice was SQLDBA or nothing (version 6), Oracle has come a long way with its database monitoring tools. Server Manager, Enterprise Manager, and the numerous other Oracle-provided monitoring tools make the task of monitoring databases easier.

However, there are still limitations. Many of these tools only monitor the top level of the data dictionary. They can tell the DBA how many users, tables, and indexes are active, but they provide little information about deeper operations, such as user activity or table activity.

Several companies offer excellent monitoring tools: Precise, with its Q and Precise*SQL packages, the Quest product suite, Patrol from BMC, ECO Tools, and the many CA offerings spring to mind. These tools are liberating for some DBAs, but others are crippled by their lack of knowledge about the underlying structures of the data dictionary. Every DBA needs to understand the data dictionary before he or she can manage these complex, feature-laden tools.

Tools are only as effective as the person using them, and a DBA has to be able to dig into the data dictionary to find and correct problems. Some may believe great tools make great works, but try giving the best materials and tools to ineffective or inexperienced workers. The result may be better than with poor materials and tools, but it will probably still be unsatisfactory. As with all things, when using Oracle, knowledge means power - the power to solve problems, or better yet, to prevent them from happening in the first place.

In the past few years, the author has interviewed dozens of candidates for Oracle DBA and developer positions. Some had great resumes, but they were nevertheless uncomfortable under the Oracle hood. Many were clueless about the workings of the data dictionary or the V$ tables.

The data dictionary tables (usually suffixed with a dollar sign ($)) are owned by the SYS user, and normally should not be accessed, except when the supporting views don't have the required data. Oracle has instead provided DBA_, USER_, and ALL_ views of these tables. They should be used whenever possible. Oracle has also provided the dynamic performance tables (DPTs), which provide running statistics and internals information. These DPTs all begin with V$ or, in their pristine form, V_$. The DPTs are documented in the Oracle reference manual for your version of Oracle. In RAC environments, if you wish to see all RAC instance data, use the GV$ views which contain data for all RAC instances for a specific database.

The data dictionary views are created by the catalog.sql script, located in the $ORACLE_HOME/rdbms/admin directory. The catalog.sql script is a required readme file. The script has numerous remarks and comments that will significantly improve your understanding of the data dictionary views. But be forewarned, the catalog.sql script is over 200 pages.

Using the Data Dictionary

Detailed information about the system, the data dictionary, and the processes of the Oracle database are provided in the above tables, views, and DPTs. The DBA can gather just about any information on the data desired by using the scripts contained in this book to access the data dictionary objects. Most of the reports provided in the following sections utilize these objects, either directly or indirectly, via the $tables, V$ DPTs, or DBA_ views.

The data dictionary objects can also be queried interactively during a DBA user session to find the current status of virtually any system parameter. Using dynamic SQL against the DBA_ views can shorten tasks, such as switching users from one temporary tablespace to another, or dropping a set of tables, by a factor of 10 or more.

When only SQLDBA was available, it was often easier to monitor with scripts than with the screens Oracle provided. The SVRMGR product, with its GUI interface, was an improvement, as was the Enterprise Manager. However, these still don't provide the flexibility available from user-generated scripts. The Performance Pack can be customized to add user-generated monitoring queries. However, the Performance Pack is a cost add-on (and a performance cost) to the DBA system tools.

The DBA must bear in mind that the above methods lack adequate report capabilities. For example, unless you utilize a web interface, the OEM reports are difficult to print and view. To remedy this shortcoming, DBAs must be prepared to create SQL, SQL*Plus, and PL/SQL reports that provide exactly the information they require. This chapter discusses these reports and provides examples of the scripts used to generate them. It is suggested that the DBA review the contents of the V$ and DBA_ views, as listed in either the *Oracle, Oracle8i,* or *Oracle9i Administrator's Guide* (Release 1 (9.0.1), June 2001, Part No. A90117-01, Oracle Corporation). Additional information is contained in the *Oracle8, Oracle8i, or Oracle9i Reference* (Release 1 (9.0.1), June 2001, Part No. A90190-02, Oracle Corporation).

Instance Internals Scripts

We begin the chapter by providing scripts to perform the following tasks:

- Monitoring Control Files and Initialization Parameters
- Monitoring Control Files
- Monitoring Database Initialization Parameters
- Monitoring Undocumented Initialization Parameters
- Monitoring Locks and Latches
- Monitoring Sessions Causing Blocked Locks
- Monitoring DDL and DML Locks
- Monitoring Internal Locks
- Monitoring Events
- Workspaces in Oracle9*i*

Monitoring Control Files and Initialization Parameters

The control files have traditionally been a mysterious element within Oracle. Everyone was aware of them, but had little idea what they were for or how to monitor them. Although initialization parameters were easy to monitor, no one did so. Now, with Oracle8, Oracle8*i*, and Oracle9*i,* it is much easier to monitor control files and initialization parameters, which are critical to database health and well-being. From a SQLPLUS session you can use the SHOW PARAMETER <name> command (even with a partial name) to show any parameter and its value. You can also use SHOW USER to show your current user name and SHOW PARAMETER with no arguments to show all parameters and their current settings. The *v$parameter* view should be used to view if these are default or altered values.

Monitoring Control Files

Oracle7 (from release 7.3 on) and Oracle8 provide the *v$controlfile* view to help keep track of the control files. Oracle8 provides the *v$controlfile_record* view that is used with Recovery Manager. In Oracle9*i*, the *v$controlfile_record* view becomes the *v$controlfile_record_section* view. The script below can be used to monitor control file status. Its output is also documented.

🖫 **con_file.sql**

```
-- ************************************************
--
--    Copyright © 2003 by Rampant TechPress Inc.
--
--    Free for non-commercial use.
--    For commercial licensing, e-mail info@rampant.cc
--
-- ************************************************
COLUMN name     FORMAT a60 HEADING 'Con|File|Location'
WORD_WRAPPED
COLUMN status   FORMAT a7  HEADING 'Con|File|Status'
SET LINES 78 FEEDBACK OFF VERIFY OFF
ttitle 'Control File Status'
SPOOL con_file.lis

SELECT
    name,
    status
```

```
FROM
    v$controlfile;

SPOOL OFF
SET VERIFY ON FEEDBACK ON
TTITLE OFF
CLEAR COLUMNS
```

Here is a sample listing:

```
Con                                                            Con .
File                                                           File
Location                                                       Status
--------------------------------------------------------------  ------
/var/oracle/OraHome2/oradata/diogenes1/control01.ctl
/var/oracle/OraHome2/oradata/diogenes1/control02.ctl
/var/oracle/OraHome2/oradata/diogenes1/control03.ctl
```

Note that the Control File status should always be blank. If it shows a status, it's an indication that the control file is corrupt. This is unlikely because the database can't start if the file is corrupt. You should confirm that the files are on separate disks or disk arrays.

In versions of Oracle prior to 8, the control files were usually less than 1 megabyte in size. From Oracle8 on, they can be tens of megabytes in size due to the extra backup material monitored. Be careful to allow for this in the file systems.

The *v$controlfile_record_section* gives statistics on each type of record contained in the control file. A script to monitor this table is shown below.

🖫 **con_rec.sql**

```
--*************************************************
--
--    Copyright © 2003 by Rampant TechPress Inc.
--
--    Free for non-commercial use.
--    For commercial licensing, e-mail info@rampant.cc
--
```

```
**************************************************
COLUMN type             FORMAT a18      HEADING 'Record Type'
COLUMN record_size      FORMAT 999999   HEADING 'Record|Size'
COLUMN records_used     FORMAT 999999   HEADING 'Records|Used'
COLUMN first_index      FORMAT 9999999  HEADING 'First|Index'
COLUMN last_index       FORMAT 9999999  HEADING 'Last|Index'
COLUMN last_recid       FORMAT 999999   HEADING 'Last|Record|ID'
SET LINES 80 PAGES 58 FEEDBACK OFF VERIFY OFF
ttitle 'Control File Records'
SPOOL con_rec.lis

SELECT
    type,
    record_size,
    records_total,
    records_used,
    first_index,
    last_index,
    last_recid
FROM
    v$controlfile_record_section;

SPOOL OFF
CLEAR COLUMNS
SET FEEDBACK ON VERIFY ON
TTITLE OFF
```

Here is a sample listing:

| | Record | | Records | First | Last | Last Record |
Record Type	Size	RECORDS_TOTAL	Used	Index	Index	ID
DATABASE	192	1	1	0	0	0
CKPT PROGRESS	4084	4	0	0	0	0
REDO THREAD	104	1	1	0	0	0
REDO LOG	72	50	3	0	0	3
DATAFILE	180	100	12	0	0	19
FILENAME	524	351	17	0	0	0
TABLESPACE	68	100	13	0	0	7
TEMPORARY FILEN	56	100	2	0	0	2
RMAN CONFIGURA	1108	50	0	0	0	0
LOG HISTORY	36	226	8	1	8	8
OFFLINE RANGE	56	145	0	0	0	0
ARCHIVED LOG	584	13	0	0	0	0
BACKUP SET	40	204	0	0	0	0
BACKUP PIECE	736	210	0	0	0	0
BACKUP DATAFILE	116	211	0	0	0	0
BACKUP REDOLOG	76	107	0	0	0	0
DATAFILE COPY	660	210	0	0	0	0
BACKUP CORRUPTI	44	185	0	0	0	0
COPY CORRUPTION	40	204	0	0	0	0
DELETED OBJECT	20	408	0	0	0	0
PROXY COPY	852	306	0	0	0	0
RESERVED4	1	8168	0	0	0	0

The control file records report can tell you the number of data files, redo logs, archived logs, and a host of other information about the database. The Records Used column indicates how many of a particular type have been assigned for the database.

🖥 Code Depot User ID = reader, Password = Nova

Monitoring Database Initialization Parameters

Among the most critical aspects of the database are the data initialization parameters. Many administrators are diligent about database backups but neglect to document the settings of their initialization parameters. Some DBAs, or should we say DBBSs (database babysitters) don't even know the location of the init<SID>.ora (pfile) or spfile file.

In Oracle9*i,* the *v$parameter* file provides the value and status of any documented initialization file parameter in effect for the current session. Previously, it was only for the instance. Oracle9*i* also added the *v$parameter2, v$system_parameter,* and *v$system_parameter2* views. The *v$system_parameter* view shows the instance-wide parameter values. The *v$parameter2* and *v$system_parameter2* views show the same parameters as their non-numbered counterparts. There is an exception when a multi-value string (such as *control_file* or *rollback_segment*) has an individual listing for each value of the string, differentiated by an *ordinal* column listing the order that the substring occurred within the master string.

A simple script to generate a nearly ready-for-prime-time init<SID>.ora file is provided below. Of course, with Oracle9*i*, you can use the *create pfile* command if you have a current *spfile* to generate a parameter file listing (and vica-versa). An example of output from this script is shown below.

💾 init_ora_rct.sql

```
--**************************************************
--
--    Copyright © 2003 by Rampant TechPress Inc.
--
--    Free for non-commercial use.
--    For commercial licensing, e-mail info@rampant.cc
--
--  **************************************************

SET NEWPAGE 0 VERIFY OFF
SET ECHO OFF FEEDBACK OFF TERMOUT OFF PAGES 300 LINES 80 HEADING
OFF
COLUMN name  FORMAT a80 WORD_WRAPPED
DEFINE OUTPUT = 'init.ora'
SPOOL &OUTPUT

SELECT '# Init.ora file FROM v$system_parameter' name FROM dual
UNION
SELECT '# generated on:'||sysdate name FROM dual
UNION
SELECT '# script by MRA 10/14/01 ' name FROM dual
UNION
SELECT '#' name FROM dual
UNION
SELECT name||' = '||value name  FROM v$system_parameter
WHERE value IS NOT NULL and Isdefault='FALSE';

SPOOL OFF
CLEAR COLUMNS
SET NEWPAGE 0 VERIFY OFF
SET TERMOUT ON PAGES 22 LINES 80 HEADING ON
SET TERMOUT ON
UNDEF OUTPUT
PAUSE Press Enter to continue
```

Here is a sample listing:

```
#
# Init.ora file FROM v$system_parameter
# generated on:14-OCT-01
# script by MRA 10/14/01
```

```
background_dump_dest =
/var/oracle/OraHome2/admin/diogenes1/bdump
compatible = 9.0.0
control_files =
/var/oracle/OraHome2/oradata/diogenes1/control01.ctl,
/var/oracle/OraHome2/oradata/diogenes1/control02.ctl,
/var/oracle/OraHome2/oradata/diogenes1/control03.ctl

core_dump_dest = /var/oracle/OraHome2/admin/diogenes1/cdump
db_block_size = 8192
db_cache_size = 67108864
db_domain = diogenes
db_name = diogenes1
dispatchers = (PROTOCOL=TCP)(SER=MODOSE),
(PROTOCOL=TCP)(PRE=oracle.aurora.server.GiopServer),
(PROTOCOL=TCP)(PRE=oracle.aurora.server.SGiopServer)

fast_start_mttr_target = 300
instance_name = diogenes1
java_pool_size = 117440512
large_pool_size = 1048576
open_cursors = 300
processes = 150
remote_login_passwordfile = EXCLUSIVE
resource_manager_plan = SYSTEM_PLAN
shared_pool_size = 117440512
sort_area_size = 524288
timed_statistics = TRUE
undo_management = AUTO
undo_tablespace = UNDOTBS
user_dump_dest = /var/oracle/OraHome2/admin/diogenes1/udump
```

Notice that the *where* clause in the query for the *init.ora* re-creation script restricts the return values to only those that have been changed from their default settings (isdefault='FALSE'). If the query is not restricted, it will return all hundred-plus parameters.

In Oracle9i the database may be using an *spfile*. An *spfile* is a file that Oracle can both read from and write to during operation, allowing dynamic reconfiguration of many parameters, which is persistent across shutdowns and startups. A normal *pfile* can be generated using the command:

```
CREATE PFILE[=<location>] FROM SPFILE[=<location>];
```

If the files are in the default location ($ORACLE_HOME/dbs) then the optional ='location' full path specifications for the file locations aren't required. The inversion of the command is also allowed to generate an *spfile* from a normal *pfile:*

```
CREATE SPFILE[='location'] FROM PFILE=[<'location'>];
```

Oracle10g Simplified Initialization Parameters

Initialization parameters are now divided into two groups, basic and advanced. In the vast majority of cases, it is necessary to set and tune only the basic parameters, of which there are 20 to 30, to get reasonable performance from the database. In rare situations, modification of the advanced parameters may be needed to achieve optimal performance.

- **Lost parameters** - Oracle 10g has deprecated 25 old parameters.

- **New Oracle10g Parameters** - Oracle 10g has introduced 20 new parameters.

In Oracle9i (9.2.0.3), there are 258 parameters in the *v$parameter* view. In Oracle 10g (10.1.0.0), there are 253 parameters in the *v$parameter* view. There are 233 parameters in both Oralce9i Release 2 and Oracle 10g Release 1.

Old Parameters

Twenty-five of the 258 parameters no longer exist in Oracle 10g's *v$parameter* view, these are:

NAME	VALUE	DESCRIPTION
dblink_encrypt_login	FALSE	enforce password for distributed login always be encrypted
hash_join_enabled	TRUE	Enable/disable hash join
log_parallelism	1	Number of log buffer strands
max_rollback_segments	37	max. number of rollback segments in SGA cache
mts_circuits	0	max number of circuits
mts_dispatchers	[NULL]	specifications of dispatchers
mts_listener_address	[NULL]	address(es) of network listener
mts_max_dispatchers	5	max number of dispatchers
mts_max_servers	20	max number of shared servers
mts_multiple_listeners	FALSE	Are multiple listeners enabled?
mts_servers	0	number of shared servers to start up
mts_service	devbill	service supported by dispatchers
mts_sessions	0	max number of shared server sessions
optimizer_max_permutations	2000	optimizer maximum join permutations per query block
oracle_trace_collection_name	[NULL]	Oracle TRACE default collection name

NAME	VALUE	DESCRIPTION
oracle_trace_collection_path	?/otrace/ admin/cdf	Oracle TRACE collection path
oracle_trace_collection_size	5242880	Oracle TRACE collection file max. size
oracle_trace_enable	FALSE	Oracle Trace enabled/disabled
oracle_trace_facility_name	oracled	Oracle TRACE default facility name
oracle_trace_facility_path	?/otrace/ admin/fdf	Oracle TRACE facility path
Partition_view_enabled	FALSE	enable/disable partitioned views
row_locking	always	row-locking
Serializable	FALSE	serializable
transaction_auditing	FALSE	transaction auditing records generated in the redo log
undo_suppress_errors	FALSE	Suppress RBU errors in SMU mode

New Oracle10g Parameters

There are twenty new parameters in Oracle 10g Release 1:

NAME	VALUE	DESCRIPTION
create_stored_outlines	[NULL]	create stored outlines for DML statements
Db_allowed_logon_ version	8	Minimum database logon protocol allowed
Db_flashback_retention_ target	1440	Maximum Flashback Database log retention time in minutes.

NAME	VALUE	DESCRIPTION
Db_recovery_file_dest	[NULL]	default database recovery file location
db_recovery_file_dest_ size	0	database recovery files size limit
ddl_wait_for_locks	FALSE	Disable NOWAIT DML lock acquisitions
instance_type	RDBMS	type of instance to be executed
ldap_directory_access	[NULL]	RDBMS's LDAP access option
log_archive_config	[NULL]	log archive config parameter
osm_disk_repair_time	14400	seconds to wait before dropping a failing disk
osm_diskgroups	[NULL]	disk groups to mount automatically
osm_diskstring	[NULL]	disk set locations for discovery
osm_power_limit	1	number of processes for disk rebalancing
plsql_optimize_level	1	PL/SQL optimize level
plsql_warnings	[NULL]	plssql warnings settings
resumable_timeout	0	set resumable_timeout
skip_unusable_indexes	TRUE	skip unusable indexes if set to TRUE
smtp_out_server	[NULL]	utl_smtp server and port configuration parameter
sp_name	GRID	Service Provider Name
streams_pool_size	0	size in bytes of the streams pool

Let's take a close look at these 20 new Oracle10g parameters.

The create_stored_outlines parameter

The *create_stored_outlines* parameter determines whether Oracle automatically creates and stores an outline for each query submitted during the session.

Values:

- True - Enables automatic outline creation for subsequent queries in the same session. These outlines receive a unique system-generated name and are stored in the DEFAULT category. If a particular query already has an outline defined for it in the DEFAULT category, then that outline will remain and a new outline will not be created.

- False - Disables automatic outline creation during the session. This is the default.

- *Catalog_name* – Enables the same behavior as true except that any outline created during the session is stored in the *catalog_name* category.

The following statement sets the default outline category for a session:

```
SQL> alter session set create_stored_outlines = 'true';
```

The db_flashback_retention_target parameter

The *db_flashback_retention_target* parameters specifies the upper limit (in minutes) on how far back in time the database may be flashed back. How far back one can flashback a database depends on how much flashback data Oracle has kept in the recovery area.

The following statement changes the flashback time from the default of 1 day to two days.

```
SQL> alter system set db_flashback_retention_target = 2880;
```

The db_recovery_file_dest parameter

The *db_recovery_file_dest* parameter specifies the default location for the recovery area. The recovery area contains multiplexed copies of the following files:

- Control files
- Online redo logs
- Archived redo logs
- Flashback logs
- RMAN backups

Specifying this parameter without also specifying the *db_recovery_file_dest_size* initialization parameter is not allowed.

The db_recovery_file_dest_size parameter

The *db_recovery_file_dest_size* parameter specifies (in bytes) the hard limit on the total space to be used by target database recovery files created in the recovery area location.

Disabling this parameter without also disabling *db_recovery_file_dest* will produce an error.

The ddl_wait_for_locks parameter

The *ddl_wait_for_locks* parameter specifies whether DDL statements (such as ALTER TABLE ... ADD

COLUMN) wait and complete instead of timing out if the statement is not able to acquire all required locks.

Values:

- True - DDL statements wait until the statement acquires all required locks

- False - DDL statements time out if the statement cannot obtain all required locks

The ldap_directory_access parameter

The *ldap_directory_access* specifies whether Oracle refers to Oracle Internet Directory for user authentication information. If directory access is turned on, then this parameter also specifies how users are authenticated.

Values:

- NONE - Oracle does not refer to Oracle Internet Directory for Enterprise User Security information.

- PASSWORD - Oracle tries to connect to the enterprise directory service using the database password stored in the database wallet. If that fails, then the Oracle Internet Directory connection fails and the database will not be able to retrieve enterprise roles and schema mappings upon enterprise user login.

- SSL - Oracle tries to connect to Oracle Internet Directory using SSL.

The log_archive_config parameter

The *log_archive_config* parameter enables or disables the sending of redo logs to remote destinations and the receipt of remote redo logs, and specifies the service provider names (SP_NAME) for each database in the Data Guard configuration.

Values:

- SEND - Enables the sending of redo logs to remote destinations

- NOSEND - Disables the sending of redo logs to remote destinations

- RECEIVE - Enables the receipt of remotely archived redo logs

- NORECEIVE - Disables the receipt of remotely archived redo logs

- DG_CONFIG - Specifies a list of up to 9 service provider names (defined with the SP_NAME initialization parameter) for all of the databases in the Data Guard configuration.

- NODG_CONFIG - Eliminates the list of service provider names previously specified with the DG_CONFIG option

With DG_CONFIG, you can dynamically add database to the Data Guard configuration while in maximum availability or maximum protection mode without shutting down databases.

The following four parameters are related to Automated Storage Management instance (ASM).

The instance_type *parameter*

The *instance_type* parameter specifies whether the instance is a database instance or an Automated Storage Management instance.

Values:

- RDBMS - The instance is a database instance.
- OSM - The instance is an Automated Storage Management instance.

The osm_diskgroups *parameter*

The *osm_diskgroups* parameter specifies a list of names of disk groups to be mounted by an Automated Storage Management instance at instance startup or when an ALTER DISKGROUP ALL MOUNT statement is issued.

Automated Storage Management automatically adds a disk group to this parameter when a disk group is successfully mounted, and automatically removes the disk group when it is dismounted (except for dismounts at instance shutdown).

The osm_diskstring *parameter*

The *osm_diskstring* parameter specifies an operating system-dependent value used by Automated Storage Management to limit the set of disks considered for discovery.

When a new disk is added to a disk group, each Automated Storage Management instance that has the disk group mounted must be able to discover the new disk using the value of *osm_diskstring*.

In most cases, the default value will be sufficient. Using a more restrictive value may reduce the time required for Automated Storage Management to perform discovery, and thus improve disk group mount time or the time for adding a disk to a disk group. It may be necessary to dynamically change *osm_diskstring* before adding a disk so that the new disk will be discovered.

An attempt to dynamically modify *osm_diskstring* will be rejected and the old value retained if the new value cannot be used to discover a disk that is in a disk group that is already mounted.

The osm_disk_repair_time parameter

The *osm_disk_repair_time* parameter specifies the number of seconds to permit a disk that was automatically put in failing state following an IO error to remain in its disk group. After this time has elapsed, ASM automatically drops the disk from its disk group.

You should set the value large enough for administrators to detect and repair the failing disk. A value of zero implies an infinite time-out period.

The osm_power_limit parameter

The *osm_power_limit* parameter specifies the maximum power on an Automated Storage Management instance for disk rebalancing. The sum of the power for all disk groups rebalances on an instance cannot exceed this value. The higher the limit, the faster rebalancing will complete. Lower values will take longer, but consume fewer processing and I/O resources.

If the POWER clause of a rebalance operation is not specified, then the default power will be the value of *osm_power_limit*.

The *plsql_optimize_level* parameter

The *plsql_optimize_level* parameter specifies the optimization level that will be used to compile PL/SQL library units. The higher the setting of this parameter, the more effort the compiler makes to optimize PL/SQL library units.

Generally, setting this parameter to 2 pays off in better execution performance. If, however, the compiler runs slowly on a particular source module or if optimization does not make sense for some reason (for example, during rapid turnaround development), then setting this parameter to 1 will result in almost as good a compilation with less use of compile-time resources.

The value of this parameter is stored persistently with the library unit.

The plsql_warnings *parameter*

The *plsql_warnings* parameter enables or disables the reporting of warning messages by the PL/SQL compiler, and specifies which warning messages to show as errors.

Examples

```
PLSQL_WARNINGS='ENABLE:SEVERE','DISABLE:INFORMATIONAL';
PLSQL_WARNINGS='DISABLE:ALL';
PLSQL_WARNINGS='DISABLE:5000','ENABLE:5001', 'ERROR:5002';
PLSQL_WARNINGS='ENABLE:(5000,5001,5002)', 'DISABLE:(6000,6001)';
```

value_clause

- Multiple value clauses may be specified, enclosed in quotes and separated by commas. Each value clause is composed of a qualifier, a colon (:), and a modifier.

Qualifier values:

- ENABLE - Enable a specific warning or a set of warnings

- DISABLE - Disable a specific warning or a set of warnings

- ERROR - Treat a specific warning or a set of warnings as errors

Modifier values:

- ALL - Apply the qualifier to all warning messages

- SEVERE - Apply the qualifier to only those warning messages in the SEVERE category

- INFORMATIONAL - Apply the qualifier to only those warning messages in the INFORMATIONAL category

- PERFORMANCE - Apply the qualifier to only those warning messages in the PERFORMANCE category

The resumable_timeout parameter

The *resumable_timeout* parameter enables or disables resumable statements and specifies resumable timeout at the system level.

Setting the *resumable_timeout* initialization parameter, you can enable resumable space allocation system wild and specify a timeout interval by setting the *resumable_timeout* initialization parameter.

For example, the following setting of the *resumable_timeout* parameter in the initialization parameter file causes all sessions to initially be enabled for resumable space allocation and sets the timeout period to 1 hour:

```
RESUMABLE_TIMEOUT = 3600
```

If this parameter is set to 0, then resumable space allocation is disabled initially for all sessions. This is the default.

You can use the ALTER SYSTEM SET statement to change the value of this parameter at the system level. For example, the following statement will disable resumable space allocation for all sessions:

```
ALTER SYSTEM SET RESUMABLE_TIMEOUT=0;
```

Within a session, a user can issue the ALTER SESSION SET statement to set the *resumable_timeout* initialization parameter and enable resumable space allocation, change a timeout value, or to disable resumable mode.

Using ALTER SESSION to enable and disable Resumable Space Allocation, a user can enable resumable mode for a session, using the following SQL statement:

```
ALTER SESSION ENABLE RESUMABLE;
```

To disable resumable mode, a user issues the following statement:

```
ALTER SESSION DISABLE RESUMABLE;
```

The skip_unusable_indexes parameter

The *skip_unusable_indexes* parameter enables or disables the use and reporting of tables with unusable indexes or index partitions.

Values:

- True - Disables error reporting of indexes and index partitions marked UNUSABLE. This setting allows all operations (inserts, deletes, updates, and selects) on tables with unusable indexes or index partitions.

  Note: If an index is used to enforce a UNIQUE constraint on a table, then allowing insert and update operations on the table might violate the constraint. Therefore, this setting does not disable error reporting for unusable indexes that are unique

- False- Enables error reporting of indexes marked UNUSABLE. This setting does not allow inserts, deletes, and updates on tables with unusable indexes or index partitions.

The smtp_out_server parameter

The *smtp_out_server* parameter specifies the SMTP host and port to which UTL_MAIL delivers out-bound E-mail. Multiple servers may be specified, separated by commas.

If the first server in the list is unavailable, then UTL_MAIL tries the second server, and so on.

If *smtp_out_server* is not specified, then the SMTP server name defaults to the value of DB_DOMAIN, the port number defaults to 25, and the SMTP domain defaults to the suffix of DB_DOMAIN.

The sp_name parameter

The *sp_name* parameter replaces *lock_name_space*, which is now deprecated. *sp_name* takes precedence over *lock_name_space*.

The streams_pool_size parameter

The *streams_pool_size* parameter specifies (in bytes) the size of the Streams pool, from which memory is allocated for Streams. If this parameter is not specified or is set to 0, then up to 10% of the shared pool is allocated for Streams.

Now that we have revirewed the new Oracle10g parameters let's examine some dictionary scripts for extracting Oracle parameters.

Extracting initialization parameters

A simple script to generate a nearly ready-for-prime-time init<SID>.ora file is provided below. Of course, with Oracle9*i*, you can use the *create pfile* command if you have a current *spfile* to generate a parameter file listing (and vica-versa). An example of output from this script is shown below.

🖫 init_ora_rct.sql

```
--************************************************
--
--     Copyright © 2003 by Rampant TechPress Inc.
--
--     Free for non-commercial use.
--     For commercial licensing, e-mail info@rampant.cc
--
--  ************************************************

SET NEWPAGE 0 VERIFY OFF
SET ECHO OFF FEEDBACK OFF TERMOUT OFF PAGES 300 LINES 80 HEADING
OFF
COLUMN name   FORMAT a80 WORD_WRAPPED
DEFINE OUTPUT = 'init.ora'
SPOOL &OUTPUT

SELECT '# Init.ora file FROM v$system_parameter' name FROM dual
UNION
SELECT '# generated on:'||sysdate name FROM dual
UNION
SELECT '# script by MRA 10/14/01 ' name FROM dual
UNION
SELECT '#' name FROM dual
UNION
SELECT name||' = '||value name  FROM v$system_parameter
WHERE value IS NOT NULL and Isdefault='FALSE';

SPOOL OFF
CLEAR COLUMNS
SET NEWPAGE 0 VERIFY OFF
SET TERMOUT ON PAGES 22 LINES 80 HEADING ON
SET TERMOUT ON
UNDEF OUTPUT
PAUSE Press Enter to continue
```

Here is a sample listing:

```
#
# Init.ora file FROM v$system_parameter
# generated on:14-OCT-01
# script by MRA 10/14/01
background_dump_dest =
/var/oracle/OraHome2/admin/diogenes1/bdump
compatible = 9.0.0
control_files =
/var/oracle/OraHome2/oradata/diogenes1/control01.ctl,
/var/oracle/OraHome2/oradata/diogenes1/control02.ctl,
/var/oracle/OraHome2/oradata/diogenes1/control03.ctl

core_dump_dest = /var/oracle/OraHome2/admin/diogenes1/cdump
db_block_size = 8192
db_cache_size = 67108864
db_domain = diogenes
db_name = diogenes1
dispatchers = (PROTOCOL=TCP)(SER=MODOSE),
(PROTOCOL=TCP)(PRE=oracle.aurora.server.GiopServer),
(PROTOCOL=TCP)(PRE=oracle.aurora.server.SGiopServer)

fast_start_mttr_target = 300
instance_name = diogenes1
java_pool_size = 117440512
large_pool_size = 1048576
open_cursors = 300
processes = 150
remote_login_passwordfile = EXCLUSIVE
resource_manager_plan = SYSTEM_PLAN
shared_pool_size = 117440512
sort_area_size = 524288
timed_statistics = TRUE
undo_management = AUTO
undo_tablespace = UNDOTBS
user_dump_dest = /var/oracle/OraHome2/admin/diogenes1/udump
```

Notice that the *where* clause in the query for the *init.ora* re-creation script restricts the return values to only those that have been changed from their default settings (isdefault='FALSE'). If the query is not restricted, it will return all hundred-plus parameters.

In Oracle9i the database may be using an *spfile*. An *spfile* is a file that Oracle can both read from and write to during operation, allowing dynamic reconfiguration of many parameters, which is persistent across shutdowns and startups. A normal *pfile* can be generated using the command:

```
CREATE PFILE[=<location>] FROM SPFILE[=<location>];
```

If the files are in the default location ($ORACLE_HOME/dbs) then the optional ='location' full path specifications for the file locations aren't required. The inversion of the command is also allowed to generate an *spfile* from a normal *pfile:*

```
CREATE SPFILE[='location'] FROM PFILE=[<'location'>];
```

Monitoring Undocumented Initialization Parameters

Undocumented initialization parameters also require monitoring. Undocumented parameters are those that are (a) undergoing testing, or (b) were too useful to eschew completely. Unfortunately, the undocumented values are a little more difficult to access.

🖫 **undoc.sql**

```
--***********************************************
--
--    Copyright © 2003 by Rampant TechPress Inc.
--
--    Free for non-commercial use.
--    For commercial licensing, e-mail info@rampant.cc
--
-- ***********************************************

COLUMN parameter              FORMAT a37
COLUMN description            FORMAT a30 WORD_WRAPPED
COLUMN "Session VALUE"        FORMAT a10
COLUMN "Instance VALUE"       FORMAT a10
SET LINES 100 PAGES 0
SPOOL undoc.lis

SELECT
    a.ksppinm  "Parameter",
    a.ksppdesc "Description",
    b.ksppstvl "Session Value",
    c.ksppstvl "Instance Value"
FROM
    x$ksppi a,
    x$ksppcv b,
```

```
    x$ksppsv c
WHERE
    a.indx = b.indx
    AND
    a.indx = c.indx
    AND
    a.ksppinm LIKE '/_%' escape '/'
;

SPOOL OFF
```

Note that this script must be run from the SYS user as
only the SYS user can access the X$ internal tables.

Monitoring Locks and Latches

Monitoring latches in Oracle involves monitoring *sleeps* a
latch can have millions of gets, misses and other stats
that are related to them, but if it has no *sleeps* then it
probably isn't a major concern. Therefore, to monitor
for latching problems, look first at sleeps as is shown in
the following script.

🖫 Latch_sleep.sql

```
--**************************************************
--
--    Copyright © 2003 by Rampant TechPress Inc.
--
--    Free for non-commercial use.
--    For commercial licensing, e-mail info@rampant.cc
--
--  **************************************************

REM
REM Script to determine sleeps for latches
REM M. R. Ault 2003
REM
col name format a30 heading 'Latch Name'
col gets format 99,999,999,999 heading 'Gets'
col misses format 9,999,999,999 heading 'Misses'
col sleeps format 999,999,999 heading 'Sleeps'
set pages 55
ttitle80 'Latches Contention Report'
spool latches_con
select name,gets,misses,sleeps from v$latch where gets>0 and
misses>0 order by gets desc
/
```

```
spool off
clear columns
ttitle off
```

The output from the above script should resemble the following:

Latch Name	Gets	Misses	Sleeps
cache buffers chains	668,498,922	16,722	1,576
library cache	57,209,901	87,420	9,747
session idle bit	17,831,191	393	7
row cache objects	16,368,218	2,265	24
enqueues	7,239,390	436	14
checkpoint queue latch	6,741,674	133	55
cache buffers lru chain	5,458,113	134	2
redo allocation	5,321,254	938	105
transaction allocation	5,248,223	458	7
session allocation	4,700,939	1,920	59
shared pool	4,316,720	1,577	991
messages	3,976,313	7,147	200
enqueue hash chains	3,878,828	838	65
redo writing	3,540,931	42,259	679
undo global data	3,374,722	184	1
process queue reference	2,461,595	1,206	2
dml lock allocation	1,370,771	119	1
list of block allocation	1,290,257	45	18
multiblock read objects	639,872	23	9
cache buffer handles	234,148	3	5
latch wait list	6,730	51	4
parallel query stats	22	5	10

It can be a challenge to monitor locks in Oracle. Just for *v$lock_dpt* alone, multiple joins are usually required to get the desired information. We suggest using the *catblock.sql* script, as it creates several useful views for locks. The *catblock.sql* script is located in the $ORACLE_HOME/rdbms/admin directory on UNIX, and in the c:\orant\rdbms\admin directory on NT. The script creates *dba_kgllock*. *dba_lock*, *dba_lock_internal*, *dba_dml_locks*, *dba_ddl_locks*, *dba_waiters*, and *dba_blockers*.

It is best to set *echo* ON, since many releases contain errors that must be corrected before it will run properly. In early Oracle7 releases, there were also permissions problems with some of the lock views, which required that they be queried from SYS or INTERNAL only.

OEM contains a detailed lock screen in the GUI, as well as an HTML-based report for locking. The OEM Lock Manager GUI is shown in Figure 1.1.

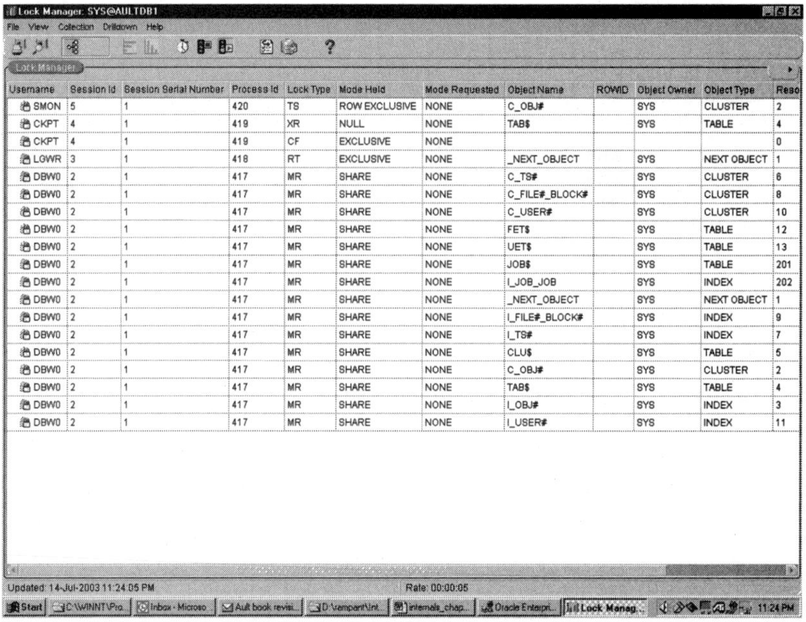

Username	Session Id	Session Serial Number	Process Id	Lock Type	Mode Held	Mode Requested	Object Name	ROWID	Object Owner	Object Type	Reso
SMON	5	1	420	TS	ROW EXCLUSIVE	NONE	C_OBJ#		SYS	CLUSTER	2
CKPT	4	1	419	XR	NULL	NONE	TAB$		SYS	TABLE	4
CKPT	4	1	419	CF	EXCLUSIVE	NONE					0
LGWR	3	1	418	RT	EXCLUSIVE	NONE	_NEXT_OBJECT		SYS	NEXT OBJECT	1
DBW0	2	1	417	MR	SHARE	NONE	C_TS#		SYS	CLUSTER	6
DBW0	2	1	417	MR	SHARE	NONE	C_FILE#_BLOCK#		SYS	CLUSTER	8
DBW0	2	1	417	MR	SHARE	NONE	C_USER#		SYS	CLUSTER	10
DBW0	2	1	417	MR	SHARE	NONE	FET$		SYS	TABLE	12
DBW0	2	1	417	MR	SHARE	NONE	UET$		SYS	TABLE	13
DBW0	2	1	417	MR	SHARE	NONE	JOB$		SYS	TABLE	201
DBW0	2	1	417	MR	SHARE	NONE	I_JOB_JOB		SYS	INDEX	202
DBW0	2	1	417	MR	SHARE	NONE	_NEXT_OBJECT		SYS	NEXT OBJECT	1
DBW0	2	1	417	MR	SHARE	NONE	I_FILE#_BLOCK#		SYS	INDEX	9
DBW0	2	1	417	MR	SHARE	NONE	I_TS#		SYS	INDEX	7
DBW0	2	1	417	MR	SHARE	NONE	CLU$		SYS	TABLE	5
DBW0	2	1	417	MR	SHARE	NONE	C_OBJ#		SYS	CLUSTER	2
DBW0	2	1	417	MR	SHARE	NONE	TAB$		SYS	TABLE	4
DBW0	2	1	417	MR	SHARE	NONE	I_OBJ#		SYS	INDEX	3
DBW0	2	1	417	MR	SHARE	NONE	I_USER#		SYS	INDEX	11

Figure 1.1 *Figure OEM Lock Manager screen. Monitoring Sessions Waiting for Locks*

The *catblock.sql* script is located in the $ORACLE_HOME/rdbms/admin directory on UNIX or Linux. It provides access to the *dba_waiters* view. The *dba_waiters* view gives information on sessions waiting for locks held by other sessions. By joining *v$session* with *dba_waiters*, detailed information is obtained about the locks and sessions that are waiting. A report on this information is shown below.

```
--*********************************************
--
--    Copyright © 2003 by Rampant TechPress Inc.
--
--    Free for non-commercial use.
--    For commercial licensing, e-mail info@rampant.cc
--
-- *********************************************

COLUMN busername          FORMAT a10      HEADING 'Holding|User'
COLUMN wusername          FORMAT a10      HEADING 'Waiting|User'
COLUMN bsession_id                        HEADING 'Holding|SID'
COLUMN wsession_id                        HEADING 'Waiting|SID'
COLUMN mode_held          FORMAT a10      HEADING 'Mode|Held'
COLUMN mode_requested     FORMAT 999999   HEADING 'Mode|Requested'
COLUMN lock_id1           FORMAT 999999   HEADING 'Lock|ID1'
COLUMN lock_id2           FORMAT a15      HEADING 'Lock|ID2'
COLUMN type                               HEADING 'Lock|Type'

SET LINES 132 PAGES 59 FEEDBACK OFF ECHO OFF
ttitle 'Processes Waiting on Locks Report'
SPOOL waiters

SELECT
   holding_session bsession_id,
   waiting_session wsession_id,
   b.username busername,
   a.username wusername,
   c.lock_type type,
   mode_held,
   mode_requested,
   lock_id1,
   lock_id2
FROM
   sys.v_$session b,
   sys.dba_waiters c,
   sys.v_$session a
WHERE
   c.holding_session=b.sid
   and
   c.waiting_session=a.sid
;

SPOOL OFF
PAUSE press Enter to continue
CLEAR COLUMNS
SET LINES 80 PAGES 22 FEEDBACK ON
TTITLE OFF
```

In the script above, the *lock_id1* and *lock_id2* columns map into the object upon which the lock is being held. An example of the report is shown below.

Holding Mode SID Requested	Waiting Lock SID ID1	Holding Lock User ID2	Waiting User	Lock Type	Mode Held
7 Exclusive	14 Exclusive	DBAUTIL 65580	SYSTEM 279	Transaction	

Monitoring Sessions Causing Blocked Locks

We have seen that the *catblock.sql* script must be run in order to create the *dba_blockers* view. The *dba_blockers* view indicates all sessions that are currently causing blocks that aren't blocked themselves. The script below looks at the other side of the coin; it reports on the sessions that are causing blocks by joining against *v$session* and *dba_locks*.

🖫 **blockers.sql**

```
--*************************************************
--
--     Copyright © 2003 by Rampant TechPress Inc.
--
--     Free for non-commercial use.
--     For commercial licensing, e-mail info@rampant.cc
--
-- *************************************************

COLUMN username          FORMAT a10     HEADING 'Holding|User'
COLUMN session_id                       HEADING 'SID'
COLUMN mode_held         FORMAT a10     HEADING 'Mode|Held'
COLUMN mode_requested    FORMAT a10     HEADING 'Mode|Requested'
COLUMN lock_id1          FORMAT a10     HEADING 'Lock|ID1'
COLUMN lock_id2          FORMAT a10     HEADING 'Lock|ID2'
COLUMN type                             HEADING 'Lock|Type'

SET LINES 132 PAGES 59 FEEDBACK OFF ECHO OFF
ttitle 'Sessions Blocking Other Sessions Report'
SPOOL blockers

SELECT
    a.session_id,
    username,
    type,
    mode_held,
    mode_requested,
```

```
      lock_id1,
      lock_id2
FROM
   sys.v_$session b,
   sys.dba_blockers c,
   sys.dba_lock a
WHERE
   c.holding_session=a.session_id
   AND
   c.holding_session=b.sid
;
SPOOL OFF
PAUSE press Enter to continue
CLEAR COLUMNS
SET LINES 80 PAGES 22 FEEDBACK ON
```

Here is a sample listing of the output:

```
          Holding    Lock       Mode        Mode       Lock      Lock
      SID User       Type       Held        Requested  ID1       ID2
--------- ---------- ---------- ----------  ---------- --------- -----
        7 DBAUTIL    USER       Row-S (SS)  None       31299     0
        7 DBAUTIL    USER       Exclusive   None       65580     279
```

Monitoring DDL and DML Locks

Other types of locks are the Data Definition (DDL) and
Data Manipulation (DML) locks. The *dba_dml_locks* and
dba_ddl_locks views are both created by the *catblock.sql*
script and are used to monitor DML and DDL locks.
Let's look at two scripts that report on DDL and DML
locks, respectively.

🖫 ddl_lock.sql

```
--*********************************************
--
--    Copyright © 2003 by Rampant TechPress Inc.
--
--    Free for non-commercial use.
--    For commercial licensing, e-mail info@rampant.cc
--
-- *********************************************

COLUMN owner           FORMAT a7    HEADING 'User'
COLUMN session_id      FORMAT 9999  HEADING 'SID'
COLUMN mode_held       FORMAT a7    HEADING 'Lock|Mode|Held'
COLUMN mode_requested  FORMAT a7    HEADING 'Lock|Mode|Request'
COLUMN type            FORMAT a20   HEADING 'Type|Object'
```

```
COLUMN name              FORMAT a21      HEADING 'Object|Name'

SET FEEDBACK OFF ECHO OFF PAGES 48 LINES 79
ttitle 'Report on All DDL Locks Held'
SPOOL ddl_lock

SELECT
   NVL(owner,'SYS') owner,
   session_id,
   name,
   type,
   mode_held,
   mode_requested
FROM
   sys.dba_ddl_locks
ORDER BY 1,2,3
;
SPOOL OFF
PAUSE press Enter/return to continue
CLEAR COLUMNS
SET FEEDBACK ON PAGES 22 LINES 80
TTITLE OFF
```

Here is a sample listing:

User Request	SID	Object Name	Type Object	Lock Mode Held	Lock Mode
SYS	11	DBMS_SESSION	Body	Null	None
SYS	11	DBMS_STANDARD	Table/Procedure/Type	Null	None
SYS	12	DATABASE	18	Null	None
SYS	12	DBMS_SESSION	Table/Procedure/Type	Null	None
SYS	12	DBMS_SESSION	Body	Null	None
SYS	12	DBMS_STANDARD	Table/Procedure/Type	Null	None
SYS	13	DATABASE	18	Null	None
SYS	13	DBMS_SESSION	Table/Procedure/Type	Null	None
SYS	13	DBMS_SESSION	Body	Null	None
SYS	13	DBMS_STANDARD	Table/Procedure/Type	Null	None
SYS	14	DATABASE	18	Null	None
SYS	14	DBMS_APPLICATIO	Body	Null	None
SYS	14	DBMS_APPLICATION	Table/Procedure/Type	Null	None
SYS	14	DBMS_SESSION	Table/Procedure/Type	Null	None
SYS	14	DBMS_SESSION	Body	Null	None
SYS	14	DBMS_STANDARD	Table/Procedure/Type	Null	None
SYSTEM	8	SYSTEM	18	Null	None
SYSTEM	11	SYSTEM	18	Null	None
SYSTEM	12	SYSTEM	18	Null	None
SYSTEM	13	SYSTEM	18	Null	None
SYSTEM	14	SYSTEM	18	Null	None

Here is the DML lock script.

```
--***********************************************
--
--     Copyright © 2003 by Rampant TechPress Inc.
--
--     Free for non-commercial use.
--     For commercial licensing, e-mail info@rampant.cc
--
-- ***********************************************

COLUMN owner           FORMAT a8      HEADING 'User'
COLUMN session_id                     HEADING 'SID'
COLUMN mode_held       FORMAT a10     HEADING 'Mode|Held'
COLUMN mode_requested  FORMAT a10     HEADING 'Mode|Requested'

SET FEEDBACK OFF ECHO OFF PAGES 59 LINES 80
ttitle 'Report on All DML Locks Held'
SPOOL dml_lock

SELECT
   NVL(owner,'SYS') owner,
   session_id,
   name,
   mode_held,
   mode_requested
FROM
   sys.dba_dml_locks
ORDER BY 2
;

SPOOL OFF
PAUSE press Enter to continue
CLEAR COLUMNS
SET FEEDBACK ON PAGES 22 LINES 80
TTITLE OFF
```

When contention is suspected, a quick look at these DDL and DML reports can tell the DBA if a session is holding a lock on the table or object involved. Be cautious, these reports contain volatile information and are useful only for pinpoint monitoring of a specific problem.

Monitoring Internal Locks

The *internal* lock is the final one we will look at. The database's internal processes generate internal locks. The *catblock.sql* script creates the *dba_internal_locks* view.

🖫 int_lock.sql

```
--*************************************************
--
--    Copyright © 2003 by Rampant TechPress Inc.
--
--    Free for non-commercial use.
--    For commercial licensing, e-mail info@rampant.cc
--
--  *************************************************

COLUMN username        FORMAT a10      HEADING 'Lock|Holder'
COLUMN session_id                      HEADING 'User|SID'
COLUMN lock_type       FORMAT a27      HEADING 'Lock Type'
COLUMN mode_held       FORMAT a10      HEADING 'Mode|Held'
COLUMN mode_requested  FORMAT a10      HEADING 'Mode|Requested'
COLUMN lock_id1        FORMAT a30      HEADING 'Lock/Cursor|ID1'
COLUMN lock_id2        FORMAT a10      HEADING 'Lock|ID2'

PROMPT 'ALL is all types or modes'
ACCEPT lock PROMPT 'Enter Desired Lock Type: '
ACCEPT mode PROMPT 'Enter Lock Mode: '
SET LINES 132 PAGES 59 FEEDBACK OFF ECHO OFF VERIFY OFF
BREAK ON username
ttitle 'Report on Internal Locks Mode: &mode Type: &lock'
SPOOL int_locks

SELECT
   NVL(b.username,'SYS') username,
   session_id,lock_type,mode_held,
   mode_requested,lock_id1,lock_id2
FROM
   sys.dba_lock_internal a,
   sys.v_$session b
WHERE
   UPPER(mode_held) like UPPER('%&mode%')
OR
   UPPER('&mode')='ALL'
AND
   UPPER(lock_type) like UPPER('%&lock%')
OR
   UPPER(mode_held) like UPPER('%&mode%')
OR
   UPPER('&mode')='ALL'
AND
   UPPER('&lock')='ALL'
AND
```

```
    a.session_id=b.sid
ORDER BY 1,2
;
SPOOL OFF
PAUSE press Enter to continue
SET LINES 80 PAGES 22 FEEDBACK ON VERIFY ON
CLEAR COLUMNS
CLEAR BREAKS
UNDEF LOCK
UNDEF MODE
```

It is wise to remain cautious here too. The report can be several pages long in an idle instance. An excerpt from the report is shown in below.

Lock Holder	User SID	Lock Type	Mode Held	Mode Requested	Lock/Cursor	Lock ID1	Lock ID2
DBAUTIL	7	Cursor Definition Pin	Share	None		table_1_0_139_0_0_	57BFE99C
	7	Cursor Definition Lock	Null	None		table_1_0_139_0_0_	57BFE99C
	7	Cursor Definition Lock	Null	None	SELECT ATTRIBUTE FROM V$CONT EXT WHERE NAMESPACE = 'LBAC$L ABELS'		57B96CF0
	7	Cursor Definition Lock	Null	None	SELECT POL#, PACKAGE FROM LBA C$POL WHERE BITAND(FLAGS,1) = 1 ORDER BY PACKAGE		57B7E728
	7	Cursor Definition Lock	Null	None	commit		57B5ABC0
	7	Cursor Definition Lock	Null	None	SELECT POL#, PACKAGE FROM LBA C$POL WHERE BITAND(FLAGS,1) = 1 ORDER BY PACKAGE		57B96EE4
	7	Body Definition Lock	Null	None	SYS.DBMS_SESSION		57B879E8
	7	Body Definition Lock	Null	None	LBACSYS.LBAC_CACHE		57BA1D8C
	7	Cursor Definition Lock	Null	None	SELECT MAX(TAG#) FROM LBAC$L AB		57B7C038
	7	Cursor Definition Lock	Null	None	select pol#, usr_name, usr_lab els, package, privs from lbac$ user_logon where usr_name = :u sername		57B91108

Monitoring Waits

Waits occur when Oracle experiences contention for a specific resource. Tuning should involve monitoring waits, latches, and locks. We have already looked at latches and locks, lets look at the third member of this trio, waits. The *v$waitstat* DPT is the place to start.

The *v$waitstat* table is the usual source of wait information for the average tuner. This table has a very basic structure:

```
EXADB>DESC v$waitstat

Name                             Null?    Type
-------------------------------- -------- ------------
CLASS                                     VARCHAR2(18)
COUNT                                     NUMBER
TIME                                      NUMBER
```

The class column contains the name of the particular type of wait. The count column gives the total number of these types of waits that have occurred since the last database startup. The final column, time, gives the total elapsed time in centa-seconds (1/100 seconds) that the waits have consumed according to Oracle's internal determinations.

A typical select on a large instance may look like so:

```
EXADB>SELECT * FROM v$waitstat WHERE count>0;

CLASS              COUNT      TIME
------------------ ---------- ----------
data block         101069     123495
segment header     70         55
unused             241        21
undo header        10012      6678
undo block         191        51
```

Unfortunately, without a bit of decryption these numbers don't really tell us a lot. Admittedly a number like 101069 tends to boggle one, however when placed in the proper context it may not be as bad as it initially appears. You must remember that these 101069 waits generated only 123495 centa-seconds of wait time or 1.22 centa-seconds per wait event.

To put these waits in context, you must be aware what the CLASS column is actually referring to. Table 1 defines what the CLASS column is referencing.

CLASS	DEFINITION
bitmap block	This tells how many bitmap block waits have happened. Bitmap blocks are used in locally managed tablespaces and for locally managed space management in Oracle9i (automated freelist and pctfree/pctuser initrans/maxtrans management)
bitmap index block	This tells how many waits happened in bitmap index blocks
data block	This tells how many data blocks themselves experienced waits
extent map	For locally managed tablespaces this tells how many extant map waits have occurred.
free list	This tells you how many waits there have been on free lists in the database.
save undo block	A save undo segment is generated when a tablespace is taken offline in an emergency situation, this tells how many waits have occurred on a save undo segment block (undo means rollback).
save undo header	This tells how many waits have occurred in a save undo header.
segment header	A database segment corresponds to a table, index, cluster, etc. This wait tells how many waits there have been on a segment header entry.
sort block	This wait is for sort blocks.
System undo block	A system undo segment is the SYSTEM rollback segment in the SYSTEM tablespace. This shows waits on the system rollback segment blocks.
System undo header	This shows waits on the system rollback segment header.

CLASS	DEFINITION
undo block	This one statistics carries the load for all normal rollback segment block waits.
undo header	This one statistic carries the load for all normal rollback segment header blocks.
Unused	This statistic carries information on waits on unused blocks.

Table 1: *Wait Classes and Their Definitions*

Table 2 shows the actions that are used to rectify block waits based on block types.

BLOCK TYPE	POSSIBLE ACTIONS
segment header	Increase of number of FREELISTs. Use FREELIST GROUPs (even in single instance this can make a difference).
Freelist blocks	Add more FREELISTS. In case of Parallel Server make sure that each instance has its own FREELIST GROUP(s).
Undo Waits	Generally speaking most of these waits are self-explanatory. For example, if you have block waits for undo segments you may need larger rollback segments, if you experience header waits for rollback segments, you may need more rollback segments. This takes care of 6 of the waits shown above.
Sort waits	Waits for sort blocks could indicate insufficient sort area size or sort segments in the sort tablespace.

Table 2: *Block Type and Action List*

Generally it is rare to see waits on any of the bitmap statistics, segment statistics , unused or extent statistics. If you do, they are usually a small number and of such short duration that they mean little if anything to over all tuning.

This leaves us with data block waits.

Data Block Waits

Data block waits are caused by a number of conditions:

- Insufficient freelists or freelist groups

- Bad initrans value

- Bad settings for PCTFREE/PCTUSED (continued rows)

- Too many rows per block

- Unselective indexes

- Right-hand indexes

But how can we determine which object is experiencing which problems? First, we need to find out specifically where the blocks are that are having the problems. This can be found out by using the *x$kcbfwait* and *v$datafile* tables in a report that is run from the *sys* user such as:

🖫 **Waits_file.sql**

```
--************************************************
--
--    Copyright © 2003 by Rampant TechPress Inc.
--
--    Free for non-commercial use.
--    For commercial licensing, e-mail info@rampant.cc
--
--    ************************************************

REM
REM Waits per Datafile report
REM M. Ault 2003
REM
col name format a66 heading 'Data File Name'
col count format 999,999,999 heading 'Wait|Count'
col file# heading 'File#' format 9,999
col wait_time heading 'Time'
col ratio heading 'Time|Count' format 999.99
set pages 47
compute sum of count on report
break on report
ttitle 'Waits Per Datafile'
```

```
set lines 132
spool waits_file
SELECT file#, name, count, time wait_time,
time/count ratio
FROM x$kcbfwait, v$datafile
WHERE indx + 1 = file#
AND time>0
Order By count DESC
/
spool off
clear columns
clear computes
ttitle off
set pages 22 lines 80
```

An example output from this query is shown below.

File#	Data File Name	Wait Count	Time	Time Count
67	/data/EXADB/oradata02/dimension.dbf	12,867	82558	6.42
158	/data/EXADB/oradata06/dimension2.dbf	12,508	99476	7.95
209	/data/EXADB/oradata07/dimension3.dbf	12,193	91256	7.48
1	/data/EXADB/oradata01/PRDsystem.dbf	8,880	3183	.36
203	/data/EXADB/oradata0a/rbs_all_08.rbs	6,310	4340	.69
68	/data/EXADB/oradata0b/btr_u128m_2002.dbf	722	16456	22.79
182	/data/EXADB/oradata06/km_u128m_D008.dbf	694	2291	3.30
79	/data/EXADB/oradata06/btr_trn.dbf	628	864	1.38

The report shown above was shortened just to show the heavy hitters. Once you have the data file names you can find the objects located in each file by a query against the *dba_extents* view.

```
SELECT distinct owner, segment_name, segment_type
    FROM dba_extents
  WHERE file_id= &FILE_ID
  ;
```

So, in this case we want to look at file number 67:

```
EXADB>col segment_name format a30
EXADB>col owner format a10
EXADB>/
Enter value for file_id: 67
```

OWNER	SEGMENT_NAME	SEGMENT_TYPE
DIMENSION	AUD_FACTOR_CHANGES	TABLE
DIMENSION	DIM_BRAND	TABLE
DIMENSION	DIM_CARRIER	TABLE

```
DIMENSION   DIM_COMMITMENT                  TABLE
DIMENSION   DIM_CONSUMING_ACCOUNT           TABLE
DIMENSION   DIM_CONTRACT                    TABLE
DIMENSION   DIM_CUSTOMER                    TABLE
DIMENSION   DIM_DAILY_CALENDAR              TABLE
DIMENSION   DIM_DAILY_CALENDAR_BKUP         TABLE
DIMENSION   DIM_GL_ACCOUNT                  TABLE
...
DIMENSION   VALIDATE_DIM_TABLE_XWALK_TB     TABLE
DIMENSION   VALIDATE_HIERARCHY_TB           TABLE
DIMENSION   VALIDATE_HIERARCHY_TMP_TB       TABLE

103 rows selected.
```

We have reduced our possible candidates down to 103 from a database with 2221 tables. By knowing our application we can pick out from this list the high activity tables, for example, DIM_CUSTOMER and perhaps concentrate our studies there. Another way would be to look at the items *initrans, freelists* and *continued rows* to see which have default settings or are experiencing row or block chaining. An example query to show this information would be:

```
SELECT DISTINCT a.table_name,a.ini_trans, a.freelists,
a.pct_free, a.pct_used, a.chain_cnt
FROM dba_tables a, dba_extents b
WHERE a.table_name=b.segment_name AND
b.file_id=&file_id;
```

Unfortunately this query may not help if all the tables have default settings. The next avenue to pursue would be to see which of the objects are using the most SGA space. If they are being used a majority of the time the chances are that they are the cause of most of the problems experienced. This will require a join against the *obj$* and *x$bh* views. Using these SYSTEM tables and views requires the use of the SYS user. An example query is shown in the next listing.

```
SELECT
b.name object,
a.dbarfil file#,
```

```
COUNT(a.dbablk) "Num blocks",
SUM(a.tch) "Touches"
FROM x$bh a, obj$ b
WHERE a.obj=b.dataobj#
AND a.tch>0
AND a.file#=&file_no
GROUP BY b.name,a.dbarfil
ORDER BY 4 desc
```

An example output for our troubled file number 67 is shown below:

OBJECT	FILE#	Num blocks	Touches
DIM_CUSTOMER	67	589	3955
DIM_PRODUCT	67	401	1372
DIM_DAILY_CALENDAR	67	98	1055
DIM_MSA	67	48	48
DIM_LOCATION	67	1	39
DIM_HIST_RPTLOC	67	1	14
DIM_ITEM_LOCATION	67	1	4

As you can see, it is as we expected, the DIM_CUSTOMER table has the most blocks and the most touches. We have reduced our candidates from 103 down to 6. In 8i and above the *tch* (or touch) column in the *x$bh* table tells you how many times a buffer has been touched by a user process. By seeing how many blocks and how many block touches a particular table has for a specific file, we can see the hot objects in that file that may require additional tuning efforts. Let's look at the block level storage values for the candidate tables using a select on DBA_TABLES.

```
SELECT
table_name,ini_trans, freelists, freelist_groups, chain_cnt
FROM dba_tables
WHERE table_name IN
('DIM_CUSTOMER',
'DIM_PRODUCT',
'DIM_DAILY_CALENDAR',
'DIM_MSA',
'DIM_LOCATION',
'DIM_HIST_RPTLOC',
'DIM_ITEM_LOCATION')
/
```

The results of the above query show all of the tables in question have default values:

```
TABLE_NAME                INI_TRANS   FREELISTS  FREELIST_GROUPS  CHAIN_CNT
-----------------------   ---------   ---------  ---------------  ---------
DIM_CUSTOMER                      1           1                1          0
DIM_DAILY_CALENDAR                1           1                1          0
DIM_LOCATION                      1           1                1          0
DIM_HIST_RPTLOC                   1           1                1          0
DIM_MSA                           1           1                1         71
DIM_PRODUCT                       1           1                1          0
DIM_ITEM_LOCATION                 1           1                1          0
```

The next step would be to determine which of the above six tables undergoes the most IUD (Insert Update and Delete) activities and the number of simultaneous transactions per block. This database happens to be a 16K block size data warehouse so we can expect that some of these tables could have a significant number of rows per block. Let's take a look at *dba_tables* for the information on rows per block.

```
SELECT
table_name,value/avg_row_len RPB
FROM dba_tables, v$parameter
WHERE table_name IN
('DIM_CUSTOMER',
'DIM_PRODUCT',
'DIM_DAILY_CALENDAR',
'DIM_MSA',
'DIM_LOCATION',
'DIM_HIST_RPTLOC',
'DIM_ITEM_LOCATION')
AND name='db_block_size'
/

TABLE_NAME                      RPB
------------------------------  ----------
DIM_CUSTOMER                    12.7007752
DIM_DAILY_CALENDAR              25.1674347
DIM_LOCATION                    125.068702
DIM_HIST_RPTLOC                 36.2477876
DIM_MSA                         86.2315789
DIM_PRODUCT                     12.8501961
DIM_ITEM_LOCATION               62.5343511
```

Based on the above we would examine the DIM_LOCATION, DIM_MSA and DIM_ITEM_LOCATION tables with the idea of reducing their rows per block. The other tables we would look at *ini_trans* and *freelists*. However, these aren't always the solution as is shown in the next phase of our investigation.

So what about the case where there are a large number of waits, but the wait time is not as much an issue? For example the following script generates a waits per file report.

🖫 **Waits_file.sql**

```
--*************************************************
--
--    Copyright © 2003 by Rampant TechPress Inc.
--
--    Free for non-commercial use.
--    For commercial licensing, e-mail info@rampant.cc
--
-- *************************************************

col name format a50 heading 'Data File Name'
col count format 999,999,999 heading 'Wait|Count'
col file# heading 'File#' format 9,999
col wait_time heading 'Time' *
col ratio heading 'Time|Count' format 999.99
set pages 47
compute sum of count on report
break on report
ttitle 'Waits Per Datafile'
set lines 132
spool waits_file
SELECT file#, name, count, time wait_time,
time/count ratio
FROM x$kcbfwait, v$datafile
WHERE indx + 1 = file#
AND time>0
Order By count DESC
/
spool off
clear columns
clear computes
ttitle off
set pages 22 lines 80
```

For our example database, the results look like the following:

File#	Data File Name	Wait	Wait Count	Time	Time Count
67	/data/EXADB/oradata02/dimension.dbf	43,346	114829		2.65
209	/data/EXADB/oradata07/dimension3.dbf	42,950	449439		10.46
158	/data/EXADB/oradata06/dimension2.dbf	40,677	240046		5.90

In the above situation, calculate the standard deviation (I use a cut and paste into Excel and the Excel *stdev* and *avg* functions) to determine if the time spent per wait (the last column) is abnormal. In the case of the above files, when the values for the other datafiles are taken into account the average wait is 3.74 centi-seconds, the standard deviation is +/- 5.14 centi-seconds for a range of 0-8.89 centi-seconds per wait. Of the three files in our example, only 209 shows a large deviation from this range. By using our query to find the SGA data buffers used by objects in file 209 we get:

Object Name	File Number	Num blocks	Touches
DIM_PRODUCT	209	932	117845
DIM_CUSTOMER	209	1452	73385
DIM_DAILY_CALENDAR	209	26	85
DIM_LOCATION	209	1	73
DIM_FUND_CATEGORY	209	1	34
DIM_HIST_STOCK_NUMBER	209	1	28
DIM_OWNER	209	1	24
MTV_DIM_REPORT_ON_DATE	209	1	3
DIM_HIST_RPTLOC	209	1	2
DIM_SHIPPING_METHOD	209	1	2

Given this data, we would examine DIM_PRODUCT and DIM_CUSTOMER to find problems. Further investigation showed that these tables undergo few INSERT or DELETE operations, but do undergo numerous UPDATEs, however, these UPDATE activities rarely actually change data, driving the touch count way up and possibly causing the high wait counts. In addition the process is not doing multiple simultaneous inserts into a single block, but may be doing multiple serial inserts that should not cause *freelist* or *ini_trans* contention. The solution in this case is to re-write the application code to only update what is needed.

So when monitoring waits you can see that you need to examine not just the counts of waits, but the time spent in a wait condition. You have also seen how to drill down from the basic I/O wait indications to the file and ultimately to the table or object to see the actual object that may be causing the problem. Once we have the objects that may be the cause of high wait counts we have looked at the various causes of the waits and seen an example analysis for cause. Hopefully you will come away with a better understanding of how to isolate I/O wait problems and resolve them using database statistics instead of guesswork.

Monitoring Events

Oracle is an event-driven system. This means that sessions wait for calls, locks and latches spin, and processes slumber and wake at the behest of events. The *v$session_event dpt* tracks all current events by session. The script below will generate a report on current Oracle events.

🖫 **events.sql**

```
--********************************************
--
--     Copyright © 2003 by Rampant TechPress Inc.
--
```

```
--    Free for non-commercial use.
--    For commercial licensing, e-mail info@rampant.cc
--
-- ************************************************

COLUMN sid                HEADING Sid
COLUMN event              HEADING Event              FORMAT a40
COLUMN total_waits        HEADING Total|Waits
COLUMN total_timeouts     HEADING Total|Timeouts
COLUMN time_waited        HEADING Time|Waited
COLUMN average_wait       HEADING Average|Wait
COLUMN username           HEADING User

BREAK ON username
ttitle "Session Events By User"
SPOOL events
SET LINES 132 PAGES 59 VERIFY OFF FEEDBACK OFF

SELECT
   username,
   event,
   total_waits,total_timeouts,
   time_waited,average_wait
FROM
   sys.v_$session_event a,
   sys.v_$session b
WHERE
   a.sid= b.sid
ORDER BY 1;

SPOOL OFF
PAUSE Press Enter to continue
CLEAR COLUMNS
CLEAR BREAKS
SET LINES 80 PAGES 22 VERIFY ON FEEDBACK ON
TTITLE OFF
```

Here is an example of an event report.

User	Event	Total Waits	Total Timeouts	Time Waited	Average Wait
SYSTEM	enqueue	149	149	44425	298
	control file sequential read	214	0	14	0
	log file sync	61	0	65	1
	SQL*Net message to client	462	0	1	0
	single-task message	2	0	5	2
	SQL*Net break/reset to client	4	0	0	0
	SQL*Net message from client	800	0	735778	920
	SQL*Net message to client	19	0	0	0
	db file sequential read	24987	0	10986	0
	db file sequential read	16	0	10	1
	pmon timer	167133	167130	49031711	293
	rdbms ipc message	163764	163681	49050112	300
	control file sequential read	20	0	2	0
	control file parallel write	163663	0	75411	0
	direct path read	14	0	0	0
	db file parallel write	3300	3300	8	0
	db file scattered read	596	0	750	1
	db file sequential read	248	0	232	1
	log file parallel write	3760	0	1168	0
	log file single write	4	0	0	0
	log file sequential read	4	0	2	1

```
library cache load lock            1        1       299      299
smon timer                      1640     1634  47313312    28850
direct path write                 12        0         0        0
direct path read                  14        0         0        0
control file parallel write        8        0         4        0
control file sequential read   49110        0      1069        0
async disk IO                      1        0         0        0
rdbms ipc message             166085   163858  49051891      295
```

Workspaces in Oracle9*i*

The concept of a database *workspace* was introduced with Oracle9i. A workspace is an environment for a long-term transaction that allows multiple versions of objects. The workspace can be shared among many users. The workspace environment is managed through a series of short transactions and multiple data versions that lead to a complete long-term transaction event. The process maintains atomicity, as well as concurrency.

The Workspace Manager (WKS) is installed by default in all seed and DBCA databases. (If it is needed in a manually created database, it must be installed following the guide in the Oracle9*i Application Developers Guide--Workspace Manager*, Release 1 9.0.1, PART# A88806-01, Oracle Corporation, June 2001.)

🖫 **workspace_status.sql**

```
--**************************************************
--
--    Copyright © 2003 by Rampant TechPress Inc.
--
--    Free for non-commercial use.
--    For commercial licensing, e-mail info@rampant.cc
--
--  **************************************************

COLUMN WORKSPACE FORMAT a10 HEADING 'Workspace'
COLUMN owner FORMAT a10 HEADING 'Owner'
COLUMN freeze_status FORMAT a8 HEADING 'Freeze|Status'
COLUMN resolve_status FORMAT a8 HEADING 'Resolve|Status'
COLUMN parent_workspace FORMAT a10 HEADING 'Parent|Workspace'
COLUMN freeze_mode FORMAT a8 HEADING 'Freeze|Mode'

ttitle 'Workspace Status'
```

```
spool workspace_status

select
  workspace,
  NVL(parent_workspace,'NONE') parent_workspace,
  owner,
  freeze_status,
  NVL(freeze_mode,'NONE') freeze_mode,
  resolve_status
from
  dba_workspaces
;
spool off
ttitle off
```

Here is a sample listing:

```
            Parent                 Freeze   Freeze   Resolve
Workspace   Workspace   Owner      Status   Mode     Status
----------  ----------  ---------- -------- -------- --------
LIVE        NONE        SYS        UNFROZEN NONE     INACTIVE
```

Other items, such as workspace privileges and save points, can also be monitored using the *dba_* series of views.

pga_aggregate_target in Oracle9*i*

In Oracle9i the sort and hash area parameters such as *sort_area_size*, *hash_area_size* and their associated multi-block read parameters can be turned over to Oracle for management by using the *pga_aggregate_target* and *workarea_size_policy* parameters. The *pga_aggregate_target* is set to the size of memory for the projected aggregate PGA (sort area and context areas) for all users and *workarea_size_policy* is set to AUTO to turn on automated tuning.

However, how do you know if these are set correctly? Oracle provides the *v$pga_target_advice* DPT to provide you with guidance as to the appropriateness of your setting. By using a simple select, such as the one below, you can easily see if you have set your *pga_aggregate_target* value appropriately.

🖫 pga_advice.sql

```
--*************************************************
--
--   Copyright © 2003 by Rampant TechPress Inc.
--
--   Free for non-commercial use.
--   For commercial licensing, e-mail info@rampant.cc
--
-- *************************************************

ttitle 'PGA Target Advice Report'
set lines 80 pages 47
spool pga_advice
SELECT round(PGA_TARGET_FOR_ESTIMATE/1024/1024) target_mb,
       ESTD_PGA_CACHE_HIT_PERCENTAGE cache_hit_perc,
       ESTD_OVERALLOC_COUNT FROM   v$pga_target_advice
/
spool off
ttitle off
```

The output from the above SQL select will resemble the following:

```
10/09/03      PGA Target Advice Report          Page 1

TARGET_MB CACHE_HIT_PERC ESTD_OVERALLOC_COUNT
--------- -------------- --------------------
       13             31                 2046
       25             31                 1999
       38             32                  926
       50             34                  591
       60             36                  461
       70             37                  353
       80             38                  251
       90             38                  168
      100             39                  100
      150             45                    8
      200             47                    0
      300             58                    0
      400             59                    0

13 rows selected.
```

In the above report we see overallocation values, this indicates that our setting is too small and should be increased to at least 150 megabytes.

Conclusion

Database memory usage monitoring is a complex topic involving the watching of latches, locks waits, and events. All of these are controlled through a series of settings controlled by the documented and undocumented initialization parameters. The DBA must be aware of how to mine the Oracle DPTs, X$, and data dictionary views to obtain the required performance indicators for effective tuning to take place.

Other structures such as the shared pool and data block buffers control the flow of code and data in an Oracle system. In the next chapter we examine the shared pool, Oracle's code repository.

Inside the Shared Pool

Structure of the Shared Pool

Tuning the shared pool is one of the least understood features of the Oracle shared global area (SGA). The generally accepted approach to tuning involves throwing memory into the pool until the problem either goes away or is masked. We will examine the shared pool in this chapter and outline a method for tuning the shared pool that uses measurement, instead of guesswork, to drive the tuning methodology. Numerous scripts for examining the shared pool are also provided.

Many people know little more about the shared pool than it is a part of the Oracle shared global area. What exactly is the shared pool? The shared pool contains several key performance-related memory areas. If the shared pool is improperly sized, then overall database performance will suffer, sometimes dramatically. Figure 2.1 diagrams the shared pool structure located inside the various Oracle SGAs.

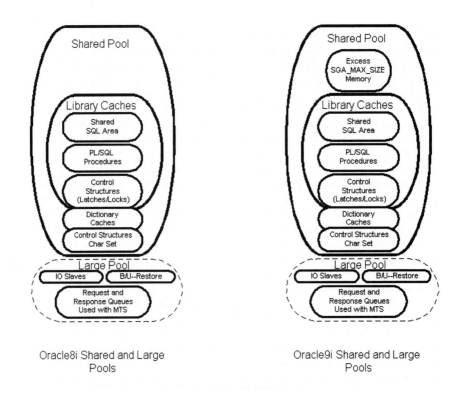

Oracle8i Shared and Large Pools

Oracle9i Shared and Large Pools

Figure 2.1: *Oracle 8i and Oracle 9i Shared Pool Structures*

You can see from an examination of the structures that the shared pool is separated into many substructures. The substructures of the shared pool fall into two broad areas, the fixed-size areas that stay relatively constant in size, and the variable-size areas that grow and shrink according to user and program requirements.

In the figure, the areas inside the library cache's substructure are variable in size, while those outside the library caches (with the exception of the request and response queues used with MTS) stay relatively fixed in size. The sizes are determined by an Oracle internal algorithm that calculates a ratio from the fixed areas, based on the overall shared pool size, a few of the initialization parameters, and empirical determinations from previous versions. In early versions of Oracle (notably 6.2 and lower versions), the dictionary caches could be sized individually, allowing finer control of this aspect of the shared pool. With Oracle 7 and all future releases from that point on, the internal algorithm for sizing the data dictionary caches took control from the DBA.

The shared pool is used for objects that can be shared among all users, such as table definitions, reusable SQL (although non-reusable SQL is also stored there), PL/SQL packages, procedures, and functions. Cursor information is also stored in the shared pool. At a minimum, the shared pool must be sized to accommodate the needs of the fixed areas plus a small amount of memory reserved for use in parsing SQL and PL/SQL statements. Otherwise, ORA-07445 errors will result.

Monitoring and Tuning the Shared Pool

The default values for the shared pool size initialization parameters are almost always too small by at least a factor of four. Unless your database is limited to the basic scott/tiger type schema and your overall physical data size is less than a couple of hundred megabytes, even the "large" parameters are far too small. What parameters control the size of the shared pool? Essentially only one, the *shared_pool_size*. The other shared pool parameters control how the variable-size areas in the shared pool are parsed out, but not overall shared pool size.

Oracle8 introduced a new area, the large pool, controlled by the *large_pool_size* parameter. In general, it is suggested that the shared pool size start at 40 megabytes and increase from there. The large pool size will depend on the number of concurrent users, the number of multi-threaded server servers, and the dispatchers and sort requirements for the application.

What should be monitored to determine if the shared pool is too small? This information can be gleaned from the data dictionary tables, specifically the *v$sgastat* and *v$sqlarea* views. The report below shows how much of the shared pool is in use at any given time.

🖫 **shared_pool_ora73.sql**

```
--*************************************************
--
--    Copyright © 2003 by Rampant TechPress Inc.
--
--    Free for non-commercial use.
--    For commercial licensing, e-mail info@rampant.cc
--
--    *************************************************
column shared_pool_used  format 9,999.99
column shared_pool_size  format 9,999.99
column shared_pool_avail format 9,999.99
column shared_pool_pct   format 999.99

@title80 'Shared Pool Summary'
spool rep_out\&db\shared_pool

select
   sum(a.bytes)/(1024*1024) shared_pool_used,
   max(b.value)/(1024*1024) shared_pool_size,
   (max(b.value)/(1024*1024))-(sum(a.bytes)/(1024*1024))
   shared_pool_avail,
   (sum(a.bytes)/max(b.value))*100 shared_pool_pct
from
   v$sgastat a,
   v$parameter b
where
   a.name in ( 'reserved stopper','table definiti',
      'dictionary cache', 'library cache', 'sql area',
```

```
          'PL/SQL DIANA', 'SEQ S.O.')
and
   b.name='shared_pool_size';

spool off
ttitle off
```

The script above should be run periodically during times of normal and high usage of your database. If the *shared_pool_pct* value stays in the high nineties, then you may need to increase the size of the shared pool, however, this isn't always the case. The *select where* clause in the script above should be modified in Oracle8 and subsequent releases to:

⊟ shared_pool.sql

```
--*********************************************
--
--    Copyright © 2003 by Rampant TechPress Inc.
--
--    Free for non-commercial use.
--    For commercial licensing, e-mail info@rampant.cc
--
-- *********************************************

select
   sum(a.bytes)/(1024*1024) shared_pool_used,
   max(b.value)/(1024*1024) shared_pool_size,
   max(b.value)/(1024*1024))-((sum(a.bytes)/(1024*1024))
shared_pool_avail,
   (sum(a.bytes)/max(b.value))*100 shared_pool_pct
from
   v$sgastat a,
   v$parameter b
where
   a.pool = 'shared pool'
and
   a.name != 'free memory'
and
   b.name='shared_pool_size';
```

The results will be similar to Figure 2.2.

```
SHARED_POOL_USED  SHARED_POOL_SIZE  SHARED_POOL_AVAIL  SHARED_POOL_PCT
----------------  ----------------  -----------------  ---------------
        3.66              38.15              34.49              9.60
```

Figure 2.2: *Example output of the Shared Pool Script*

All too often, the only thing monitored is the amount of the shared pool that is filled. It is also important to know how it is filled, with good reusable SQL or bad throw away SQL. You must know how the space is being used before you can decide whether the shared pool should be increased in size, decreased in size, or kept the same with a periodic flush schedule. How can we determine the contents of the shared pool and whether it is being properly reused or not? Let's consider a few reports that help provide an answer.

The first report shows how individual users are utilizing the shared pool. Before the report can be run, a summary view of the *v$sqlarea* view must be created. The code for the *sql_summary* view is shown in below.

sql_summary.sql

```
-- **********************************************
--
--     Copyright © 2003 by Rampant TechPress Inc.
--
--     Free for non-commercial use.
--     For commercial licensing, e-mail info@rampant.cc
--
--     **********************************************
create or replace view
    sql_summary
as
select
    username,
    sharable_mem,
    persistent_mem,
    runtime_mem
from
    sys.v_$sqlarea a,
    dba_users b
```

```
where
  a.parsing_user_id = b.user_id;
```

Once the *sql_summary* view is created, the following script is used to generate a summary report of the SQL areas in use by the connections. The report shows the distribution of SQL areas, and can indicate whether users are hogging a disproportionate amount of the shared pool area. Usually, a user that is hogging a large volume of the shared pool is not using good SQL coding techniques, and is generating a large number of non-reusable SQL areas.

🖫 sqlsum.sql

```
--*********************************************
--
--     Copyright © 2003 by Rampant TechPress Inc.
--
--     Free for non-commercial use.
--     For commercial licensing, e-mail info@rampant.cc
--
--  *********************************************
column areas                                   heading Used|Areas
column sharable    format 999,999,999          heading Shared|Bytes
column persistent  format 999,999,999          heading Persistent|Bytes
column runtime     format 999,999,999          heading Runtime|Bytes
column username    format a15                  heading "User"
column mem_sum     format 999,999,999          heading Mem|Sum

ttitle "Users SQL Area Memory Use"
spool sqlsum
set pages 59 lines 80
break on report

compute sum of sharable on report
compute sum of persistent on report
compute sum of runtime on report
compute sum of mem_sum on report

select
   username,
   sum(sharable_mem) Sharable,
   sum( persistent_mem) Persistent,
   sum( runtime_mem) Runtime ,
   count(*) Areas,
   sum(sharable_mem+persistent_mem+runtime_mem) Mem_sum
from
```

```
     sql_summary
group by username
order by 2;

spool off
pause Press enter to continue
clear columns
clear breaks
set pages 22 lines 80
ttitle off
```

A sample output from the script is shown below. In the
sample report, no one user is really hogging the SQL
area. If a particular user is hogging an SQL area, the
script will show which areas they are and what is in
them. This report on the actual SQL area contents can
then be used to help teach the user how to better
construct reusable SQL statements.

User	Shared Bytes	Persistent Bytes	Runtime Bytes	Used Areas	Mem Sum
AJONES	408,211,332	12,876,752	58,737,832	13814	479,825,916
SYS	7,458,619	86,912	350,088	2791	7,895,619
PRECISE	45,392,274	1,155,440	12,562,016	322	59,109,730
DWPROC	6,710,324	239,128	1,194,792	205	8,144,244
DSSUSER	4,985,220	174,304	742,136	97	5,901,660
NETSPO	5,907,293	86,032	657,384	51	6,650,709
...					
DEMERY	59,205	1,752	6,760	1	67,717
BSNMP	14,416	816	5,840	1	21,072
sum	489,039,559	14,826,608	75,968,544	17427	579,834,711

In the sample output we see that the *ajones* user holds the
most SQL areas. The application DBA user, *dwproc*,
holds a great deal less. Usually, the application owner
will hold the largest section of memory in a well-
designed system, followed by ad-hoc users using
properly designed SQL. In a situation where users aren't
using properly designed SQL statements, the ad-hoc
users will usually have the largest number of SQL areas
and hog the most memory. This is the case in the sample
report. Practice has shown that if a shared pool contains
greater than 7,000 to 10,000 SQL areas, the pool latch

has difficulty in keeping up and performance suffers. Again, the script shows the actual in-memory SQL areas for a specific user.

The script below shows the sample output from a report run against a user on the test system, *graphics_dba*.

🖫 **sqlmem.sql**

```
--***********************************************
--
--    Copyright © 2003 by Rampant TechPress Inc.
--
--    Free for non-commercial use.
--    For commercial licensing, e-mail info@rampant.cc
--
-- ***********************************************
column sql_text          format a60    heading Text word_wrapped
column sharable_mem                     heading Shared|Bytes
column persistent_mem                   heading Persistent|Bytes
column loads                            heading Loads
column users             format a15    heading "User"
column executions                         heading "Executions"
column users_executing                    heading "Used By"

ttitle "Users SQL Area Memory Use"
spool sqlmem
set long 2000 pages 59 lines 132
break on users

compute sum of sharable_mem on users
compute sum of persistent_mem on users
compute sum of runtime_mem on users

select username users, sql_text, Executions, loads,
users_executing,
 sharable_mem, persistent_mem
from   sys.v_$sqlarea a, dba_users b
where  a.parsing_user_id = b.user_id
 and b.username like upper('%&user_name%')
order by 3 desc,1;
spool off
pause Press enter to continue
clear columns
clear computes
clear breaks
set pages 22 lines 80
```

The following page shows a sample listing:

Shared Per. User	Text	Executions	Loads	Used By	Bytes	Bytes
GRAPHICS_DBA	BEGIN dbms_lob.read (:1, :2, :3, :4); END;	2121	1	0	10251	488
	alter session set nls language= 'AMERICAN' nls territory= 'AMERICA' nls_currency= '$' nls_iso_currency= 'AMERICA' nls_numeric_characters= '.,' nls_calENDar= 'GREGORIAN' nls_date_format= 'DD-MON-YY' nls_date_language= 'AMERICAN' nls_sort= 'BINARY'	7	1	0	3975	408
	BEGIN :1 := dbms_lob.getLength (:2); END;	6	1	0	9290	448
	SELECT TO_CHAR(image_seq.nextval) FROM dual	6	1	0	6532	484
	SELECT graphic_blob FROM internal_graphics WHERE graphic_id=10	2	1	0	5863	468
	SELECT RPAD(TO_CHAR(graphic_id),5)||':' ||RPAD(graphic_desc,30)||' : '||RPAD(graphic_type,10) FROM internal_graphics ORDER BY graphic_id	1	1	0	7101	472
	SELECT graphic_blob FROM internal_graphics WHERE graphic_id=12	1	1	0	6099	468
	SELECT graphic_blob FROM internal_graphics WHERE graphic_id=32	1	1	0	6079	468
	SELECT graphic_blob FROM internal_graphics WHERE graphic_id=4	1	1	0	6074	468
	SELECT graphic_blob FROM internal_graphics WHERE graphic_id=8	1	1	0	5962	468
******************* sum					67226	4640

Be warned that the script can generate a report of several hundred pages for a user with a large number of SQL areas (e.g., the *ajoshi* user in the previous report). What are the specific things to check in a user's SQL areas? First, check whether bind variables are used; bind variable usage is shown by the inclusion of variables such as ":1" or ":B" in the SQL text. Notice how the first four statements in the sample report use bind variables and are consequently reusable. Non-bind variables mean hard-coded values such as 'Missing' or '10' are used. Notice that most of the remaining statements in the report do not use bind variables, even though many of the SQL statements are nearly identical. This is one of the leading causes of shared pool misuse and results in useful SQL being drowned in tons of non-reusable garbage SQL.

The problem with non-reusable SQL is that it must still be checked by any new SQL inserted into the pool (actually its hash value is scanned). While a hash value scan may seem trivial, if the shared pool contains tens of thousands of SQL areas it can cause a performance bottleneck. How can we determine, without running a report for each of possibly hundreds of users, if we have garbage SQL in the shared pool?

The script below provides details on reuse of the SQL area by individual users. The view can be tailored to your environment if the limit on reuse (currently set at 1) is too restrictive. For example, in a recent tuning assignment, resetting the value to 12 resulted in nearly 70 percent of the SQL being rejected as garbage. In DSS or data warehouse systems, where rollups are performed by the month, bi-monthly or weekly values of 12, 24, or 52 might be advisable. The report below uses the view created from the script above.

💾 sql_garbage.sql

```
--*********************************************
--
--    Copyright © 2003 by Rampant TechPress Inc.
--
--    Free for non-commercial use.
--    For commercial licensing, e-mail info@rampant.cc
--
--   *********************************************
REM View to sort SQL into GOOD and GARBAGE
REM
CREATE OR REPLACE VIEW sql_garbage AS
SELECT    b.username users,
          SUM(a.sharable_mem+a.persistent_mem) Garbage,
          TO_NUMBER(null) good
FROM      sys.v_$sqlarea a, dba_users b
WHERE     (a.parsing_user_id = b.user_id and a.executions<=1)
GROUP BY b.username
   UNION
SELECT DISTINCT b.username users,
          TO_NUMBER(null) garbage,
          SUM(c.sharable_mem+c.persistent_mem) Good
FROM      dba_users b, sys.v_$sqlarea c
WHERE     (b.user_id = c.parsing_user_id and c.executions>1)
GROUP BY b.username;

column garbage format a14 heading 'Non-Shared SQL'
column good format a14 heading 'Shared SQL'
column good_percent format a14 heading 'Percent Shared'
column users format a14 heading users
column nopr noprint
set feedback off
ttitle 'Shared Pool Utilization'
spool sql_garbage

select 1 nopr, a.users users,
       to_char(a.garbage,'9,999,999,999') garbage,
       to_char(b.good,'9,999,999,999') good,
       to_char((b.good/(b.good+a.garbage))*100,'9,999,999.999')
        good_percent
from   sql_garbage a, sql_garbage b
where a.users=b.users
       and a.garbage is not null and b.good is not null
union
select 2 nopr, '-------------' users,
          '--------------' garbage,
          '-------------' good,
          '-------------' good_percent
from    dual
union
```

```
select 3 nopr, to_char(count(a.users)) users,
       to_char(sum(a.garbage),'9,999,999,999') garbage,
       to_char(sum(b.good),'9,999,999,999') good,
       to_char(((sum(b.good)/(sum(b.good)+sum(a.garbage)))*100),
       '9,999,999.999') good_percent
from   sql_garbage a, sql_garbage b
where  a.users=b.users
and    a.garbage is not null and b.good is not null
order by 1,3 desc
/
spool off
```

The next report script indicates which users aren't making good use of reusable SQL.

users	Non-Shared SQL	Shared SQL	Percent Shared
AJONES	371,387,006	1,007,366	.271
NETSPO	10,603,456	659,999	5.860
DCHUN	6,363,158	151,141	2.320
DSSUSER	5,363,057	824,865	13.330
MRCHDXD	4,305,330	600,824	12.246
DWPROC	2,690,086	4,901,400	64.564
CWOOD	946,199	239,604	20.206
TMANCEOR	877,644	93,323	9.611
GCMATCH	604,369	1,637,788	73.045
MAULT	445,566	3,737,984	89.350
PRECISE	205,564	46,342,150	99.558
BKUEHNE	154,754	35,858	18.812
SYS	146,811	9,420,434	98.465
SMANN	102,460	8,523,746	98.812
MRCHPHP	56,954	59,069	50.911
MRCHAEM	42,465	65,017	60.491
16	404,553,888	78,358,468	16.226

Notice that the *ajones* user only shows 0.271% shared SQL use, based on memory footprints. From the report, we would expect a low reuse value for *ajones* based on the information provided in earlier reports.

A final report shows SQL that is being generated over and over again, based on the first 90 characters. Of course, you can look at longer or shorter pieces of code by simply changing the call to the *substr()* function.

```
--*************************************************
--
--      Copyright © 2003 by Rampant TechPress Inc.
--
--      Free for non-commercial use.
--      For commercial licensing, e-mail info@rampant.cc
--
--    *********************************************

set lines 140 pages 55 verify off feedback off
col num_of_times heading 'Number|Of|Repeats'
col SQL heading 'SubString width - &&chars Characters'
col username format a15 heading 'User'
ttitle 'Similar SQL'
spool similar_sql&&chars
select b.username,substr(a.sql_text,1,&&chars) SQL,
count(a.sql_text) num_of_times from v$sqlarea a, dba_users b
where a.parsing_user_id=b.user_id
group by b.username,substr(a.sql_text,1,&&chars) having
count(a.sql_text)>&&num_repeats
order by count(a.sql_text) desc
/
spool off
undef chars
undef num_repeats
clear columns
set lines 80 pages 22 verify on feedback on
ttitle off
```

An example report generated by this script is shown below.

Number of Repeats	User	SubString - 90 Characters
142	SYS	INSERT INTO MONT3_TBL_SLA_FAILURES_LOG (ERROR_CODE,ERROR_TEXT,ERROR_FIELDS,ERROR_DATE) VAL
91	BO	update OBJ_M_TIMESTAMP set M_TMS_N_ENTITYTYPE = 2 , M_TMS_N_ENTITYID = 16 , M_TMS_N_BEGINT
83	BO	select pj.BATCH_ID, pj.DOCUMENT_ID, pj.USER_SUBMIT_ID, pj.PRIORITY, pj.FREQUENCY, pj.BEGIN
21	DWOWNER	SELECT ds.segment_name, ds.segment_type, ds.tablespace_name, ds.owner, f.file#, e.block#
21	SYS	INSERT INTO FTIN1_TBL_PMC_DATA_LOG (ERROR_CODE,ERROR_TEXT,ERROR_FIELDS,ERROR_DATE) VALUES (
21	DWOWNER	select fe.ts#, fs.file_id, fe.block#, fe.length FROM sys.dba_free_space fs, sys.fet$ fe, s
14	DWOWNER	SELECT tablespace_name, initial_extent, next_extent, min_extents, max_extents, pct
12	SYS	INSERT INTO FTIN1_TBL_SLA_FAILURES_LOG (ERROR_CODE,ERROR_TEXT,ERROR_FIELDS,ERROR_DATE) VAL
11	SYS	INSERT INTO FTIN1_TBL_NPO_DATA_LOG (ERROR_CODE,ERROR_TEXT,ERROR_FIELDS,ERROR_DATE) VALUES (
8	BO	select M_GENPAR_N_ID from OBJ_M_GENPAR where M_GENPAR_N_ID = 500 and M_GENPAR_N_APPLID = 9
7	SYS	GRANT SELECT ON DBA_
6	BO	select M_ACTL_N_ID, M_ACTOR_N_ID, M_ACTL_N_FATLINKID, M_ACTL_N_ACTORTYPE, M_ACTL_N_INFO, M
5	SYS	GRANT SELECT ON V_$S
4	BO	select M_ACTOR_N_ID, M_ACTOR_N_STATUS, M_ACTOR_N_LEVEL, M_ACTOR_N_AUTID, M_ACTOR_N_ENDING,
4	DWOWNER	SELECT tablespace_name, initial_extent, next_extent, min_extent, max_extent, pct_i
4	SYS	GRANT SELECT ON V_$L
4	SYS	alter session set nls_language= 'AMERICAN' nls_territory= 'AMERICA' nls_currency= '$' nls
4	SYS	INSERT INTO MES_TRANSACTION_LOG_INTERIM (TRANSACTION_KEY,LOT_KEY,PLANT_LOCATION,ACTUAL_DAT
4	SYS	GRANT SELECT ON dba_
4	GTRMAP1	select decode(transaction_name,'START',operation_name,'COMPLETE',from operation_name) oper
4	BO	select M_DOC_N_ID, M_RES_N_STATUS, M_DOC_N_REPOID, M_DOC_C_NAME, M_ACTOR_C_NAME, M_DOC_N_D

Conclusions about the shared pool

We have examined reports that show both gross and detailed shared pool usage, and whether or not shared areas are being reused. What can we do with this data? Ideally, we will use the results to size our shared pool properly. Here are a few general guidelines for shared pool sizing:

Guideline 1

If gross usage of the shared pool in a non-ad-hoc environment exceeds 95% (rises to 95% or greater and stays there), establish a shared pool size large enough to hold the fixed size portions. Then, pin reusable packages and procedures and increase the shared pool by 20% increments, until usage drops below 90% on average.

Guideline 2

If the shared pool shows a mixed ad-hoc and reuse environment, establish a shared pool size large enough to hold the fixed size portions. Pin the reusable packages and establish a comfort level above this required pool fill level, then establish a routine flush cycle to filter non-reusable code from the pool.

Guideline 3

If the shared pool shows that no reusable SQL is being used, establish a shared pool large enough to hold the fixed size portions, plus a few megabytes (usually not more than 40). Allow the least recently used (LRU) algorithm to manage the shared pool.

Using guidelines 1, 2, and 3, start a standard-sized system at around 40 megabytes. Notice that guideline 2 recommends a routine flush cycle be instituted. This is counter to the Oracle Support recommendation in their shared pool white papers, however, Oracle works from the assumption that proper SQL is being generated and that the SQL present in the shared pool is going to be resused. In a mixed environment, where there is a mixture of reusable and non-reusable SQL, the non-reusable SQL will act as a drag against the other SQL unless it is periodically removed by flushing. Shown below is a PL/SQL package that can be used by the *dbms_job* job queues to periodically flush the shared pool when it exceeds a specified percentage.

💾 Flush_it_proc.sql

```
--************************************************
--
--     Copyright © 2003 by Rampant TechPress Inc.
--
--     Free for non-commercial use.
--     For commercial licensing, e-mail info@rampant.cc
--
-- ************************************************

CREATE OR REPLACE PROCEDURE flush_it(
    p_free IN NUMBER, num_runs IN NUMBER) IS
--
CURSOR get_share IS
SELECT
  LEAST(MAX(b.value)/(1024*1024),SUM(a.bytes)/(1024*1024))
   FROM v$sgastat a, v$parameter b
 WHERE (a.pool='shared pool'
 AND a.name <> ('free memory'))
 AND b.name = 'shared_pool_size';
--
CURSOR get_var IS
 SELECT  value/(1024*1024)
 FROM v$parameter
 WHERE name = 'shared_pool_size';
--
CURSOR get_time IS
 SELECT sysdate FROM dual;
--
-- Following cursors from Steve Adams Nice_flush
```

```
--
  CURSOR reused_cursors IS
    SELECT address || ',' || hash_value
    FROM sys.v_$sqlarea
    WHERE executions > num_runs;
  cursor_string varchar2(30);
--
  CURSOR cached_sequences IS
    SELECT  sequence_owner, sequence_name
    FROM  sys.dba_sequences
    WHERE cache_size > 0;
  sequence_owner varchar2(30);
  sequence_name varchar2(30);
--
  CURSOR candidate_objects IS
    SELECT kglnaobj, decode(kglobtyp, 6, 'Q', 'P')
    FROM sys.x_$kglob
    WHERE inst_id = userenv('Instance') AND
      kglnaown = 'SYS' AND kglobtyp in (6, 7, 8, 9);
  object_name varchar2(128);
  object_type char(1);
--
-- end of Steve Adams Cursors
--
  todays_date       DATE;
  mem_ratio         NUMBER;
  share_mem         NUMBER;
  variable_mem      NUMBER;
  cur               INTEGER;
  sql_com    VARCHAR2(60);
  row_proc   NUMBER;
--
BEGIN
 OPEN get_share;
 OPEN get_var;
 FETCH get_share INTO share_mem;
 FETCH get_var INTO variable_mem;
 mem_ratio:=share_mem/variable_mem;
 IF mem_ratio>p_free/100 THEN
 --
 -- Following keep sections from Steve Adams nice_flush
 --
 BEGIN
  OPEN reused_cursors;
  LOOP
    FETCH reused_cursors INTO cursor_string;
    EXIT WHEN reused_cursors%notfound;
    sys.dbms_shared_pool.keep(cursor_string, 'C');
  END LOOP;
 END;
 BEGIN
  OPEN cached_sequences;
  LOOP
    FETCH cached_sequences INTO sequence_owner, sequence_name;
    EXIT WHEN cached_sequences%notfound;
    sys.dbms_shared_pool.keep(sequence_owner || '.' ||
sequence_name, 'Q');
  END LOOP;
 END;
```

```
  BEGIN
   OPEN candidate_objects;
   LOOP
     FETCH candidate_objects INTO object_name, object_type;
     EXIT WHEN candidate_objects%notfound;
     sys.dbms_shared_pool.keep('SYS.' || object_name,
object_type);
   END LOOP;
  END;
  --
  -- end of Steve Adams section
  --
   cur:=DBMS_SQL.OPEN_CURSOR;
   sql_com:='ALTER SYSTEM FLUSH SHARED_POOL';
   DBMS_SQL.PARSE(cur,sql_com,dbms_sql.v7);
   row_proc:=DBMS_SQL.EXECUTE(cur);
   DBMS_SQL.CLOSE_CURSOR(cur);
   OPEN get_time;
   FETCH get_time INTO todays_date;
   INSERT INTO dba_running_stats VALUES
     (
     'Flush of Shared Pool',1,35,todays_date,0
     );
   COMMIT;
  END IF;
END flush_it;
```

An example of a command to perform a flush once
every 30 minutes, but only when the pool reaches 95%
full would be:

```
VARIABLE x NUMBER;
BEGIN
dbms_job.submit(
:X,'BEGIN flush_it(95,24); END;',SYSDATE,'SYSDATE+(30/1440)');
END;
/
COMMIT;
```
(Always commit after assigning a job or the job will not be run and
queued)

There has been some discussion whether this really does
help performance. A test on a production instance was
run, where on day 1, there was no automated flushing,
and on day 2, automated flushing was utilized. Figure
2.3 is a series of graphs of performance indicators, flush
cycles, and users.

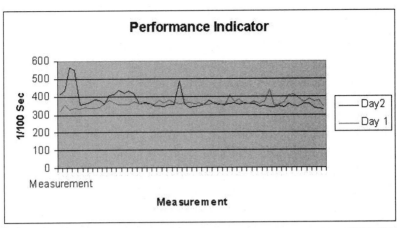

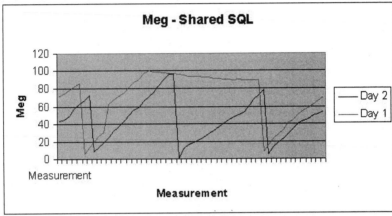

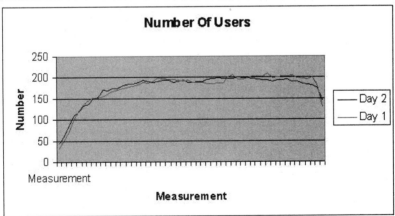

Figure 2.3 *Graphs Showing Effects of Flushing*

Oracle Internals Monitoring & Tuning Scripts

Notice the overall trend of the performance indicator between day 1 and day 2 in the graphs. On day 1 (the day with an initial flush, as indicated by the steep plunge on the pool utilization graph, followed by the buildup to maximum and the flattening of the graph), the performance indicator shows an upward trend. The performance indicator is a measure of how long the database takes to do a specific set of tasks (from the Q Diagnostic tool from Savant Corporation). An increase in the performance indicator shows a net decrease in performance. On day 2, the overall trend is downward, with the average value less than the average value from day 1. Overall, flushing improved the performance by 10 to 20 percent, as indicated by the performance indicator. Depending on the environment, improvements of up to 40-50 percent have been observed.

One factor complicating the analysis was several large batch jobs run on day 2, which weren't run on day 1. The results still show that flushing has a positive effect on performance, when the database is a mixed SQL environment with a large percentage of non-reusable SQL areas.

If the shared pool has already been over-allocated, guideline 3 may actually result in a decrease in the size of the shared pool. In this situation, the shared pool has become a cesspool filled with garbage SQL. After allocating enough memory for dictionary objects and other fixed areas, and ensuring that the standard packages and such are pinned, only maintain a few megabytes beyond this amount of memory for SQL statements. Since none of the code is being reused, the

---

hash search overhead should be reduced as much as possible; this is done by reducing the size of the available SQL area memory, so that the number of kept statements are as few as possible.

Pinning PL/SQL Packages in the Shared Pool

With all the rules discussed so far, the memory is usually allocated beyond that needed for fixed-size areas and pinned objects. How are the objects to be pinned determined? Generally speaking, any package, procedure, function, or cursor that is used frequently by the application should be pinned into the shared pool when the database is started. In current versions of Oracle the simple act of pinning a package, procedure or function using the *dbms_shared_pool* package will call it into memory.

The *dbms_shared_pool* package may have to be created in earlier releases of Oracle. The *dbms_shared_pool* package is built using the *dbmspool.sql* and *prvtpool.plb* scripts located in (UNIX) $ORACLE_HOME/rdbms/admin or (NT) x:\orant\rdbms\admin (where x: is the home drive for the install).

How are the packages, procedures, and functions to be pinned determined? Actually, Oracle has made this easy by providing the *v$db_object_cache* view. This view shows all the objects in the pool, and more importantly, how they are being utilized. The script below provides a list of objects that have been loaded more than once, and have executions greater than one. A sample output is also provided. A rule of thumb is that if an object is being frequently executed and frequently reloaded, it should be pinned into the shared pool.

🖫 Gen_keep.sql

```
--**********************************************
--
--     Copyright © 2003 by Rampant TechPress Inc.
--
--     Free for non-commercial use.
--     For commercial licensing, e-mail info@rampant.cc
--
-- **********************************************

set lines 132 feedback off verify off
set pages 0
spool keep_them.sql
select  'execute
dbms_shared_pool.keep('||chr(39)||OWNER||'.'||name||chr(39)||','
||

chr(39)||decode(type,'PACKAGE','P','PROCEDURE','P','FUNCTION','P
','SEQUENCE','Q',
                             'TRIGGER','R')||chr(39)||')'
from
 v$db_object_cache
where
 type not in ('NOT LOADED','NON-
EXISTENT','VIEW','TABLE','INVALID TYPE','CURSOR','PACKAGE BODY')
 and executions>loads and executions>1 and kept='NO'
order by owner,namespace,type,executions desc
/
spool off
```

The output from the above script is shown below.

```
execute dbms_shared_pool.keep('SYS.DICTIONARY_OBJ_OWNER','P')
execute dbms_shared_pool.keep('SYS.DICTIONARY_OBJ_NAME','P')
execute dbms_shared_pool.keep('SYS.PLITBLM','P')
execute dbms_shared_pool.keep('SYS.DBMS_STANDARD','P')
```

Triggers, cursors, packages, and procedures or functions can all be pinned. Note, only the package has to be pinned, not the package and package body.

Another criteria for determining whether an object should be pinned into the shared pool is its size. The *dbms_shared_pool.sizes* procedure searches the shared pool for any objects larger (in kilobytes) than the argument passed. Generally, the larger the size, the more likely that the object is a package, and it should probably be kept in the pool. Smaller objects tend to be individual queries and can be aged out of the pool. Remember, that the *dbms_shared_pool* procedure is not generally loaded automatically when an instance is built; the *dbmspool.sql* and *prvtpool.plb* scripts must be run from *internal* or *sys* users for it to be created. The use of *dbms_shared_pool.sizes* is shown below.

```
SQL> set serveroutput on size 4000;
SQL> execute sys.dbms_shared_pool.sizes(10);
SIZE(K) KEPT    NAME
------- ------  -------------------------------------------------------
139             SYS.STANDARD                    (PACKAGE)
56              SYS.DBMS_SHARED_POOL             (PACKAGE BODY)
31              SELECT TO_CHAR(SHARABLE_MEM / 1000 ,'999999') SZ,DECODE(KEPT_VE
                RSIONS,0,'          ',RPAD('YES(' || TO_CHAR(KEPT_VERSIONS)  |
                | ')' ,6)) KEEPED,RAWTOHEX(ADDRESS) || ',' || TO_CHAR(HASH
                _VALUE) NAME,SUBSTR(SQL_TEXT,1,354) EXTRA   FROM V$SQLAREA
                WHERE SHARABLE_MEM > :b1 * 1000   UNION SELECT TO_CHAR(SH
                ARABLE_MEM / 1000 ,'999999') SZ,DECODE(KEPT,'YES','YES
                (004D7F84,2008220828)           (CURSOR)
30              SYS.STANDARD                    (PACKAGE BODY)
27              SYS.DBMS_SHARED_POOL            (PACKAGE)
17              SYS.V$SQLAREA               (VIEW)
16              SYS.V$DB_OBJECT_CACHE       (VIEW)
15              insert into idl_ub2$(obj#,part,version,piece#,length,piece) val
                ues(:1,:2,:3,:4,:5,:6)
                (0027BA44,-512326869)           (CURSOR)
```

The 'set serveroutput' command in line 1 limits the size of the output buffer to 4000 bytes. This command is required. Perhaps in the future Oracle will incorporate the use of *util_file*, which would simply generate a report listing that could be reviewed as desired.

The script above indicates there is one large package in shared memory. A keep issued against this package would retain it. The results of this action are shown below.

```
SQL> execute dbms_shared_pool.keep('sys.standard');
PL/SQL procedure successfully completed.
SQL> execute dbms_shared_pool.sizes(130);
```

```
SIZE(K) KEPT   NAME
------- ------ ------------------------------------------------------
139     YES    SYS.STANDARD            (PACKAGE)
```

The keep issued against large packages, retaining them in memory, mitigates shared pool fragmentation resulting in the ORA-04031 error. Pinning the packages so they don't age out prevents smaller queries, cursors, and procedures from using the package space. If the packages are not pinned, they must seek a space large enough to reinstall themselves, leading to the ORA-04031 error. This error is supposedly eliminated in Oracle8, by changing the way the shared memory area is used. However, there have been some reports of errors on versions as late as 9.2.0.4.

Guideline 4

Determine the usage patterns of packages, procedures, functions, triggers, and cursors. Pin those that are frequently used.

The Shared Pool and the MTS

Using the Oracle multi-threaded server option (MTS) may require a dramatic increase in the size of the shared pool. This increase is due to the addition of the user global areas required for sorting and message queues. When using MTS, the *v$sgastat* values for MTS-related memory areas should be monitored, and the shared pool memory allocations adjusted accordingly.

Note: When using Oracle 8 and later version with MTS, the large pool feature should be used to pull the user global areas (UGA) and multi-threaded server queues

---

out of the shared pool area. This prevents the fragmentation problems that have been reported in shared pools. Large pool areas should also be used with parallel query and DML as well as when RMAN is used.

Large Pool Sizing

Sizing the large pool can be complex. If configured, the large pool must be at least 600 kilobytes in size. 600k is usually enough for most MTS applications. However, if PQO is also used in an Oracle8 environment, then the size of the large pool will increase dramatically. The *v$sgastat* dynamic performance view has a new column in Oracle8, *pool*. The *pool* column in the *v$sgastat* view contains the pool area where that particular type of object is being stored. By issuing a summation select against the *v$sgastat* view, a DBA can quickly determine the size of the large pool area currently being used.

```
SELECT name, SUM(bytes) FROM V$SGASTAT WHERE pool='LARGE POOL'
GROUP BY ROLLUP(name);
```

The select above should be used when an "ORA-04031: Unable to allocate 16084 bytes of shared memory ("large pool", "unknown object", "large pool hea", "PX large pool")" error is received with a configured large pool (the number of bytes specified may differ). When the select is run, the resulting summary number of bytes indicates the current size of the pool, and shows how close it is to the maximum, as specified in the initialization parameter *large_pool_size*. Generally, increasing the *large_pool* by up to 100% will eliminate the ORA-04031 errors.

Oracle8i allows the large pool to be sized automatically. If *parallel_automatic_tuning* is set to *true*, or if *parallel_max_servers* is set to a non-zero value, then the *large_pool_size* will be calculated. However, it can be over-ridden with an entry, manually specified, in the initialization file. Indeed, if an ORA-27102: Out of Memory error is received when either of these parameters (or both) is set, the *large_pool_size* must be manually set or the value for *parallel_max_servers* must be reduced. The following formula determines the set point for the *large_pool_size*, if it is not set manually:

```
(DOP^2*(4I-1)+2*DOP*3+4*DOP(I-1))*PEMS*USERS
Where
    DOP - Degree of Parallel calculated from #CPU/NODE * #NODES
    I - Number of threads/CPU
    PEMS - Parallel execution message size - set with
PARALLEL_EXECUTION_MESSAGE_SIZE
        initialization parameter, usually defaults to 2k or 4k
but can be larger.
    USERS - Number of concurrent users using parallel query
```

A 2k PEMS with 4 concurrent users results in a steadily increasing value for DOP. The memory size is a quadratic function ranging from around 4 MB for 10 CPUs, to 120 MB with 70 CPUs. This memory requirement is demonstrated in Figure 2.4.

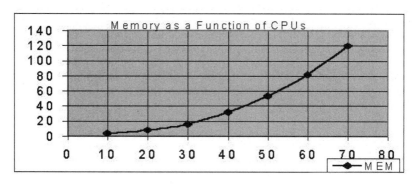

Figure 2.4 *Memory as a Function of CPUs*

On a NT4.0 Oracle8i, 8.1.3 test system there are 2 CPUs, set first at 2 threads per CPU (DOP of 4), and then at 4 threads per CPU (DOP of 8), with a message buffer of 4k. Multiple tests were performed, increasing the *parallel_max_servers* initialization parameter to see what the resulting increase in *large_pool_size* would be. The results were as follows:

```
PARALLEL_MAX_SERVERS DOP 4 LARGE_POOL_SIZE  DOP 8 LARGE_POOL_SIZE
4                           685,024 bytes           685,024 bytes
                            857,056 bytes           857,056 bytes
16                        1,151,968 bytes         1,545,184 bytes
```

Notice that for a small number of CPUs, the increase in the large pool size resulting from an increase in parallel max servers isn't affected by changes in the number of parallel threads, until the value of the threads is large with respect to the number of CPUs.

For non-PQO systems, a general rule of thumb is to allocate 5K of memory in the large pool area for each MTS user.

Guideline 5

With Oracle7, the shared pool size should be increased when using MTS to accommodate MTS messaging, queuing, and UGA requirements. In Oracle8, use the large pool to prevent MTS from affecting the shared pool areas. If using PQO, Oracle9 requires the large pool.

In current releases of Oracle the entire SQL statement is used to generate the statement hash value. You should never see duplicate hashes in 8i, 9i and subsequent releases. A script to monitor for duplicate hash values is shown below.

🖫 shared_hash.sql

```
--***************************************************
--
--    Copyright © 2003 by Rampant TechPress Inc.
--
--    Free for non-commercial use.
--    For commercial licensing, e-mail info@rampant.cc
--
-- ***************************************************

Rem:
rem: FUNCTION: Shows by user who has possible
rem:           SQL reuse problems
rem:
column total_hash                          heading 'Total
Hash|Values'
column same_hash                           heading 'SQL
With|Same Hash'
column u_hash_ratio        format 999.999   heading 'SQL
Sharing|Hash'
ttitle 'Shared Hash Value Report'
spool shared_hash.lst
break on report
compute sum of total_hash on report
compute sum of same_hash on report
select
     a.username,
     count(b.hash_value) total_hash,
     count(b.hash_value)-count(unique(b.hash_value)) same_hash,
(count(unique(b.hash_value))/count(b.hash_value))*100
u_hash_ratio
from
     dba_users a,
     v$sqlarea b
where
     a.user_id=b.parsing_user_id
group by
     a.username;
clear computes
```

The script above produces a report similar to a previous one.

The report below shows which users are generating SQL that hash to the same values. Once a user is isolated, the script below can be run to find the bad SQL statements.

USERNAME	Total Hash Values	SQL With Same Hash	SQL Sharing Hash
AULTM	129	0	100.000
DCARS	6484	0	100.000
MCNAIRT	20	0	100.000
PASSMAP	2	0	100.000
QDBA	109	0	100.000
RCAPS	270	0	100.000
RCOM	342	0	100.000
REPORTS1	28	0	100.000
SECURITY_ADMIN	46	0	100.000
SYS	134	0	100.000
sum	7564	0	

🖫 sqlmem.sql

```
--***********************************************
--
--    Copyright © 2003 by Rampant TechPress Inc.
--
--    Free for non-commercial use.
--    For commercial licensing, e-mail info@rampant.cc
--
-- ***********************************************

rem
rem FUNCTION: Generate a report of SQL Area Memory Usage
rem           showing SQL Text and memory catagories
rem
rem sqlmem.sql
rem
column sql_text        format a60    heading Text word_wrapped
column sharable_mem                  heading Shared|Bytes
column persistent_mem                heading Persistent|Bytes
column loads                         heading Loads
column users           format a15    heading "User"
column executions                heading "Executions"
column users_executing              heading "Used By"
start title132 "Users SQL Area Memory Use"
spool rep_out\&db\sqlmem
set long 2000 pages 59 lines 132
break on users
compute sum of sharable_mem on users
compute sum of persistent_mem on users
compute sum of runtime_mem on users
select username users, sql_text, Executions, loads,
users_executing,
sharable_mem, persistent_mem
from sys.v_$sqlarea a, dba_users b
where a.parsing_user_id = b.user_id
and b.username like upper('%&user_name%')
order by 3 desc,1;
spool off
```

Oracle Internals Monitoring & Tuning Scripts

```
pause Press enter to continue
clear columns
clear computes
clear breaks
set pages 22 lines 80
ttitle off
```

If you see duplicate hash values, a fast way to find the
duplicate hash values is to do a self-join, filtering out the
duplicate hash values. This may sound easy, but
remember, the *v$* tables have no rowids, so the classic
methods cannot be used. Another column will have to
be found that is different when the *hash_value* column in
v$sqlarea is the same. Consider the select that follows:

```
select
   a.hash_value
from
   v$sqlarea a,
   v$sqlarea b
where
   a.hash_value=b.hash_value
and
   a.FIRST_LOAD_TIME != b.FIRST_LOAD_TIME
```

This select should indicate the problem hash values. It is
then a simple matter to go back to the *v$sqlarea* table and
isolate the actual text. Long statements require special
care to make sure that bind variables are used to prevent
this hashing problem. Another remedy for long
statements is to use views to store values at an
intermediate state, thus reducing the size of the variable
portion of the SQL.

Guideline 6

Use bind variables, PL/SQL (procedures or functions),
and views to reduce the size of large SQL statements in
order to prevent hashing problems.

The Shared Pool and the MTS   **91**

Disk IO and the Shared Pool

The Pcode versions of all current SQL commands that haven't been aged out of the shared pool are contained in the shared SQL area. Numerous statistics are available via the *v$sqlarea* DPT. The text of SQL statements in the shared pool can be retrieved (at least the first tens of bytes) from the *v$sqltext* DPT.

The report below displays the SQL statements with the greatest amount of disk reads (these will probably be the ones you will want to review and tune).

🖫 **sqldrd.sql**

```
--*************************************************
--
--      Copyright © 2003 by Rampant TechPress Inc.
--
--      Free for non-commercial use.
--      For commercial licensing, e-mail info@rampant.cc
--
--  *************************************************
DEFINE access_level = 1000 (NUMBER)
COLUMN parsing_user_id FORMAT 9999999 HEADING 'User Id'
COLUMN executions   FORMAT 9999     HEADING 'Exec'
COLUMN sorts                FORMAT 99999     HEADING 'Sorts'
COLUMN command_type         FORMAT 99999     HEADING 'CmdT'
COLUMN disk_reads   FORMAT 999,999,999 HEADING 'Block Reads'
COLUMN sql_text     FORMAT a40      HEADING 'Statement'
WORD_WRAPPED
SET LINES 130 VERIFY OFF FEEDBACK OFF
ttitle 'SQL Statements With High Reads'
SPOOL sqldrd.lis

SELECT
    parsing_user_id,
    executions,
    sorts,
    command_type,
    disk_reads,
    sql_text
FROM
    v$sqlarea
WHERE
    disk_reads > &&access_level
ORDER BY
```

```
     disk_reads;

SPOOL OFF
SET LINES 80 VERIFY ON FEEDBACK ON
```

The following is sample output from this script.

```
User
Id    Exec Sorts CmdT Block Reads Statement
----  ---- ----- ---- ----------- --------------------------------------
   0   403     0    3          11 select f.file#, f.block#, f.ts#,
                                   f.length from fet$ f, ts$ t where
                                   t.ts#=f.ts# and t.dflextpct!=0

   0    11     0    3          11 select order#,columns,types from
                                   access$ where d_obj#=:1

   0    12     0    3          12 select /*+ index(idl_ub1$ i_idl_ub11)
                                   +*/ piece#,length,piece from idl_ub1$
                                   where obj#=:1 and part=:2 and
                                   version=:3 order by piece#

   5    34     0    3          13 SELECT NAME,VALUE   FROM V$SYSSTAT
                                        WHERE NAME = 'db block gets'

   0    12     0    3          14 select /*+ index(idl_ub2$ i_idl_ub21)
                                   +*/ piece#,length,piece from idl_ub2$
                                   where obj#=:1 and part=:2 and
                                   version=:3 order by piece#

   0    17     0    3          27 select file#, block#, ts# from seg$
                                   where type# = 3

   0     1     1    3          79 select distinct d.p_obj#,d.p_timestamp
                                   from sys.dependency$ d, obj$ o where
                                   d.p_obj#>=:1 and d.d_obj#=o.obj# and
                                   o.status!=5

   5    34     0   47          90 DECLARE job BINARY_INTEGER := :job;
                                   next_date DATE := :mydate;   broken
                                   BOOLEAN := FALSE; BEGIN hitratio;
                                   :mydate := next_date; IF broken THEN :b
                                   := 1; ELSE :b := 0; END IF; END;
```

The sample report above was generated to force a read count of 10. Usually, disk reads will be in the range specified by the define statement. By tuning those statements which show large amounts of disk reads, the overall performance of the application is increased.

In Oracle9i the *v$sqlarea* DPT has been expanded to include timing data related to total elapsed time and elapse CPU time. These timing statistics help the DBA to monitor for SQL that is using the majority of time for its parsing and execution. The following select shows

how to pull the top X SQL statements from the *v$sqlarea*
DPT.

```
SELECT * FROM (
SELECT
sql_text,
ceil(cpu_time/greatest(executions,1)) ave_cpu_time,
ceil(elapsed_time/greatest(executions,1)) ave_elapsed_time,
ceil(disk_reads/greatest(executions,1)) ave_disk_reads,
persistent_mem per_mem, runtime_mem run_mem,
ceil(sorts/greatest(executions,1)) ave_sorts,
ceil(parse_calls/greatest(executions,1)) ave_parse_calls,
ceil(Buffer_gets/greatest(executions,1)) ave_buffer_gets,
ceil(rows_processed/greatest(executions,1)) ave_row_proc,
ceil(Serializable_aborts/greatest(executions,1)) ave_ser_aborts
FROM
v$sqlarea
WHERE
Disk_reads/greatest(executions,1)>&&disk_reads
OR
Cpu_time/greatest(executions,1)>&&cpu_time
OR
Elapsed_time/greatest(executions,1)>&&elapsed_time
order by elapsed_time, cpu_time, disk_reads)
where rownum<&&num_sql
/
```

An example result from the above SELECT would
resemble:

SQL	AVG CPU Time	AVG Elap Time	AVG Disk Reads	Per. Mem	Run. Mem	AVG Sorts	AVG Parse Calls	AVG Buff Gets	AVG Rows Proc	AVG Ser. Aborts
SELECT INET_ADDRESS, PORT, LISTENER, PRESENTATION, OPTIONS FROM AURORADYNREG	0	10000	2	792	6520	0	1	31	2	0
select schema, classname from aurora$startup$classes$	0	10000	2	624	5344	0	1	19	2	0
SELECT max(version) FROM "SYS"."JAVA$POLICY$SHARED$TABLE"	0	5000	1	568	1656	0	1	11	1	0
SELECT /* DBA_UTIL. GET_DELTA */ :b4-a.value FROM dba_running_stats a WHERE a.name=:b3 and a.meas_date between :b1-35/1440 and :b1-25/1440	82	82	0	648	2880	0	1	3	0	0

By monitoring not only disk reads, but other performance characteristics such as CPU and total elapsed time, the DBA gets a full picture of SQL code usage and problem areas. Notice how the script calculates the average value per execution for the aggregated values stored in *v$sqlarea*.

Monitoring Library and Data Dictionary Caches

Much of this chapter has discussed the shared SQL area of the shared pool. Let's wrap up with a high-level look at the library and data dictionary caches. The library cache area is monitored via the *v$librarycache* view and contains the SQL area, PL/SQL area, table, index, and cluster cache areas. The data dictionary caches contain cache areas for all data dictionary related definitions.

The script below generates a report on the library caches. The items of particular interest in the report are the various ratios, which are shown further down.

🖫 **libcache.sql**

```
--********************************************
--
--    Copyright © 2003 by Rampant TechPress Inc.
--
--    Free for non-commercial use.
--    For commercial licensing, e-mail info@rampant.cc
--
--  ********************************************

rem FUNCTION: Generate a library cache report
column namespace                      heading "Library Object"
column gets            format 9,999,999 heading "Gets"
column gethitratio     format 999.99    heading "Get Hit%"
column pins            format 9,999,999 heading "Pins"
column pinhitratio     format 999.99    heading "Pin Hit%"
column reloads         format 99,999    heading "Reloads"
column invalidations   format 99,999    heading "Invalid"
```

```
column db format a10
set pages 58 lines 80
ttitle "Library Caches Report"
define output = lib_cache
spool &output

select
    namespace,
    gets,
    gethitratio*100 gethitratio,
    pins,
    pinhitratio*100 pinhitratio,
    reloads,
    invalidations
from
    v$librarycache;

spool off
pause Press enter to continue
set pages 22 lines 80
ttitle off
undef output
```

Look at the example output below. All Get Hit% (gethitratio in the view) are greater than 80-90 percent. This is the desired range. Notice that the Pin Hit% is also greater than 90%. This is also to be desired.

Library Object	Gets	Get Hit%	Pins	Pin Hit%	Reloads	Invalid
SQL AREA	5,628,059	98.31	28,080,373	99.26	20,566	20,322
TABLE/PROCEDURE	7,140,597	99.15	16,876,602	97.79	74,252	0
BODY	263,096	99.75	259,497	93.32	16,645	0
TRIGGER	5,288	96.41	5,342	92.25	147	0
INDEX	530,725	97.12	530,685	94.40	0	0
CLUSTER	3,967	98.89	4,266	98.05	0	0
OBJECT	0	100.00	0	100.00	0	0
PIPE	792,503	100.00	792,578	100.00	0	0

8 rows selected.

The other tuning goals are to reduce reloads to as small a value as possible (this is done by proper sizing and pinning), and to reduce invalidations. Invalidations happen when, for one reason or another, an object becomes unusable. However, if you must use flushing of the shared pool reloads, invalidations may occur as objects are swapped in and out of the shared pool. Proper pinning can reduce the number of objects reloaded and invalidated.

Guideline 7

If no flushing is used, increase the shared pool size to reduce reloads and invalidations and increase hit ratios.

The data dictionary caches used to be tuned individually through several initialization parameters. Now they are internally controlled. The script below can be used to monitor the overall hit ratio for the data dictionary caches.

💾 **ddcache.sql**

```
--***************************************************
--
--    Copyright © 2003 by Rampant TechPress Inc.
--
--    Free for non-commercial use.
--    For commercial licensing, e-mail info@rampant.cc
--
--    ***************************************************

ttitle "DD Cache Hit Ratio"
spool ddcache
SELECT
    (SUM(getmisses)/SUM(gets))*100 RATIO
FROM
    v$rowcache;
spool off
pause Press enter to continue
ttitle off
```

Here is the output from the script above:

```
    RATIO
---------
 1.273172
```

The reported ratio should always be less than 1. The ratio corresponds to the number of times out of 100 that the database engine searched the cache without finding anything. A dictionary cache miss is more expensive than a data block buffer miss, so if the ratio approaches 1, increase the size of the shared pool. If the ratio is close to 1, the internal algorithm isn't allocating enough memory to the data dictionary caches.

Guideline 8

If the data dictionary cache ratio is greater than 1.0, increase the size of the shared pool.

Shared Pool Advisor in Oracle9*i*

Oracle9i also provides the *v$shared_pool_advice* DPT which like its other advisor views provides estimates as to the effects of increasing or decreasing the monitored parameter, in this case, *shared_pool_size*. A script to pull information form the *v$shared_pool_advice* view is shown below:

🖫 shared_pool_adv.sql

```
--*************************************************
--
--    Copyright © 2003 by Rampant TechPress Inc.
--
--    Free for non-commercial use.
--    For commercial licensing, e-mail info@rampant.cc
--
--  *************************************************
ttitle 'Shared Pool Advice'
spool shared_pool_adv
select shared_pool_size_for_estimate est_size,
shared_pool_size_factor factor,
estd_lc_size, estd_lc_time_saved, estd_lc_memory_object_hits
hits
from v$shared_pool_advice
/
spool off
ttitle off
```

An example output from this script is shown below.

Shared Pool Advice

EST_SIZE	FACTOR	ESTD_LC_SIZE	ESTD_LC_TIME_SAVED	HITS
24	.5	1	21	671
32	.6667	1	21	671
40	.8333	1	21	671
48	1	1	21	671
56	1.1667	1	21	671
64	1.3333	1	21	671
72	1.5	1	21	671
80	1.6667	1	21	671
88	1.8333	1	21	671
96	2	1	21	671

10 rows selected.

As you can see this view provides data that can be used in sizng the shared pool, however, I have found it fairly difficult to understand the application of the data to tuning the pool and prefer my own methods.

Shared Pool Summary

This chapter has covered a lot of territory. It should be clear that simply increasing the size of the shared pool is an insufficient approach to a tuning problem. Examine the shared pool in detail and tune what needs to be tuned; don't just throw memory at a problem until it submerges. Indeed, in some cases, increasing the size of the shared pool may harm performance, while decreasing the size may be advisable. The chapter provides seven general guidelines for tuning the shared pool. The shared pool is vital to the proper performance of the Oracle database - it must be properly tuned or it will drown in bad performance.

In the next chapter, we'll look at the data buffer areas and how to tune them.

Data Buffer Internals Scripts

The buffer cache memory area stores data from tables, indexes, rollback segments, clusters, and sequences. All data must go through the Oracle db block buffers (except for special types of sorts) to get to disk or to get to the user from disk. By ensuring that enough buffers are available for transient storage of these data items, execution speed can be increased by reducing disk reads.

Oracle7 and early Oracle8 releases only had the "normal" buffer areas. With Oracle8i, and subsequent releases, the buffer area is subdivided into KEEP and RECYCLE buffer areas. In 9i and subsequent releases you may further subdivide the default cache area into multiple sub-areas with various block sizes (2, 4, 8, 16 and 32K blocksize) Later in the chapter, we will examine how these areas interact and how they should be tuned and sized.

Classic DB Block Buffer Tuning

The relationship between "logical", or cache hits, versus "physical", or disk hits, is indicated by several statistics, including "db block gets", "consistent gets" (their sum is logical reads), and "physical reads" from the *v$sysstat* table. The statistic called the "hit ratio" is determined by the simple formula:

```
logical reads = db_block_gets+consistent_gets
hit ratio(%) = ((logical reads - physical reads) / logical
reads) * 100 .
```

If the hit ratio is less than 80 to 90 percent in a loaded and running database, the allocated buffers may be insufficient. If the hit ratio is too low, increase the *init.ora* parameter *db_block_buffers*. However, a high hit ratio does not always indicate a healthy buffer area.

Monitoring the Hit Ratio

The PL/SQL procedure shown below can be used to periodically load the hit ratio, usage, and number of users into a table for later review. The script can be run at any interval the DBA chooses, with minor changes. The script provides valuable information about peak usage times and the hit ratio during those times. By adding columns, other statistics can be gathered as desired. A script suitable for this is shown later in the section.

Many DBAs make the common mistake of monitoring only the cumulative hit ratio. Remember, all the statistics are cumulative therefore any ratio or calculated value will also be cumulative. The statistics can be monitored over discrete time periods by placing them in a holding table, as the StatsPack reports do, and then calculating deltas and applying the ratios to the deltas. For instantaneous or period hit ratio a table must be created to store this information in order to derive instantaneous or period hit ratios. The structure of the table is shown below.

```
CREATE TABLE
   hit_ratios
(
   check_date        date,
   check_hour            number,
   db_block_gets     number,
   consistent            number,
```

```
phy_reads          number,
hitratio           number,
period_hit_ratio   number,
period_usage       number,
users              number)
STORAGE (INITIAL 10K NEXT 10K PCTINCREASE 0);
```

A unique index on *check_date, check_hour* should also be
created to prevent duplicate entries. The sample SQL
script shown below can be used to run a PL/SQL
procedure to gather the hit ratio and usage from
SQL*Plus. This is done through the use of UNIX cron
or a Windows scheduler, such as WINAT (available in
the NT Toolkit).

🖫 run_b_hratio.sql

```
--************************************************
--
--    Copyright © 2003 by Rampant TechPress Inc.
--
--    Free for non-commercial use.
--    For commercial licensing, e-mail info@rampant.cc
--
--    ************************************************
REM PURPOSE :RUN PL/SQL PROCEDURE TO LOAD HIT RATIO AND USAGE
DATA
REM USE       :FROM RUN_B_HRATIO.COM
REM Limitations    : None
REM Revisions:
REM Date    Modified By    Reason For change
REM 10-JUL-1992    M. AULT INITIAL CREATE
REM 22-Jun-1997
execute hitratio;
exit
```

The procedure below can be scheduled to run hourly
using the Oracle job queues. If you want it to run with
more or less frequency, the PL/SQL procedure can be
modified. If the decision is made to run the script as
needed on a manual basis, the command is executed in
the SQLPLUS environment. In this case, a small file
consisting of an EXECUTE command should be built;

this file is the one actually run by the batch scheduling program. The file should look something like the script shown above.

💾 Hit_ratio_proc.sql

```
--*************************************************
--
--   Copyright © 2003 by Rampant TechPress Inc.
--
--   Free for non-commercial use.
--   For commercial licensing, e-mail info@rampant.cc
--
-- *************************************************
CREATE OR REPLACE PROCEDURE HITRATIO IS
    c_date   DATE;
    c_hour   NUMBER;
    h_ratio       NUMBER;
    con_gets      NUMBER;
    db_gets       NUMBER;
    p_reads       NUMBER;
    stat_name     CHAR(64);
    temp_name     CHAR(64);
    stat_val      NUMBER;
    users   NUMBER;
BEGIN
  SELECT TO_CHAR(sysdate,'DD-MON-YY') INTO c_date FROM DUAL;
  SELECT TO_CHAR(sysdate,'HH24') INTO c_hour FROM DUAL;
  SELECT
    name, value
  INTO
    temp_name, stat_val
  FROM
    v$sysstat
  WHERE
    NAME = 'db block gets';
  db_gets:=stat_val;
  dbms_output.put_line(temp_name||'='||to_char(db_gets));
  SELECT
    name, value
  INTO
    temp_name, stat_val
  FROM
    v$sysstat
  WHERE
    name = 'consistent gets';
  con_gets:=stat_val;
  dbms_output.put_line(temp_name||'='||to_char(con_gets));
  SELECT
    name, value
  INTO
    temp_name, stat_val
  FROM
```

```
      v$sysstat
  WHERE
    name = 'physical reads';
  p_reads:=stat_val;
  dbms_output.put_line(temp_name||'='||to_char(p_reads));
  SELECT COUNT(*)
  INTO users
  FROM v$session
  WHERE username IS NOT NULL;
  dbms_output.put_line('Users='||to_char(users));
    H_RATIO := (((DB_GETS+CON_GETS-
p_reads)/(DB_GETS+CON_GETS))*100);
    dbms_output.put_line('h_ratio='||to_char(h_ratio));
    INSERT INTO  hit_ratios
      VALUES
(c_date,c_hour,db_gets,con_gets,p_reads,h_ratio,0,0,users);
  COMMIT;
  UPDATE hit_ratios SET period_hit_ratio =
    (SELECT ROUND((((h2.consistent-
h1.consistent)+(h2.db_block_gets-h1.db_block_gets)-
      (h2.phy_reads-h1.phy_reads))/((h2.consistent-
h1.consistent)+
      (h2.db_block_gets-h1.db_block_gets)))*100,2)
    FROM hit_ratios h1, hit_ratios h2
    WHERE h2.check_date = hit_ratios.check_date
    AND h2.check_hour = hit_ratios.check_hour
    AND ((h1.check_date = h2.check_date AND h1.check_hour+1 =
h2.check_hour)
    OR(h1.check_date+1 = h2.check_date AND h1.check_hour =
'23' AND h2.check_hour='0')))
  WHERE period_hit_ratio = 0;
  COMMIT;
  UPDATE hit_ratios SET period_usage =
    (SELECT ((h2.consistent-h1.consistent)+(h2.db_block_gets-
h1.db_block_gets))
    FROM hit_ratios h1, hit_ratios h2 where h2.check_date =
hit_ratios.check_date
      AND h2.check_hour = hit_ratios.check_hour
      AND ((h1.check_date = h2.check_date AND h1.check_hour+1 =
h2.check_hour)
      OR (h1.check_date+1 = h2.check_date
      AND h1.check_hour = '23' and h2.check_hour='0')))
  WHERE period_USAGE = 0;
  COMMIT;
  EXCEPTION
    WHEN ZERO_DIVIDE THEN
    INSERT INTO  hit_ratios  VALUES
(c_date,c_hour,db_gets,con_gets,p_reads,0,0,0,users);
    COMMIT;
END;
/
```

The procedure above is designed for hourly monitoring
of the hit ratio. The script can be called from a standard
SQL script similar to the first script shown. Once the

script completes, it is rescheduled to run the next hour. Of course, it is easier to use the *dbms_job* package that allows Oracle to execute the procedure automatically.

The next script demonstrates how this is done. To use a job queue, the initialization parameters *job_queue_processes* and *job_queue_interval* have to be set, and the instance restarted. The hit ratio for the previous hour is calculated, as is the cumulative hit ratio and the usage as a function of read/write activity.

```
DECLARE
jobno NUMBER;
BEGIN
dbms_job.submit (jobno, 'HITRATIO;',sysdate,'sysdate+1');
dbms_output.put_line(TO_CHAR(jobno));
END;
```

Note: There must be a semi-colon at the end of the 'HITRATIO' statement.

⊟ hrsumm.sql

```
--************************************************
--
--    Copyright © 2003 by Rampant TechPress Inc.
--
--    Free for non-commercial use.
--    For commercial licensing, e-mail info@rampant.cc
--
-- ************************************************

REM
REM NAME      :HRSUMM.SQL
REM FUNCTION:GENERATE SUMMARY REPORT OF PERIOD HIT RATIOS AND
USAGE
REM FUNCTION:BETWEEN TWO DATES
REM USE       :FROM SQLPlus
REM Limitations    : None
REM Revisions:
REM Date    Modified By    Reason For change
REM 10-JUL-1992    M.AULT  INITIAL CREATE
REM 23-Jun-1997 M.AULT      Verify against 8
REM
SET VERIFY OFF PAGES 58 NEWPAGE 0
ttitle "HIT RATIO AND USAGE FOR &&CHECK_DATE1 TO &&CHECK_DATE2"
DEFINE output = hrsumm.lis
SPOOL &output
```

```
SELECT
    check_date,
    check_hour,
    period_hit_ratio,
    period_usage,
    users
FROM
    hit_ratios
WHERE
    check_date BETWEEN '&&check_date1' AND '&&check_date2'
ORDER BY
    check_date,check_hour;
SPOOL OFF
PAUSE Press return to continue
```

Here is a sample listing of the output from the script shown above:

CHECK_DAT	CHECK_HOUR	PERIOD_HIT_RATIO	PERIOD_USAGE	USERS
22-JUN-97	13			1
22-JUN-97	15			2
22-JUN-97	16	97.76	2098	2
22-JUN-97	17	100	1066	2
22-JUN-97	18	100	1098	2
22-JUN-97	19	100	1067	2
22-JUN-97	20	100	1096	2
22-JUN-97	21	100	1066	2
22-JUN-97	22	100	1096	2
22-JUN-97	23	100	1067	2
23-JUN-97	0	100	1096	2
23-JUN-97	1	100	1073	2
23-JUN-97	2	100	1096	2
23-JUN-97	3	100	1067	2
23-JUN-97	4	100	1324	2
23-JUN-97	5	100	1067	2

16 rows selected.

Note: The hit ratios of 100 are a result of the way the system treats purely internal (V$) requests and an artifact of the calculation process.

The problem with sporadic monitoring of hit ratios is that the DBA may catch the system at a low point, or just when the database usage has switched from one user to another on a different application. All of this can contribute to incorrect hit ratio results. The use of a periodic script to monitor hit ratios tends to even out these fluctuations and provides a more accurate statistic.

Another problem with the hit ratio as it is described in the Oracle manuals, is that it is a running average, a cumulative value. This results in low readings when the database is started and high readings after it has been running.

Using decode and pad statements, the hit ratio data can be plotted on any printer as a graph. This technique can be used to plot just about any data set, if the numbers are normalized to between zero and one hundred. As you can see in the following listing, the cumulative hit ratio graph stayed fairly constant for the period, while the actual or period hit ratio varied between 18.78 and 92.95 percent. In fact, the cumulative hit ratio will reach a steady, slowly increasing value, shortly after startup.

🖫 hratio_report.sql

```
--*******************************************
--
--     Copyright © 2003 by Rampant TechPress Inc.
--
--     Free for non-commercial use.
--     For commercial licensing, e-mail info@rampant.cc
--
--  *******************************************

rem host SET TERM/WID=132 REM: For VMS only, won't work under
UNIX
SET LINES 131 NEWPAGE 0 VERIFY OFF PAGES 180 SPACE 0 FEEDBACK
OFF COLUMN HR FORMAT 99
ttitle "Period HR for &&check_date1 TO &&check_date2"
DEFINE output = 'phrgrph.lis'
SPOOL &output

SELECT
  check_hour hr,
  DECODE(ROUND(period_hit_ratio),0,'o',NULL) zchk0,
  DECODE(ROUND(period_hit_ratio),1,'o',NULL) chk1,
  DECODE(ROUND(period_hit_ratio),2,'o',NULL) chk2,
```

```
DECODE(ROUND(period_hit_ratio),3,'o',NULL) chk3,
DECODE(ROUND(period_hit_ratio),4,'o',NULL) chk4,
DECODE(ROUND(period_hit_ratio),5,'o',NULL) chk5,
DECODE(ROUND(period_hit_ratio),6,'o',NULL) chk6,
DECODE(ROUND(period_hit_ratio),7,'o',NULL) chk7,
DECODE(ROUND(period_hit_ratio),8,'o',NULL) chk8,
DECODE(ROUND(period_hit_ratio),9,'o',NULL) chk9,
DECODE(ROUND(period_hit_ratio),10,'o',NULL) chk10,
DECODE(ROUND(period_hit_ratio),11,'o',NULL) chk11,
DECODE(ROUND(period_hit_ratio),12,'o',NULL) chk12,
DECODE(ROUND(period_hit_ratio),13,'o',NULL) chk13,
DECODE(ROUND(period_hit_ratio),14,'o',NULL) chk14,
DECODE(ROUND(period_hit_ratio),15,'o',NULL) chk15,
DECODE(ROUND(period_hit_ratio),16,'o',NULL) chk16,
DECODE(ROUND(period_hit_ratio),17,'o',NULL) chk17,
DECODE(ROUND(period_hit_ratio),18,'o',NULL) chk18,
DECODE(ROUND(period_hit_ratio),19,'o',NULL) chk19,
DECODE(ROUND(period_hit_ratio),20,'o',NULL) chk20,
DECODE(ROUND(period_hit_ratio),21,'o',NULL) chk21,
DECODE(ROUND(period_hit_ratio),22,'o',NULL) chk22,
DECODE(ROUND(period_hit_ratio),23,'o',NULL) chk23,
DECODE(ROUND(period_hit_ratio),24,'o',NULL) chk24,
DECODE(ROUND(period_hit_ratio),25,'o',NULL) chk25,
DECODE(ROUND(period_hit_ratio),26,'o',NULL) chk26,
DECODE(ROUND(period_hit_ratio),27,'o',NULL) chk27,
DECODE(ROUND(period_hit_ratio),28,'o',NULL) chk28,
DECODE(ROUND(period_hit_ratio),29,'o',NULL) chk29,
DECODE(ROUND(period_hit_ratio),30,'o',NULL) chk30,
DECODE(ROUND(period_hit_ratio),31,'o',NULL) chk31,
DECODE(ROUND(period_hit_ratio),32,'o',NULL) chk32,
DECODE(ROUND(period_hit_ratio),33,'o',NULL) chk33,
DECODE(ROUND(period_hit_ratio),34,'o',NULL) chk34,
DECODE(ROUND(period_hit_ratio),35,'o',NULL) chk35,
DECODE(ROUND(period_hit_ratio),36,'o',NULL) chk36,
DECODE(ROUND(period_hit_ratio),37,'o',NULL) chk37,
DECODE(ROUND(period_hit_ratio),38,'o',NULL) chk38,
DECODE(ROUND(period_hit_ratio),39,'o',NULL) chk39,
DECODE(ROUND(period_hit_ratio),40,'o',NULL) chk40,
DECODE(ROUND(period_hit_ratio),41,'o',NULL) chk41,
DECODE(ROUND(period_hit_ratio),42,'o',NULL) chk42,
DECODE(ROUND(period_hit_ratio),43,'o',NULL) chk43,
DECODE(ROUND(period_hit_ratio),44,'o',NULL) chk44,
DECODE(ROUND(period_hit_ratio),45,'o',NULL) chk45,
DECODE(ROUND(period_hit_ratio),46,'o',NULL) chk46,
DECODE(ROUND(period_hit_ratio),47,'o',NULL) chk47,
DECODE(ROUND(period_hit_ratio),48,'o',NULL) chk48,
DECODE(ROUND(period_hit_ratio),49,'o',NULL) chk49,
DECODE(ROUND(period_hit_ratio),50,'o',NULL) chk50,
DECODE(ROUND(period_hit_ratio),51,'o',NULL) chk51,
DECODE(ROUND(period_hit_ratio),52,'o',NULL) chk52,
DECODE(ROUND(period_hit_ratio),53,'o',NULL) chk53,
DECODE(ROUND(period_hit_ratio),54,'o',NULL) chk54,
DECODE(ROUND(period_hit_ratio),55,'o',NULL) chk55,
DECODE(ROUND(period_hit_ratio),56,'o',NULL) chk56,
DECODE(ROUND(period_hit_ratio),57,'o',NULL) chk57,
DECODE(ROUND(period_hit_ratio),58,'o',NULL) chk58,
DECODE(ROUND(period_hit_ratio),59,'o',NULL) chk59,
DECODE(ROUND(period_hit_ratio),60,'o',NULL) chk60,
DECODE(ROUND(period_hit_ratio),61,'o',NULL) chk61,
```

```
    DECODE(ROUND(period_hit_ratio),62,'o',NULL) chk62,
    DECODE(ROUND(period_hit_ratio),63,'o',NULL) chk63,
    DECODE(ROUND(period_hit_ratio),64,'o',NULL) chk64,
    DECODE(ROUND(period_hit_ratio),65,'o',NULL) chk65,
    DECODE(ROUND(period_hit_ratio),66,'o',NULL) chk66,
    DECODE(ROUND(period_hit_ratio),67,'o',NULL) chk67,
    DECODE(ROUND(period_hit_ratio),68,'o',NULL) chk68,
    DECODE(ROUND(period_hit_ratio),69,'o',NULL) chk69,
    DECODE(ROUND(period_hit_ratio),70,'o',NULL) chk70,
    DECODE(ROUND(period_hit_ratio),71,'o',NULL) chk71,
    DECODE(ROUND(period_hit_ratio),72,'o',NULL) chk72,
    DECODE(ROUND(period_hit_ratio),73,'o',NULL) chk73,
    DECODE(ROUND(period_hit_ratio),74,'o',NULL) chk74,
    DECODE(ROUND(period_hit_ratio),75,'o',NULL) chk74,
    DECODE(ROUND(period_hit_ratio),76,'o',NULL) chk76,
    DECODE(ROUND(period_hit_ratio),77,'o',NULL) chk77,
    DECODE(ROUND(period_hit_ratio),78,'o',NULL) chk78,
    DECODE(ROUND(period_hit_ratio),79,'o',NULL) chk79,
    DECODE(ROUND(period_hit_ratio),80,'o',NULL) chk80,
    DECODE(ROUND(period_hit_ratio),81,'o',NULL) chk81,
    DECODE(ROUND(period_hit_ratio),82,'o',NULL) chk82,
    DECODE(ROUND(period_hit_ratio),83,'o',NULL) chk83,
    DECODE(ROUND(period_hit_ratio),84,'o',NULL) chk84,
    DECODE(ROUND(period_hit_ratio),85,'o',NULL) chk85,
    DECODE(ROUND(period_hit_ratio),86,'o',NULL) chk86,
    DECODE(ROUND(period_hit_ratio),87,'o',NULL) chk87,
    DECODE(ROUND(period_hit_ratio),88,'o',NULL) chk88,
    DECODE(ROUND(period_hit_ratio),89,'o',NULL) chk89,
    DECODE(ROUND(period_hit_ratio),90,'o',NULL) chk90,
    DECODE(ROUND(period_hit_ratio),91,'o',NULL) chk91,
    DECODE(ROUND(period_hit_ratio),92,'o',NULL) chk92,
    DECODE(ROUND(period_hit_ratio),93,'o',NULL) chk93,
    DECODE(ROUND(period_hit_ratio),94,'o',NULL) chk94,
    DECODE(ROUND(period_hit_ratio),95,'o',NULL) chk95,
    DECODE(ROUND(period_hit_ratio),96,'o',NULL) chk96,
    DECODE(ROUND(period_hit_ratio),97,'o',NULL) chk97,
    DECODE(ROUND(period_hit_ratio),98,'o',NULL) chk98,
    DECODE(ROUND(period_hit_ratio),99,'o',NULL) chk99,
    DECODE(ROUND(period_hit_ratio),100,'o',NULL) chk100
FROM hit_ratios
WHERE check_date BETWEEN '&&check_date1' AND '&&check_date2'
ORDER BY check_date,check_hour;
SPOOL OFF
PAUSE 'Press return to continue'
```

If the hit ratio for periods of high usage is lower than 70 to 90 percent, increase the *db_block_buffers* INIT.ORA parameter. As can be seen from the listing, when database usage was minimal, the hit ratio hovered at 18-20%, once usage increased above 10,000 to 20,000, the hit ratio leapt to greater than 90%, as would be expected.

If *db_block_buffers* is set too high, the instance may exceed the shared memory size on UNIX or NT. Another possible result is that the entire Oracle process could be swapped out due to memory contention with other processes. In either case, it is not a desirable condition. To avoid exceeding the shared memory area size, be sure these operating system values (on UNIX) are set to high when the instance is created. To avoid swapping, be aware of how much memory can be accessed, talk with your system administrator to determine this.

However, hit ratios are not the best way to tune the buffer cache, they are only one measurement and are susceptible to skew if, for example, a non-selective index is cached and repeatedly selected against. A better indication of buffer usage and problems areas is the *x$bh* and *v$bh* set of internal tables. An example report against the *x$bh* table is shown below.

🖫 **Xbh_status.sql**

```
--******************************************************
--
--      Copyright © 2003 by Rampant TechPress Inc.
--
--      Free for non-commercial use.
--      For commercial licensing, e-mail info@rampant.cc
--
-- ******************************************************
col name for a30
break on pool skip 1
tttitle 'X$BH Buffer Status'
spool xbh_buffer_usage
select 'KEEP' POOL, o.name, count(buf#) BLOCKS
from sys.obj$ o, x$bh x
where o.dataobj# = x.obj
and x.state !=0
and o.owner# !=0
and buf# >= (select min(b.START_BUF#) from x$kcbwbpd a, X$KCBWDS
b
  where a.bp_name = 'KEEP'
```

```
 and b.set_id between a.BP_LO_SID and a.BP_HI_SID
 and a.bp_size > 0)
and buf# <= (select max(b.END_BUF#) from x$kcbwbpd a, X$KCBWDS b
 where a.bp_name = 'KEEP'
 and b.set_id between a.BP_LO_SID and a.BP_HI_SID
 and a.bp_size > 0)
group by 'KEEP',o.name
union all
select 'DEFAULT' POOL, o.name, count(buf#) BLOCKS
from sys.obj$ o, x$bh x
where o.dataobj# = x.obj
and x.state !=0
and o.owner# !=0
and buf# >= (select min(b.START_BUF#) from x$kcbwbpd a, X$KCBWDS
b
 where a.bp_name = 'DEFAULT'
 and b.set_id between a.BP_LO_SID and a.BP_HI_SID
 and a.bp_size > 0)
and buf# <= (select max(b.END_BUF#) from x$kcbwbpd a, X$KCBWDS b
 where a.bp_name = 'DEFAULT'
 and b.set_id between a.BP_LO_SID and a.BP_HI_SID
 and a.bp_size > 0)
group by 'DEFAULT',o.name
union all
select 'RECYCLE' POOL, o.name, count(buf#) BLOCKS
from sys.obj$ o, x$bh x
where o.dataobj# = x.obj
and x.state !=0
and o.owner# !=0
and buf# >= (select min(b.START_BUF#) from x$kcbwbpd a, X$KCBWDS
b
 where a.bp_name = 'RECYCLE'
 and b.set_id between a.BP_LO_SID and a.BP_HI_SID
 and a.bp_size > 0)
and buf# <= (select max(b.END_BUF#) from x$kcbwbpd a, X$KCBWDS b
 where a.bp_name = 'RECYCLE'
 and b.set_id between a.BP_LO_SID and a.BP_HI_SID
 and a.bp_size > 0)
group by 'RECYCLE',o.name
/
clear breaks
clear columns
ttitle off
```

A simpler script against the *v$bh* DPT is shown below.

🖫 Vbh_status.sql

```
--*************************************************
--
--    Copyright © 2003 by Rampant TechPress Inc.
--
--    Free for non-commercial use.
--    For commercial licensing, e-mail info@rampant.cc
--
```

```
-- ************************************************

Set echo off
ttitle off
undef tb
set newpage 1 verify off feedback off
rem HEADER
***********************************************************
rem
rem  File:   BUFFER_USAGE.SQL
rem  Date:   April 17, 2000
rem  Created By:  Steven P. Karniotis / Compuware Corporation
rem  Modified by: Mike Ault TUSC
rem  Description:
rem    Creates a report showing database block buffer usage by
category.
rem
***********************************************************
rem COLUMNS
***********************************************************
rem
column total_buffers new_value tb noprint
select value total_buffers from v$parameter where
name='db_block_buffers';
column buffer_state  format a30 heading "State of|Database
Buffer" justify center
column buffer_count  format 999,990 heading "Buffer|Count"
justify center
column percent format 999.99 heading "Percent|Of Buffer" justify
center
rem COMPUTES and BREAKS
*******************************************
rem
compute sum of buffer_count on report
break on report
rem Set up header and spool file
***********************************
rem
ttitle 'Database Block Buffer Usage'
spool buffer_usage
rem Do SELECT
***********************************************************
rem
select decode(status,'free', 'Free', 'xcur', 'Read and
Modified',
                   'cr','Read and Not Modified', 'read',
'Currently Being Read',
                   'Other')  buffer_state,
      count(*) buffer_count
  from v$bh
 group by decode(status,'free', 'Free', 'xcur', 'Read and
Modified',
                   'cr','Read and Not Modified', 'read',
'Currently Being Read',
                   'Other');
rem Clear all settings
***********************************************
rem
spool off
```

```
ttitle off
clear breaks
clear columns
clear computes
```

An example output from the second script is shown
below.

```
            State of            Buffer
       Database Buffer          Count
----------------------------    --------
Currently Being Read                   4
Read and Modified                186,791
Read and Not Modified              4,840
                                --------
sum                              191,635
```

The buffer should be sized such that there are a few
percent of buffers free at least some of the time. In the
example report, there are no free buffers, if this
condition is the normal status then the DBA would be
wise to add buffers until some free buffers are shown at
least once in a while.

A script to monitor all pools and their buffer state is
shown below:

🖫 All_buff_pools.sql

```
--************************************************
--
--    Copyright © 2003 by Rampant TechPress Inc.
--
--    Free for non-commercial use.
--    For commercial licensing, e-mail info@rampant.cc
--
-- ************************************************

Col state format a35
ttitle 'Buffer State - All Pools'
spool all_pool_buffers
select
count(*) COUNT,
kcbwbpd.bp_name,
decode(state,0,'FREE - Not Currently Used',1, decode(lrba_seq,
  0,'XCUR:FRBL - Exclusive: Freeable','XCUR:RECR - Exclusive:
```

```
Recreatable'),
  2,'SCUR - Shared Current',
  3,'CR - Consistent Read: Recreatable',
  4,'READ - Being Read from Disk',
  5,'MREC - Media Recover',
  6,'IREC - Instance Recovery') STATE
from sys.x$bh bh, sys.x$kcbwbpd kcbwbpd, sys.x$kcbwds kcbwds
where kcbwds.set_id >= kcbwbpd.bp_lo_sid
and kcbwds.set_id <= kcbwbpd.bp_hi_sid
and kcbwbpd.bp_size != 0
and bh.set_ds=kcbwds.addr
group by kcbwbpd.bp_name,
decode(state,0,'FREE - Not Currently Used',1, decode(lrba_seq,
  0,'XCUR:FRBL - Exclusive: Freeable','XCUR:RECR - Exclusive:
Recreatable'),
  2,'SCUR - Shared Current',
  3,'CR - Consistent Read: Recreatable',
  4,'READ - Being Read from Disk',
  5,'MREC - Media Recover',
  6,'IREC - Instance Recovery')
order by 1 desc
/
spool off
ttitle off
clear columns
```

The output of the above script should resemble the following if you have multiple pools defined.

```
       COUNT BP_NAME              STATE
---------- -------------------- -------------------------------
      3878 DEFAULT              FREE - Not Currently Used
      3798 DEFAULT              XCUR:FRBL - Exclusive: Freeable
       139 DEFAULT              XCUR:RECR - Exclusive:
Recreatable
        17 DEFAULT              CR - Consistent Read:
Recreatable
       101 KEEP                 FREE - Not Currently Used
      2245 KEEP                 XCUR:FRBL - Exclusive: Freeable
       101 KEEP                 XCUR:RECR - Exclusive:
Recreatable
        10 KEEP                 CR - Consistent Read:
Recreatable
      1154 RECYCLE              FREE - Not Currently Used
      1002 RECYCLE              XCUR:FRBL - Exclusive: Freeable
        10 RECYCLE              XCUR:RECR - Exclusive:
Recreatable
         7 RECYCLE              CR - Consistent Read:
Recreatable
```

Using *v$db_cache_advice*

Oracle9i provides enhanced functionality in the form of the *v$db_cache_advice* DPT. This view provides the DBA with advice on buffer pool sizing, an example script to view the information in this DPT is shown below:

🖫 **buff_adv.sql**

```
--*************************************************
--
--    Copyright © 2003 by Rampant TechPress Inc.
--
--    Free for non-commercial use.
--    For commercial licensing, e-mail info@rampant.cc
--
-- *************************************************
col id format 999 heading 'ID'
col name format a10 heading 'Name'
col block_size format 9,999,999 heading 'Blk.Size'
col advice_status heading 'Adv'
col size_for_estimate heading 'Size in|Meg' format 9,999,999
col estd_physical_reads heading 'Physical Reads|Saved' format
999,999,999,999
set lines 80 pages 47
ttitle 'Buffer Pool Advisor'
spool buffer_adv
select
id,name,block_size,advice_status,size_for_estimate,estd_physical
_reads from v$db_cache_advice
/
spool off
clear columns
ttitle off
```

An example report generated by the above script would look like:

```
Fri Oct 10                                              page    1
                        Buffer Pool Advisor

                                    Size in  Physical Reads
      ID Name        Blk.Size Adv       Meg           Saved
    ---- ---------- ---------- --- ---------- ----------------
       3 DEFAULT         4,096 ON          4           5,885
       3 DEFAULT         4,096 ON          8           3,665
       3 DEFAULT         4,096 ON         12           3,631
       3 DEFAULT         4,096 ON         16           3,631
```

```
3 DEFAULT     4,096 ON          20         3,631
3 DEFAULT     4,096 ON          24         3,631
3 DEFAULT     4,096 ON          28         3,631
3 DEFAULT     4,096 ON          32         3,631
3 DEFAULT     4,096 ON          36         3,631
3 DEFAULT     4,096 ON          40         3,631
3 DEFAULT     4,096 ON          44         3,631
3 DEFAULT     4,096 ON          48         3,631
3 DEFAULT     4,096 ON          52         3,631
3 DEFAULT     4,096 ON          56         3,631
3 DEFAULT     4,096 ON          60         3,631
3 DEFAULT     4,096 ON          64         3,631
3 DEFAULT     4,096 ON          68         3,631
3 DEFAULT     4,096 ON          72         3,631
3 DEFAULT     4,096 ON          76         3,631
3 DEFAULT     4,096 ON          80         3,631

20 rows selected.
```

The above report tells us that even if we increase our buffers to 80 meg for this small instance, we will see physical reads saved. The view will contain entries for all sections of the buffer pool, including those with different block sizes.

Tuning the Multi-part Oracle Buffer Cache

In versions of Oracle higher than 8, the database block buffer has been split into three possible areas, the default, keep, and recycle buffer pool. It is not required that the three pools be used. Only the default pool, configured with the *db_block_buffers* initialization parameter, must be present, the others are subordinate to this main pool.

Use of the Default Pool

If the data in a table, index, or cluster is specified to reside in the KEEP or RECYCLE pool, then it is placed in the default pool when it is accessed. This is standard Oracle7 behavior. If no special action is taken to use the other pools, this is also standard Oracle8 and Oracle8i behavior. The initialization parameters *db_block_buffers* and *db_block_lru_latches* must be set if multiple pools are to be used:

```
DB_BLOCK_BUFFERS = 2000
DB_BLOCK_LRU_LATCHES = 10
```

Note: In Oracle9i and subsequent versions the *db_block_lru_latches* parameter becomes undocumented and is set automatically by Oracle.

Use of the KEEP Pool

The KEEP database buffer pool is configured using the *buffer_pool_keep* initialization parameter like so:

```
BUFFER_POOL_KEEP = '100,2'
-- IN Oracle9i:   --
DB_KEEP_CAHCE_SIZE = xK|M
```

In the pre-Oracle9i versions, the two specified parameters are the number of buffers from the default pool assigned to the keep pool, and the number of LRU (least recently used) latches assigned to the keep pool. The minimum number of buffers assigned to the pool is 50 times the number of assigned latches. The keep pool, as its name implies, is used to store object data that shouldn't be aged out of the buffer pool, such as look-up information and specific performance-enhancing indexes. The objects are assigned to the keep pool either through their creation statement or by specifically assigning them to the pool using the ALTER command. Any blocks already in the default pool are not affected by the ALTER command, only subsequently accessed blocks are affected.

The keep pool should be sized such that it can hold all the blocks from all of the tables created with the buffer pool set to KEEP.

Use of the RECYCLE Pool

The RECYCLE database buffer pool is configured using the *buffer_pool_recycle* initialization parameter:

```
BUFFER_POOL_RECYCLE = '1000,5'
-- Post Oracle9i: --
DB_RECYCLE_CACHE_SIZE = xK|M
```

In the pre-Oracle9i parameter, the two specified parameters are the number of buffers from the default pool assigned to the recycle pool and the number of LRU (least recently used) latches assigned to the keep pool. The minimum number of buffers assigned to the pool is 50 times the number of assigned latches. The recycle pool, as its name implies, is used to store object data that should be aged out of the buffer pool rapidly, such as searchable LOB information. The objects are assigned to the recycle pool through either their creation statement or by specifically assigning them to the pool using the ALTER command. Any blocks already in the default pool are not affected by the ALTER command, only subsequently accessed blocks are affected.

As long as the recycle pool shows low block contention it is sized correctly.

Using the set points above for the default, keep, and recycle pools, the default pool in a pre-Oracle9i database would end up with 900 buffers and 3 LRU latches.

Sizing the Default Pool

The default pool holds both the keep and recycle pools; the minimum value is determined according to the following formula:

```
Default = (keep + recycle + (total_of_non-
keep_or_recycle_object_sizes/100))/DB_BLOCK_SIZE
```

Each object not explicitly assigned to the keep or recycle pool will be placed into the default pool when it is accessed. As a general rule of thumb, the data currently in use will be equal to approximately one twentieth to one hundredth of the physical database objects such as tables, clusters, and indexes. It is suggested to start at one hundredth and move up from there.

Sizing the Keep Pool

The keep buffer pool should be the total size of the data objects that are explicitly assigned to the pool. Remember, the keep pool is designed to hold objects that would have been cached in earlier versions of Oracle. Generally speaking, small indexes, lookup tables, and small active data tables are good candidates for the keep pool. To size the pool, you must have a good estimate of the size of the objects you want to keep.

Sizing the Recycle Pool

Probably the most difficult pool to size will be the recycle pool. The reason the recycle pool is difficult to size is that it is designed to hold transient data objects (such as chunks of LOB data items). The recycle pool should be sized according to the following formula:

```
Recycle = (SUM(size_non_lob_object(1-n)/20) +
(lob_chunk_size_i(1-n) * No_simul_accesses_i))
```

The first part of this formula is for non-lob objects that might be searched in large pieces, such as partitioned tables. If the partition size can be determined, then exclude the division by 20 and just use the partition size.

The second half of the formula addresses LOB (BLOB, CLOB, NCLOB) type objects that will be accessed in chunks, for searching or comparing using piece-wise logic. The specified chunk size for each assigned object times the number of expected different simultaneous accesses is used to derive the area size required.

The sum of the above two numbers should give a size for the recycle pool.

Tuning the Three Pools

New methods of tuning the shared pool must be examined, since the classic method of tuning is not available in Oracle8i. This means becoming familiar with what Oracle has provided for tuning the new pools. A new script, *catperf.sql*, offers several new views for tuning the Oracle buffer pools. These views are:

- *v$buffer_pool* - Provides static information on pool configuration.

- *v$buffer_pool_statistics* - Provides pool-related statistics.

- *v$dbwr_write_histogram* - Provides summary information on DBWR write activities.

- ***v$dbwr_write_log*** - Provides write information for each buffer area.

Of the four new views, the *v$buffer_pool_statistics* view seems the most useful for tuning the buffer pool. This view contains statistics such as *buffer_busy_waits*, *free_buffer_inspected*, *dirty_buffers_inspected,* and physical write-related data for each of the pool areas.

If a buffer pool shows an excessive number of *dirty_buffers_inspected* and high amounts of *buffer_busy_waits,* then it probably needs to be increased in size.

Remember that the latches are assigned to the pools sequentially and to the DBRW processes round robin, when configuring LRU latches and DBWR processes. The number of LRU processes should be equal to or a multiple of the value of DBWR processes, to ensure that the DBRW load is balanced across the processes.

Conclusion

The multiple buffer pools provided by Oracle allow tighter control of the data objects. By proper use of the default, keep, and recycle pools, a DBA should be able to improve overall database performance.

While some tools, such as the X$ tables that were used in the past to tune the Oracle buffer pool have been eliminated, several new views are now provided to allow multiple pool tuning.

The next chapter will take a look at some special undocumented initialization parameters.

Undocumented Oracle Parameters

Introduction

Every version of Oracle has varying numbers of undocumented initialization parameters, in addition to the documented ones. These undocumented initialization parameters are usually only used in emergencies and only under the direction of a senior DBA or Oracle support. Source 2.5 shows a script for getting the undocumented initialization parameters out of a 7.3, 8.0, 8.1 or 9.x instance. The undocumented parameters for an Oracle9*i* (9.0.1) database are shown in the appendix.

🖫 undoc.sql

```
--***********************************************
--
--    Copyright © 2003 by Rampant TechPress Inc.
--
--    Free for non-commercial use.
--    For commercial licensing, e-mail info@rampant.cc
--
--    ***********************************************

COLUMN parameter            FORMAT a37
COLUMN description          FORMAT a30 WORD_WRAPPED
COLUMN "Session Value"      FORMAT a10
COLUMN "Instance Value"     FORMAT a10
SET LINES 100
SET PAGES 0
SPOOL undoc.lis

SELECT
   a.ksppinm  "Parameter",
   a.ksppdesc "Description",
   b.ksppstvl "Session Value",
   c.ksppstvl "Instance Value"
FROM
   x$ksppi a,
```

```
   x$ksppcv b,
   x$ksppsv c
WHERE
   a.indx = b.indx
   AND
   a.indx = c.indx
   AND
   a.ksppinm LIKE '/_%' escape '/'
/

SPOOL OFF
SET LINES 80 PAGES 20
CLEAR COLUMNS
```

Note that each undocumented parameter in the table begins with an underscore (_) character. Some of you may notice that a few of these "undocumented" parameters used to be documented. Some, such as _offline_rollback_segments, may be familiar, while others will never be seen or used. Just be aware that there are more parameters than those listed in a user's manual, and that Oracle support may be needed if you see one (for example, _corrupted_rollback_segments, that may just be helpful in a sticky situation).

Inside the undocumented parameters

Most DBAs are familiar with Oracle's documented initialization parameters, and they are easy to look up and use. However, not everyone knows about the undocumented parameters, and few know how or when to use them. Oracle does not allow DBAs to use many of these parameters unless specifically directed by Oracle support. DBAs should be aware that use of certain undocumented parameters would result in an unsupported system. We will attempt to identify when parameters should be used only with Oracle guidance and where a DBA can safely utilize these high-powered tools.

The major difference between the documented and undocumented parameters is that the undocumented parameters begin with an underscore character. In many cases, the undocumented parameters were either documented in previous releases or will be in future releases. Those parameters that have been, or will be, documented are usually those that are safe to use. It is difficult to use the undocumented parameters that have never been documented, and never will be, safely. When in doubt, get guidance from Oracle support. And always back up the database before using any questionable parameters, so that a supported version can be restored.

The following 14 undocumented parameters are the most prominent:

- *_allow_resetlogs_corruption.* This may be the only way to start a db backed-up open without setting backup on tablespaces, it will result in an unsupported system. See the detailed section on using *_allow_resetlogs_corruption* that follows.

- *_corrupted_rollback_segments.* The only way to start up with corrupted public rollback segments. Can be used without fear of invalidating support.

- *_allow_read_only_corruption.* Allows the database to be opened even if it has corruption. This should only be used to export as much data from a corrupted database as is possible before re-creating a database. A database that has been opened in this manner should not be used in a normal manner, as it will not be supported.

- **_spin_count.** Sets the number of spins a process will undergo before trying to get a latch. If the CPU is not fully loaded, a high value may be best; for a fully-loaded CPU, a smaller value may help. Usually defaults to 2000. Can be changed without fear of invalidating support. Flips from undocumented to documented depending on version.

- **_log_entry_prebuild_threshold.** Formerly documented, now undocumented, it is the minimum size of entry in blocks that will be pre-built for redo log entries, and is usually set to 30.

- **_latch_spin_count.** Shows how often a latch request will be taken.

- **_db_block_write_batch.** Formerly documented, now undocumented. It is the number of blocks that the db writers will write in each batch. It defaults to 512 or DB_FILES*DB_FILE_SIMULTANEOUS_WRITES/2 up to a limit of one-fourth the value of DB_BLOCK_BUFFERS.

- **_cpu_count.** Flips from undocumented to documented. Should be set automatically, but isn't on some platforms. Set to the number of CPUs. This determines several other parameters.

- **_init_sql_file.** The initialization SQL script run by Oracle when a database is created. This should be *sql.bsq*. If it is changed, it may not be supported.

- **_trace_files_public.** Changes the privileges on trace files such that everyone can read them. Should be fine to change at will.

- *_fast_full_scan_enabled.* Enables (or disables) fast full index scans, if only indexes are required to resolve the queries. Change at will.

- *_corrupt_blocks_on_stuck_recovery.* Can sometimes get a corrupted database up. However, it probably won't be supported if done without Oracle's blessing. Immediately export the tables needed and rebuild the database if used.

- *_always_star_transformation.* Helps to tune data warehouse queries, if the warehouse is designed properly.

- *_small_table_threshold.* Sets the size definition of a small table. A small table is automatically pinned into the buffers when queried. Defaults to 2 percent in Oracle9*i.*

Niemiec lists another 26 parameters that bear mentioning:

- *_debug_sga.* Has no noticeable effect.

- *_log_buffers_debug.* Slows things down.

- *_reuse_index_loops.* The blocks to examine for index block reuse.

- *_save_escalates.* Not sure what it does; no measurable effects. According to Steve Adams, Oracle may take an exclusive lock earlier than required to save lock escalations; if this is set to FALSE, it won't. Don't mess with it.

- *_optimizer_undo_changes.* Reverts to pre-6.0.3 optimizer for IN statements. This one is required in certain versions of Oracle Applications. According to K. Gopalakrishnan of the *India Times*, this parameter has nothing to do with cost-based optimization. In Version 6, somewhere around V6.0.36, if he remembers correctly, Ed Peeler made several changes to the way the optimizer made choices. Many queries in the existing Oracle Applications at that time relied in particular on the old way the optimizer worked to be certain to come up with the intended plan. The code was written prior to hints, so many tricks were used to influence the optimizer to come up with a certain plan and were scattered throughout the code. When the new database release was made, tests showed that many critical applications processes ran catastrophically slower. Fortunately, the old optimizer code had not been stripped out yet, and a way to use the old optimizer code was allowed via the "hidden*" parameter *_undo_optimizer_changes* (probably so that Oracle could test the old versus the new optimizer internally). So Oracle released this parameter to the applications community. This was long before the cost-based optimizer even existed.

- **_dss_cache_flush.** Enables full cache flush for parallel, and the effect is not measurable.

- **_db_no_mount_lock.** Doesn't get a mount lock. No noticeable effect.

- **_affinity.** Defaults to TRUE, and enables or disables CPU affinity.

- **_corrupt_blocks_on_stuck_recovery.** Tried in a corrupt recovery and it didn't do anything. No noticeable effect.

- **_cursor_db_buffers_pinned.** Lists additional buffers a cursor can pin, however, provided no noticeable effect. The default value is max (*db_block_buffers*/processes-2, 2). One note from Oracle development says that playing around with this parameter will almost always damage performance, so it was made hidden starting in 8.0.3.

- **_db_block_no_idle_writes.** Disables writes of blocks when the database is idle, and may result in an unusable system if used. If there is an instance crash with the following Error ORA-00600: internal error code, arguments: [kcbbzo_2], [1], [25974], setting this parameter may help. A Ctrl-c during a truncate may cause the DBWR to fail with an ORA-600 [kcbbzo_2], causing the instance to crash.

- **_disable_logging.** Don't expect support if you set this one. If this parameter is set to TRUE, redo records will *not* be generated, and recovery is *not* possible if the instance crashes or is terminated with shutdown abort.

- **_io_slaves_disabled.** Disables I/O slaves, and is probably not the safest way.

- **_distributed_lock_timeout.** Sets the amount of time a lock used in a distributed transaction will be held, usually 5. Safe to reset without worry of invalidating support.

- **_row_cache_cursors.** Maximum number of cached recursive cursors used for data dictionary cache queries. This sets the size of the array in the PGA used for the data dictionary cursors. It takes 28 bytes per cached cursor. Long-running procedures that do a lot of data dictionary lookups can benefit from higher values. If the view *k$kqdpg* shows excessive overflows of the cache, a small increase may help. This view is for the current process only. The

ORADUBUG or DBMS_*SYSTEM.SET_EV* can be used to grab a trace of a different process. In the resulting trace, find the *x$kqdpg* structure, count 12 blocks, and use the hexadecimal values to get the values. Recursive calls can be caused by firing database triggers, execution of SQL statements within stored procedures, executing functions and anonymous PL/SQL blocks, and enforcement of referential integrity constraints. Setting this value higher may reduce these recursive calls.

- *_log_blocks_during_backup.* From Oracle support, but the use of this parameter is still not recommended on production systems. There is a known problem with performance on systems using certain configurations of Veritas with Solaris 2.6. Contact Veritas for further information. Use of this parameter will result in an unsupported system.

- *_db_writer_scan_depth_increment.* Controls the rate at which the scan depth increases if the database writer is idle, defaults to one-eighth the difference between the upper and lower bounds of the scan depth.

- *_db_writer_scan_depth_decrement.* Controls the rate at which the scan depth decreases if the database writer is working too hard. The *x$kvit* table gives the details of the database writer; and the details can be found using the following SELECT statement, courtesy of Steve Adams at www.ixora.com.au:

```
select
    kvitdsc,
    kvitval
from
    sys.x$kvit
```

```
where
  kvittag in ('kcbldq', 'kcbsfs')
or
   kvittag like 'kcbsd_'
;
```

- **_db_large_dirty_queue.** Defaults to one-sixteenth of the write batch size limit. Sets the frequency at which DBWR writes. Should be decreased gradually in one-block increments until buffer waits are eliminated. The cost of reducing this parameter is in CPU usage, so it shouldn't be changed without good reason.

- **_db_block_max_scan_cnt.** Defaults to one-fourth of the working set size, rounded down. If this number of blocks is scanned, then the free buffer request fails. The failure of a scan increments the dirty buffers inspected parameter in the *v$sysstat* view. If there are no free buffer waits, and there are dirty buffers inspected, then there is a potentially serious problem and the parameter should be tuned.

- **_enqueue_hash_chains.** Derived from the *processes* parameter, as is the value for *enqueue_resources*, which is directly affected by *enqueue_hash_chains*; therefore, if you explicitly set *enqueue_resources*, you will need to adjust *enqueue_hash_chains* to a prime number just less than the value of *enqueue_resources*. If the value of *_enqueue_hash* is not set to a prime number, long enqueue hash chains could develop. Unless you are receiving ORA-00052 or ORA-00053 errors, this parameter and *enqueue_resources* probably don't need adjusting. The default value is equal to *cpu_count*.

- **_enqueue_locks.** Use *v$resource_limit* to see if you need more locks or *enqueue_resources*. A lock takes 60 bytes; a resource, 72 bytes. To increase the *enqueue_locks* value in *v$resource* limit, you have to increase the *_enqueue_limit* value in *init.ora*.

- **_use_ism.** Determines if intimate shared memory is used. On some platforms this can cause problems, and *_use_ism* should be set to FALSE instead of its default of TRUE.

- **_db_block_hash_buckets.** In releases prior to 9*i*, this was set to twice the value of *db_block_buffers*. Unfortunately, this should be set to a prime number to keep the hash chains from getting out of hand; therefore, on releases prior to 9*i*, resetting this to a prime number near the value of twice the *db_block_buffers* is a good idea and will not result in loss of support. According to Steve Adams, *_db_block_hash_buckets* could be used to set both the number of hash chains and latches in previous releases. From 7.1, it was constrained to prime numbers, and used to default to *next_prime(db_block_buffers / 4)*.

  Under release 8.1, *_db_block_hash_buckets* defaults to 2 * *db_block_buffers*, and the *_db_block_hash_latches* parameter must be used to control the number of hash latches, if necessary. This parameter is constrained to binary powers so that Oracle can calculate which latch to use with a simple SHIFT operation, rather than a DIVIDE operation. The default number of hash latches depends on *db_block_buffers*. If *db_block_buffers* is less than 2052 buffers, then the default number of latches is $2 \wedge \text{trunc}(\log(2, db\_block\_buffers - 4) - 1)$.

  If *db_block_buffers* is greater than 131075 buffers, then the default number of latches is $2 \wedge \text{trunc}(\log(2,$

db_block_buffers - 4) - 6). If *db_block_buffers* is between 2052 and 131075 buffers, then there are 1024 latches by default. Sites that have used *_db_block_hash_buckets* to combat *cache buffer chains* latch contention under previous releases should allow the value to default when upgrading to Oracle 8*i*. Remember that contention for these latches is almost always a symptom of one or more blocks being very hot, due to unresolved application or SQL tuning problems. Adams may be correct; however, some have seen improvements on 8.1.7 by setting these values as in previous releases.

- **_db_block_hash_latches.** Usually set to 1024, which is usually too small. Set it to near 32K (32768) for better performance. Up to release 8.0.

- **_kgl_latch_count.** Value defaults to 7. This determines the number of latches that control the shared pool. If you need a large shared pool, or have a large number of items that are placed in the shared pool, set this to a larger prime number. According to Oracle support: In general, on systems that have multiple CPUs and/or when parsing a lot of SQL with few shared cursors, it is recommended to set it to 1. On all other systems it must be set to the default, in which case the latch contention may not be significant compared to the cost of building a new cursor for each SQL statement. However, according to Steve Adams: The default is the least prime number greater than or equal to *cpu_count*. The maximum is 67. It can safely be increased to combat library cache latch contention, as long as you stick to prime numbers. That said, it is only effective if the activity across the existing child library cache latches is evenly distributed as shown in *v$latch_children*.

Tuning the database writer with undocumented parameters

Here are some undocumented parameters for maximizing DBWR performance:

- Increase *_db_block_write_batch* (hidden parameter in Oracle8, obsolete in Oracle8*i*).

- Decrease *_db_block_max_scan_count*, *_db_writer_scan_depth*, and *_db_writer_scan_depth_increment* to decrease the dirty buffer backlog.

- Adjust *_db_writer_chunk_writes*, which controls the number of writes DBWR tries to group into one batch I/O operation.

- Adjust *_db_block_med_priority_batch_size* for regular writes.

- Adjust *_db_block_hi_priority_batch_size* for urgent writes, such as when LRUW is full or there are no free buffers or when free buffers are below limit.

Hidden Parameters with inappropriate default values

Here we attempt to list the specific conditions when the following undocumented parameters must be changed:

- ***_db_handles.*** In versions before 8.1.7.2, if set too high, this may cause ORA-04031 because of bug 1397603.

- **_db_handles_cached.** Before 8.1.7.2, may need to be set to 0.

- **_eliminate_common_subexpr.** If left set to TRUE, may cause some queries using IN clauses to return too many rows or bad answers; set to FALSE in 8.1.7.0 and 8.1.7.1.

- **_ignore_desc_in_index.** May have to set to TRUE on some platforms, such as AIX versions 8.1.6 and 8.1.7, if there are ORA-03113 and ORA-07445 errors with different management or DML operations on descending indexes. Some platforms may have to use the event setting "10612 trace name context forever, level 1" to reset it.

- **_init_sql_file.** This may have to be reset to use 32K block sizes on some platforms, as they will use the *sql.bsq.32K* file instead of the *sql.bsq* file.

- **_mv_refresh_selections.** In 8.1.7 only, and if multilevel joins are in the materialized view, setting this to TRUE may allow fast refreshes.

- **_new_initial_join_orders.** Set to TRUE when upgrading to 11.5.4 on 8.1.7.

- **_ogms_home.** Used in Oracle Parallel Server. Set explicitly or may default to /tmp, which could result in file loss and inability to start Oracle Parallel Server.

- **_sqlexec_progression_cost.** For Oracle Application 11.5.4 in 8.1.7, set to 0.

- **_unnest_subquery.** When the UNNEST hint cannot be used, it may improve performance.

- **_use_ism.** Set to FALSE on Solaris 2.6 or you may have system crashes and poor performance (depending on Oracle version may be USE_ISM).

- **_db_always_check_system_ts.** Always perform block check and checksum for SYSTEM tablespace. This defaults to TRUE. You may need to set this to FALSE after upgrade from a pre-8*i* version of Oracle. If you need to set this to FALSE to restart the database, immediately export and rebuild the database, as it detected corruption in the data dictionary (probably in the C_TS# cluster, but that is another story).

- **_db_cache_advice.** Will turn on the buffer cache sizing advisory if set to ON to help you perform cache sizing.

Immutable hidden parameters

In contrast to parameters that must be changed, there are those that should never be changed. Let's look at a few of them.

- **_compatible_no_recovery.** Usually set to 0.0.0, which defaults to the current version. If you set it to something else and the databse crashes, you may need to do a media recovery instead of just an instance recovery.

- **_allow_error_simulation.** Used by Oracle for internal testing. If you set it, there's no telling what it will do to the instance.

- **_db_block_cache_protect.** Will cause a database crash rather than let corruption get to the database. It may result in many ORA-0600 errors and other unpleasant things if set in a regular production database. This is for debugging only!

- **_ipc_fail_network.** Simulates network failure; for testing only.

- **_ipc_test_failover.** Tests transparent cluster network failover. For testing only.

- **_ipc_test_mult_nets.** Simulates multiple cluster networks. For testing only.

- **_log_buffers_corrupt.** Corrupts redo buffers after write. For testing only.

- **_mts_load_constants.** A complex set of constants that govern the multithreaded server load balancing. It contains six different values dealing with how the load is balanced across servers and dispatchers.

- **_cpu_to_io._** The multiplier for converting CPU cost to I/O cost. Change this and you will directly affect the CBO cost calculation.

- **_log_buffers_corrupt.** Corrupts redo buffers before write and is used only for testing. A sure way to bring your database to its knees is to set this to TRUE.

- **_single_process.** Run without detached processes. Iif you want single-user Oracle, this will give it to you.

- *_wait_for_sync.* Wait for checkpoint sync on commit and must always be TRUE. If set to FALSE, will cause mismatch between headers and SCN on database crash or shutdown abort.

- **_no_objects.** Tells Oracle that no objects are being used. Set to FALSE. If you set it to TRUE, Oracle will probably crash since the data dictionary uses objects.

- **_pmon_load_constants.** As with MTS, these are PMON Server load-balancing constants and directly affect the operation of PMON; don't mess with them.

This list contains only those parameters that stand out. There are many more that, if changed, will have a negative effect on how Oracle behaves. When in doubt, don't touch it! One point I should also cover is that the initialization parameter *optimizer_feature_enable* turns the value of many of the undocumented parameters from *true* to *false* or vica-versa depending on its setting, this is how Oracle turns on or off various features for example, the optimizer features.

Oracle Recovery with _allow_resetlogs_corruption

Here is a detailed example using *_allow_resetlogs_corruption* to recover a database. Recovery of a database using the undocumented parameter *_allow_resetlogs_corruption* should be regarded as a last-ditch, emergency recovery scenario only, and should not be attempted until all other avenues of recovery have been exhausted.

Note that Oracle will not support a database that has been recovered using this method unless it is subsequently exported and rebuilt.

Essentially, using *_allow_resetlogs_corruption* forces the opening of the datafiles even if their SCNs do not match up; then, on the next checkpoint, the old SCN values are overwritten. This could leave the database in an unknown state as far as concurrency.

This type of recovery is usually required when a datafile has been left in hot backup mode through several backup cycles, without an intervening shutdown and startup. Upon shutdown and startup, the database will complain that a file (usually file id#1 in the SYSTEM tablespace) needs more recovery, and asks for logs past all available archive logs and online logs.

An alternative scenario occurs when the database is recovered from a hot backup with the above scenario, or when the database asks for an archive log dated earlier than any that are available (usually for the rollback segment tablespace datafiles). This may also happen when creating a standby database using a hot backup.

A typical error stack would resemble:

```
SVRMGR> connect internal

Connected.

SVRMGR> @sycrectl

ORACLE instance started.

Total System Global Area 113344192 bytes

Fixed Size 69312 bytes

Variable Size 92704768 bytes

Database Buffers 20480000 bytes

Redo Buffers 90112 bytes

Statement processed.

ALTER DATABASE OPEN resetlogs

*
```

```
ORA-01194: file 1 needs more recovery to be consistent

ORA-01110: data file 1: '/u03/oradata/tstc/dbsyst01.dbf'
```

Or:

```
ORA-01547: warning: RECOVER succeeded but OPEN RESETLOGS would
get error below

ORA-01194: file 48 needs more recovery to be consistent

ORA-01110: data file 48: '/vol06/oradata/testdb/ard01.dbf'
```

If all available archive logs and online redo logs are applied, and the error is not corrected, then the use of the _allow_resetlogs_corruption parameter should be considered. Make sure a good backup of the database in a closed state (all files) is taken before attempting recovery using this parameter.

It cannot be emphasized enough that the database will no longer be supported by Oracle until it is rebuilt after using _allow_resetlogs_corruption for recovery.

Procedure

The following steps outline the recovery process using _allow_resetlogs_corruption:

1. If no recovery attempts have been made, shut down and back up the database (all files) as it is, to provide a fallback position should recovery fail.

2. If recovery attempts have been made, recover the database to the state just before any other recovery attempts were made.

3. Use *svrmgrl*, *sqlplus*, or an appropriate interface to start up the database in a mounted, but not open, condition:

   - STARTUP MOUNT

4. Ensure all datafiles are set to END BACKUP status:

   - SET PAGES 0 FEEDBACK OFF LINES 132

   - SPOOL alter_df.sql

   - SELECT 'alter database datafile '||file_name||' END BACKUP;' from *v$datafile*;

   - SPOOL OFF

   - @alter_df.sql

5. Alter the database into open condition:

   - ALTER DATABASE OPEN;

6. If the database asks for recovery, use an UNTIL CANCEL-type recovery and apply all available archive and online redo logs. Then issue the CANCEL and reissue the ALTER DATATBASE OPEN RESETLOGS commands.

7. If the database asks for logs that are no longer available, or the preceding still results in errors, shut down the database.

8. Insert into the initialization file the following line:

   - *_allow_resetlogs_corruption*=TRUE

9. Use *svrmgrl*, *sqlplus*, or an appropriate interface to start up the database in a mounted, but not open, condition:

   - STARTUP MOUNT

10. Ensure all datafiles are set to END BACKUP status:

- SET PAGES 0 FEEDBACK OFF LINES 132

- SPOOL alter_df.sql

- SELECT 'alter database datafile '||file_name||'' END BACKUP;' from *v$datafile*;

- SPOOL OFF

- @alter_df.sql

11. Alter the database into open condition:

- ALTER DATABASE OPEN;

12. If the database asks for recovery, use an UNTIL CANCEL-type recovery and apply all available archive and online redo logs; then issue the CANCEL and reissue the ALTER DATATBASE OPEN RESETLOGS commands. Once the database is open, immediately do a full export of the database or an export of the schemas needed to recover.

13. Shut down the database and remove the parameter *_allow_resetlogs_corruption*.

14. Rebuild the database.

15. Import to finish the recovery.

16. Implement a proper backup plan and procedure.

17. It may be advisable to perform an ANALYZE TABLE...VALIDATE STRUCTURE CASCADE on critical application tables after the recovery and before the export.

Uncommitted records that had been written to disk will possibly be marked as committed by this procedure.

Conclusion

This chapter has presented and discussed many of the undocumented Oracle parameters. These parameters should be used with extreme caution, since Oracle does not support the use of them.

The next chapter will discuss event parameters.

Oracle Event Internals

Event parameters can also be useful and are discussed in this chapter. Setting an event entails telling Oracle to generate information in the form of a trace file within the context of the event. The trace file is usually located in a directory specified by the initialization parameter *user_dump_dest*. By examining the resulting trace file, detailed information about the event traced can be deduced. The general format for an event is:

```
EVENT = "<trace class><event name><action><name><trace
name><qualifier>"
```

There are two types of events: *session-events* and *process-events*. Process-events are initialized in the parameter file; session-events are initialized with the ALTER SESSION... or ALTER SYSTEM command. When checking for posted events, the Oracle server first checks for session-events then for process-events.

Event Classes

There are four traceable event classes:

- **Class 1: "Dump something."** Traces are generated upon so-called unconditioned, immediate events. This is the case when Oracle data has to be dumped, for example, the headers of all redolog files or the contents of the controlfile. These events can not be set in the *init<SID>.ora*, but must be set using the

ALTER   SESSION   or   the
DBMS_SESSION.SET_EV() procedure.

- **Class 2: "Trap on Error."** Setting this class of (error-) events causes Oracle to generate an errorstack every time the event occurs.

- **Class 3: "Change execution path."** Setting such an event will cause Oracle to change the execution path for some specific Oracle internal code segment. For example, setting event "10269" prevents SMON from doing free-space coalescing.

- **Class 4: "Trace something."** Events from this class are set to obtain traces that are used for, among other things, SQL tuning. A common event is "10046", which will cause Oracle to trace the SQL access path on each SQL-statement.

TRACE CLASS	EVENT NAME	ACTION KEY WORD	"NAME"	TRACE NAME	TRACE QUALIFIER
Dump Something	Immediate	Trace	"name"	blockdump redohdr file_hdrs controlf systemstate	level block# level 10 level 10 level 10 level 10
Trap on error	Error number	Trace	"name"	errorstack processstate heapdump	Forever off Level n
Change execution path	Even code corresponding to path	Trace	"name"	context	Forever or level 10
Trace Something	10046	Trace	"name"	context	Forever Level n off

Table 5.1 – *Oracle Event Classifications*

The Initialization File Event Settings

The SET EVENTS commands in an *init<SID>.ora* file are usually placed there by Oracle support to perform specific functions. Generally, these alerts turn on more advanced levels of tracing and error detection than are commonly available. Source 2.6 lists some of the more common events.

The syntax to specify multiple events in the *init.ora* is:

```
EVENT="<event 1>:<event 2>: <event 3>: <event n>"
```

The events can also be split on multiple lines by using the continuation backslash character (\) at the end of each event. The next event is continued on the next line. For example:

```
EVENT="<event 1>:\
<event 2>:\
<event 3>: \
<event n>"
```

For example:

```
EVENT="\
10210 trace name context forever, level 10:\
10211 trace name context forever, level 10:\
10231 trace name context forever, level 10:\
10232 trace name context forever, level 10"
```

After setting the events in the initialization file, the instance should be stopped and restarted. Check the alert.log and verify that the events are in effect. Almost all EVENT settings can be specified at the session level using the ALTER SESSION command or a call to the DBMS_SYSYTEM.SET_EV( ) procedure. Doing so does not require an instance bounce for the EVENT to take effect.

The alert.log should show the events that are in effect; for example:

```
event = 10210 trace name context forever, level 10:10211 trace
name context for ever, level 10:10231 trace name context
forever, level 10:10232 trace name context forever, level 10
```

Example Uses of the EVENT Initialization Parameter

To enable block header and trailer checking to detect corrupt blocks:

```
event="10210 trace name context forever, level 10"  -- for tables
event="10211 trace name context forever, level 10"  -- for indexes
event="10210 trace name context forever, level 2" -- data block checking
event="10211 trace name context forever, level 2" -- index block checking
event="10235 trace name context forever, level 1" -- memory heap checking
event="10049 trace name context forever, level 2" -- memory protect
cursors
```

The undocumented parameter setting to go with the above is:

```
_db_block_cache_protect=TRUE
```

This setting will prevent corruption of the disks (at the cost of a database crash).

In order to trace a MAX_CURSORS exceeded error:

```
event="1000 trace name ERRORSTACK level 3"
```

To get an error stack related to a SQLNET ORA-03120 error:

```
event="3120 trace name error stack"
```

To work around a space leak problem:

```
event="10262 trace name context forever, level x"
```

x is the size of space leak to ignore.

To trace memory shortages:

```
event="10235 trace name context forever, level 4"
event="600 trace name heapdump, level 4"
```

To track Ora-04031 as the error occurs, take a shared pool heapdump by setting the following event in the *init.ora* file:

```
event = "4031 trace name heapdump forever, level 2"
```

For ORA-04030 errors: Take a dump by setting this event in the INIT file and analyze the trace file. This will clearly pinpoint the problem.

```
event="4030 trace name errorstack level 3"
```

The following undocumented SQL statements can be used to obtain information about internal database structures:

- To dump the control file:
  ```
  alter session set events 'immediate trace name CONTROLF
  level 10'
  ```

- To dump the file headers:
  ```
  alter session set events 'immediate trace name FILE_HDRS
  level 10'
  ```

- To dump redo log headers:
  ```
  alter session set events 'immediate trace name REDOHDR level
  10'
  ```

- To dump the system state:

```
alter session set events 'immediate trace name SYSTEMSTATE
level 10'
```

- To dump the optimizer statistics whenever a SQL statement is parsed:

```
alter session set events '10053 trace name context forever'
```

- To prevent db block corruptions:

```
event = "10210 trace name context forever, level 10"
event = "10211 trace name context forever, level 10"
event = "10231 trace name context forever, level 10"
```

- To enable the maximum level of SQL performance monitoring:

```
event = "10046 trace name context forever, level 12"
```

- To enable a memory-protect cursor:

```
event = "10049 trace name context forever, level  2"
```

- To perform data-block checks:

```
event = "10210 trace name context forever, level  2"
```

- To perform index-block checks:

```
event = "10211 trace name context forever, level  2"
```

- To perform memory-heap checks:

```
event = "10235 trace name context forever, level  1"
```

- To allow 300 bytes memory leak for each connection:

```
event = "10262 trace name context forever, level 300"
```

Notice the pattern for tracing events related to error codes: the first argument in the EVENT is the error code followed by the desired action upon receiving the code.

Example Uses of the EVENT Initialization Parameter **151**

Events at the Session Level

Events are also used at the SESSION level using the ALTER SESSION command or calls to the *dbms_system.set_ev()* procedure. The general format for the ALTER SESSION command is:

```
ALTER SESSION SET EVENTS 'ev_number ev_text level x';
```

Where:

- **Ev_number** is the event number.

- **Ev_text** is any required text (usually "trace name context forever").

- **x** is the required level setting corresponding to the desired action, file, or other required data.

For example, to provide more detailed SQL trace information:

```
ALTER SESSION SET EVENTS '10046 trace name context forever level
NN'
```

Where NN:

- 1 is the same as a regular trace.

- 4 means also dump bind variables.

- 8 means also dump wait information.

- 12 means dump both bind and wait information.

Example Uses of the ALTER SESSION Command to Set EVENT Codes

To coalesce freespace in a tablespace pre-version 7.3:

```
ALTER SESSION SET EVENTS 'immediate trace name coalesce level
XX'
```

XX is the value of ts# from ts$ table for the tablespace.

To coalesce freespace in a tablespace defined as temporary:

```
ALTER SESSION SET EVENTS 'immediate trace name drop_segments
level &x';
```

x is the value for file# from ts$ plus 1.

To get the order of LRU chains out of the db block buffers:

```
ALTER SESSION SET EVENTS 'immediate trace name buffers level x';
```

x is 1-3 for buffer header order or 4-6 for LRU chain order.

To correct transportable tablespace export hanging (reported on 8.1.6, 8.1.7 on HPUX, a known bug):

```
ALTER SESSION SET EVENT '10297 trace name context forever, level
1';
```

To cause "QKA Disable GBY sort elimination" (This affects how Oracle will process sorts):

```
ALTER SESSION SET EVENTS'10119 trace name context forever';
```

You can disable the Index FFS using the event 10156. In this case, CBO will lean toward FTS or an index scan.

You can set the event 10092 if you want to disable the hash joins completely.

It is very easy to see how SMON cleans up rollback entries by using event 10015. You can use event 10235 to check how the memory manager works internally.

There is nothing mysterious about the CBO. Event 10053 will give details on the various plans, depending on the statistics available. Be careful using this for large multitable joins, as the report can be quite lengthy! The data density, sparse characteristics, index availability, and index depth all lead the optimizer to make its decisions. The running commentary can be seen in trace files generated by the10053 event.

Seeing Which Events Are Set in a Session

For ALTER SESSION commands that set events, the undocumented *dbms_system.read_ev* procedure can be used. For example:

🖫 **read_ev.sql**

```
--*************************************************
--
--     Copyright © 2003 by Rampant TechPress Inc.
--
--     Free for non-commercial use.
--     For commercial licensing, e-mail info@rampant.cc
--
-- *************************************************
 set serveroutput on
declare
 event_level number;
begin
 for i in 10000..10999 loop
    sys.dbms_system.read_ev(i,event_level);
    if (event_level > 0) then
       dbms_output.put_line('Event '||to_char(i)||' set at
level '||
                            to_char(event_level));
    end if;
```

```
  end loop;
  end;
  /
```

To demonstrate how the PL/SQL above can be used, create the script *check_param.sql*. Note that setting the *init<sid>.ora* parameter *sql_trace* sets the event 10046. Other parameters such as *timed_statistics* and *optimizer_mode* do not set events.

Within the session issue:

```
SQL> @check_param
PL/SQL procedure successfully completed.

SQL> alter session set sql_trace=true;
SQL> alter session set events '10015 trace name context forever,
level 3';

SQL> @check_param
Event 10015 set at level 12
Event 10046 set at level 1
PL/SQL procedure successfully completed.
SQL> alter session set events '10046 trace name context forever,
level 12';

SQL> @check_param
Event 10015 set at level 12
Event 10046 set at level 12
PL/SQL procedure successfully completed.

SQL> alter session set sql_trace=false;

SQL> alter session set events '10015 trace name context off';

SQL> @check_param
PL/SQL procedure successfully completed.
```

Using DBMS_SYSTEM.SET_EV and DBMS_SYSTEM.READ_EV

There are two useful procedures related to events in the DBMS_SYSTEM package. They are SET_EV, used to set a specific event, and READ_EV, used to see the current status of an event. The procedures are defined as follows:

```
DBMS_SYSTEM.SET_EV(
SI   Binary_integer,
SE   Binary_integer,
EV   Binary_integer,
LE   Binary_integer,
NM   Binary_integer);
```

Where:

- **SI** is the Oracle SID value.

- **SE** is the Oracle serial number.

- **EV** is the Oracle event to set.

- **LE** is the event level.

- **NM** is the name.

For example:

```
EXECUTE SYS.DBMS_SYSTEM.SET_EV(sid,serial#,10046,level,'');
```

The DBMS_SYSTEM.READ_EV has the following syntax:

```
DBMS_SYSTEM.READ_EV(
IEV binary_integer,
OEV binary_integer);
```

Where:

- **IEV** is the Oracle event (in value).

- **OEV** is the Oracle event setting (out value).

For example:

```
EXECUTE sys.dbms_system.read_ev(i,event_level);
```

Oracle support has been known to give inconsistent advice regarding whether or not to use DBMS_SYSTEM

SET_EV and READ_EV. A list of the Oracle event codes is shown in Table

Source shows an example of how to use events. As with other powerful and undocumented Oracle features, make sure someone who thoroughly understands the ramifications of using the event or events is present when you attempt usage of the event codes. Improper use of events can result in database crashes and corruption.

🖫 dump_em.sql

```
--*************************************************
--
--     Copyright © 2003 by Rampant TechPress Inc.
--
--     Free for non-commercial use.
--     For commercial licensing, e-mail info@rampant.cc
--
--  *************************************************
How to dump a segment header - by Don Burleson
set heading off;
spool dump_em.sql;

select
'alter session set events ''immediate trace name blockdump level
'||
to_char((header_file*16777216)+header_block)||''';'
from
dba_segments
where
segment_name = 'VBAP';

spool off;

cat dump_em.sql
@dump_em
```

The segment header block dump will be in the user session trace file. As with the undocumented initialization parameters, events should be used only under the direction of a senior-level DBA or Oracle support.

Conclusion

This chapter discussed some topics of interest when administrating the database itself. Commands such as CREATE and ALTER DATABASE and related topics were considered. Several techniques were also presented that, when used, will ensure that database management is done correctly. The chapter also covered how to rename databases and rebuild their control files. There should now be an understanding of how Oracle databases are created, modified, and dropped. The concepts of Oracle undocumented parameters and Oracle events and their usage have also been discussed.

In the next chapter, we will look at tablespaces and file internals in depth.

Tablespace and File Internals Scripts

## CHAPTER 6

Monitoring Tablespaces

There is more to monitor in a database than just users. Tablespaces require watching because they are changing objects. They are subject to becoming filled and/or fragmented. The Oracle Administrator toolbar provides GUI-based monitoring of tablespaces via the storage manager. This is shown in Figure 6.1.Unfortunately, it provides no report output. Luckily, it is fairly easy to monitor tablespaces using the V$ and DB_ views. Figure 6.2 shows the *dba_* views that relate to tablespaces. We will examine a few scripts that provide information for assessing the status of tablespaces.

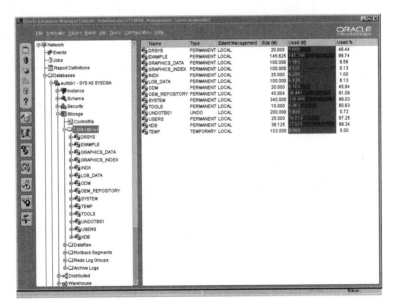

Figure 6.1 *Oracle Enterprise Manager Storage Manager screen.*

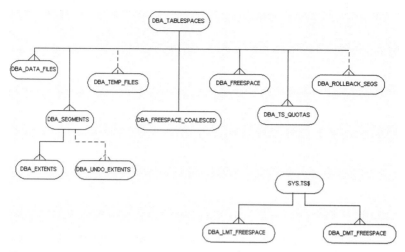

Figure 6.2 *dba_tablespaces* view cluster

Monitoring Tablespace Freespace and Fragmentation

We'll start with a report that covers two critical parameters, available space and fragmentation. The OEM GUI includes a tablespace map feature that graphically provides this information and can be printed in a report format. This is shown in Figure 6.3. An example of the OEM tablespace analysis report is shown in Figure 6.4. For a manual report, see *free_space.sql*.

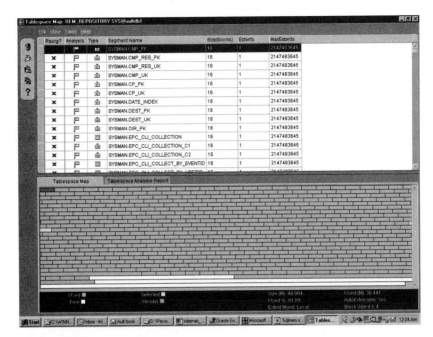

Figure 6.3 *OEM Tablespace Map*

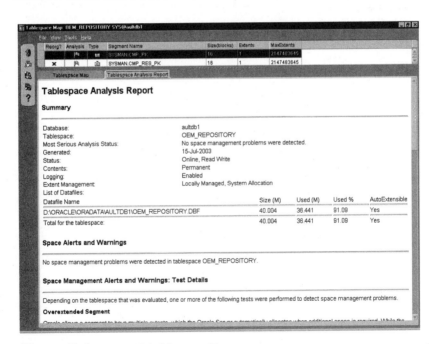

Figure 6.4 *OEM Tablespace Report*

Monitoring Tablespaces

🖫 free_space.sql

```
--*************************************************
--
--    Copyright © 2003 by Rampant TechPress Inc.
--
--    Free for non-commercial use.
--    For commercial licensing, e-mail info@rampant.cc
--
-- *************************************************
SET FEED OFF
SET FLUSH OFF
SET VERIFY OFF
set pages 58 LINES 132
COLUMN tablespace       HEADING Name              FORMAT a30
COLUMN files            HEADING '#Files'          FORMAT 9,999
COLUMN pieces           HEADING 'Frag'            FORMAT 9,999
COLUMN free_bytes       HEADING 'Free|Byte'       FORMAT
9,999,999,999
COLUMN free_blocks      HEADING 'Free|Blk'        FORMAT 999,999
COLUMN largest_bytes    HEADING 'Biggest|Bytes'   FORMAT
9,999,999,999
COLUMN largest_blks     HEADING 'Biggest|Blks'    FORMAT 999,999
COLUMN ratio            HEADING 'Percent'         FORMAT 999.999
COLUMN average_fsfi     HEADING 'Average|FSFI'    FORMAT 999.999
ttitle "FREE SPACE REPORT"
DEFINE 1 = free_spc
SPOOL &1

SELECT
    tablespace,
    COUNT(*) files,
    SUM(pieces) pieces,
    SUM(free_bytes) free_bytes,
    SUM(free_blocks) free_blocks,
    SUM(largest_bytes) largest_bytes,
    SUM(largest_blks) largest_blks,
    SUM(largest_bytes)/sum(free_bytes)*100 ratio,
    SUM(fsfi)/COUNT(*) average_fsfi
FROM
    free_space
GROUP BY
    tablespace;

SPOOL OFF
CLEAR COLUMNS
TTITLE OFF
SET FEED ON
SET FLUSH ON
SET VERIFY ON
SET PAGES 22 LINES 80
PAUSE Press Enter to continue
```

The report in *free_space.sql* uses the *free_space* view, which is based on the *dba_free_space* view. This view is shown below. The freespace report is shown in *free_space_view.sql*.

🖫 free_space.sql

```
--**********************************************
--
--     Copyright © 2003 by Rampant TechPress Inc.
--
--     Free for non-commercial use.
--     For commercial licensing, e-mail info@rampant.cc
--
-- **********************************************

REM  You must have direct select grants on the underlying tables
REM  for this view to be generated.

create or replace  view free_space (
     tablespace,
     file_id,
     pieces,
     free_bytes,
     free_blocks,
     largest_bytes,
     largest_blks,
     fsfi)
as
select
     tablespace_name,
     file_id,
     count(*),
     sum(bytes),
     sum(blocks),
     max(bytes),
     max(blocks),
     sqrt(max(blocks)/sum(blocks))*(100/sqrt(sqrt(count(blocks))
))
from
     sys.dba_free_space
group by
     tablespace_name,
     file_id;
```

```
--*************************************************
--
--    Copyright © 2003 by Rampant TechPress Inc.
--
--    Free for non-commercial use.
--    For commercial licensing, e-mail info@rampant.cc
--
--  *************************************************

rem FUNCTION: Create free_space view for use by freespc reports
rem
CREATE VIEW free_space
    (tablespace, file_id, pieces, free_bytes, free_blocks,
     largest_bytes,largest_blks, fsfi) AS
SELECT tablespace_name, file_id, COUNT(*),
    SUM(bytes), SUM(blocks),
    MAX(bytes), MAX(blocks),

SQRT(MAX(blocks)/SUM(blocks))*(100/SQRT(SQRT(COUNT(blocks))))
FROM sys.dba_free_space
GROUP BY tablespace_name, file_id, relative_fno;
```

Here is a sample listing.

Name	#Files	Frag	Free Byte	Free Blk	Biggest Bytes	Biggest Blks	Percent	Average FSFI
CWMLITE	1	1	20,905,984	2,552	20,905,984	2,552	100.000	100.000
DBAUTIL_DATA	1	1	5,939,200	725	5,939,200	725	100.000	100.000
DBAUTIL_INDEX	1	1	9,625,600	1,175	9,625,600	1,175	100.000	100.000
DRSYS	1	1	12,845,056	1,568	12,845,056	1,568	100.000	100.000
EXAMPLE	1	1	262,144	32	262,144	32	100.000	100.000
INDX	1	1	26,148,864	3,192	26,148,864	3,192	100.000	100.000
SYSTEM	1	1	540,672	66	540,672	66	100.000	100.000
TOOLS	1	3	8,192,000	1,000	7,274,496	888	88.800	71.602
UNDOTBS	1	4	208,338,944	25,432	114,098,176	13,928	54.766	52.329
UNDO_TBS2	1	1	19,595,264	2,392	19,595,264	2,392	100.000	100.000
UNDO_TBS3	1	1	19,595,264	2,392	19,595,264	2,392	100.000	100.000
USERS	1	1	25,952,256	3,168	25,952,256	3,168	100.000	100.000

Ideally, the tablespace data files will show only one extent. This means there will be one line in the report for each tablespace data file, and the biggest area will match the free area. Practically, there will be several extents if the tablespace has been used for any length of time, and the free area (which corresponds to total freespace in the tablespace) and the biggest area (which corresponds to the biggest area of contiguous free space) will not be equal.

There is probably nothing to worry about after coalescing, unless the number of extents is 20 or more, and the mismatch between the biggest area and the free area is 10 percent or more. If either of these values is exceeded, the DBA should consider using the defragmentation methods described earlier. This report does not cover temporary tablespaces that are created as CREATE TEMPORARY TABLESPACE using tempfiles.

Beginning with version 8, the tablespaces are automatically defragmented by the SMON process if the value for the default storage parameter *pctincrease* is set greater than 0. The free space fragmentation index (FSFI), from the *Oracle DBA Handbook,* by Kevin Loney (Oracle Press, 1994), shows how much freespace in a tablespace is fragmented. A high value is good (with 100 the best); a low value is bad.

If it becomes necessary to add data files to a single tablespace in a short period of time, it may be wise to extrapolate the growth and then export, drop, and re-create the tablespace to a size large enough to prevent excessive addition of data files. Oracle suggests using autoextend data files for tablespaces that are expected to grow. However, there is something to be said for manual control of tablespace growth. With autoextend, a runaway insert or other database mishap can cause the tablespace to grow unpredictably. Autoextend can work very well in a stable production environment, so long as the DBA has a firm understanding of the way the tablespaces are likely to grow.

In order to equalize disk I/O, it may be beneficial to spread data files for large databases across several drives. This must be decided on a case-by-case basis, and is database-specific. If there are several large tables that would benefit from being spread across multiple disks, consider placing them in their own tablespaces, then size the data files for the tablespaces such that the data contained in the tables is spread. For example, a single table that contains a gigabyte of data may benefit from spreading the file across several platters.

This can be done in Oracle7 by creating a table-specific tablespace on each platter that will hold the file, with each tablespace a fraction of the total size of the table. For instance, if the file will be spread across four drives, each data file would be 250 megabytes in size. Then, when the table is imported, it will be spread across the four drives.

The database treats the table as one contiguous entity, but spreading the table across the available drives increases I/O speed. Under Oracle8, Oracle8i, and Oracle9i, this can be accomplished with table partitioning. Partitioning allows a single table to be spread, by value range, across several files. Of course, with RAID 1, RAID01/10, or RAID5, the spreading is done quasi-automatically, so the only reason to partition is for use of partition elimination or the benefits of parallel query and independent partition maintenance.

Each tablespace should be created with a default storage parameter that takes into account the performance demands of the tables in the application. Estimate the size requirements for the tables as they are created, and only use the default storage for minor tables. Ideally, application developers will estimate the table size requirements.

To avoid fragmentation issues altogether, use the fixed-size extent model for tablespaces. The fixed-size extent model creates initial extent sizes for tablespace objects that are multiples of a fixed default value, and subsequent extent sizes that are equal to the default extent value for the tablespace. With fixed-extent, tablespaces are sized according to the needs of the application, usually a small, medium, and large extent. The fixed-size model permits extents that are released due to table or index maintenance to be used by any other object in the table. By allowing freed-extent reuse, fragmentation is no longer a concern in fixed-extent-size model tablespaces.

In Oracle8i and later releases consider using the locally managed tablespace option that uses a bitmap to control extent allocation and deallocation. The bitmap is located locally to the tablespace thus avoiding the I/O overhead of the dictionary managed tablespace *uet$* and *fet$* dictionary table operations. The LMT can use auto allocated or uniform allocated extent sizes.

Monitoring Tablespace Autoextend Settings

If the autoextend feature is used, database autoextend status and data file locations should be monitored, in addition to space usage and fragmentation monitoring. *dba_file_data.sql* shows SQL that will create a view monitoring autoextend data for pre-Oracle8. In pre-Oracle8 versions, the only way to get this information is to query the SYS table FILEXT$, which, unfortunately, looks like this:

```
Name                                  Null?          Type
-----------------------------------   -------------  ------
FILE#                                 NOT NULL       NUMBER
MAXEXTEND                             NOT NULL       NUMBER
INC                                   NOT NULL       NUMBER
```

This structure means that several other tables need to be joined, namely, FILE$, TS$, and V$DBFILE, in order to get back to the actual filename and tablespace. A script to create a data file view is shown in *dba_file_data.sql*

🖫 dba_file_data.sql

```
--*************************************************
--
--   Copyright © 2003 by Rampant TechPress Inc.
--
--   Free for non-commercial use.
--
--   For commercial licensing, e-mail info@rampant.cc
--
--  *************************************************

CREATE VIEW dba_file_data AS

SELECT
  a.name tablespace,a.dflminext min_extents,
  a.dflmaxext max_extents,
  a.dflinit init,a.dflincr next,
  a.dflextpct pct_increase, d.name datafile,
  b.blocks datafile_size, c.maxextend max_extend,
  c.inc ext_incr

FROM ts$ a, file$ b, filext$ c, v$dbfile d
```

```
WHERE
    a.ts#=b.ts# and b.file#=c.file# and b.file#=d.file#
/
```

This script creates the view *dba_file_data*, which will look like this when queried:

```
Name                            Null?        Type
----------------------------    --------     ------------
TABLESPACE                      NOT NULL     VARCHAR2(30)
MIN_EXTENTS                     NOT NULL     NUMBER
MAX_EXTENTS                     NOT NULL     NUMBER
INIT                            NOT NULL     NUMBER
NEXT                            NOT NULL     NUMBER
PCT_INCREASE                    NOT NULL     NUMBER
DATAFILE                                     VARCHAR2(257)
DATAFILE_SIZE                   NOT NULL     NUMBER
MAX_EXTEND                      NOT NULL     NUMBER
EXT_INCR                        NOT NULL     NUMBER
```

This view makes it easy to create a simple SELECT to fetch autoextend and data file location information from a single view, along with all of the pertinent sizing information. The Oracle Administrator Storage Manager shows this information under the data files section. In Oracle8i, the view *dba_data_files* contains the columns AUTOEXTENSIBLE (YES or NO), MAXBYTES, MAXBLOCKS, and INCREMENT_BY, which allow for report generation and monitoring of the autoextension capabilities of all data files.

Monitoring Tablespace Data Files

The DBA should also monitor the size and location of the data files associated with tablespaces under his/her control. It is necessary to have an accurate map of data files, if for no other reason than to prevent placing index tablespace data files alongside those that deal with table data. A script to document tablespace data files is shown

---

in *dbfiles.sql*. The report it produces is also show below and provides this data file map.

```
--**************************************************
--
--    Copyright © 2003 by Rampant TechPress Inc.
--
--    Free for non-commercial use.
--    For commercial licensing, e-mail info@rampant.cc
--
--  **************************************************

REM    FUNCTION:  Document  file sizes and locations
REM    Use:        From SQLPLUS
REM    MRA 05/16/99 Added autoextend monitoring
REM    MRA 10/14/99 Added temp file monitoring 9i
REM
CLEAR COMPUTES
COLUMN file_name          FORMAT A51         HEADING 'File Name'
COLUMN tablespace_name    FORMAT A15         HEADING 'Tablespace'
COLUMN meg                FORMAT 99,999.90   HEADING 'Megabytes'
COLUMN status             FORMAT A10         HEADING 'Status'
COLUMN autoextensible     FORMAT A3          HEADING 'AE?'
COLUMN maxmeg             FORMAT 99,999      HEADING
'Max|Megabytes'
COLUMN Increment_by       FORMAT 9,999       HEADING 'Inc|By'
SET LINES 130 PAGES 47 VERIFY OFF FEEDBACK OFF
ttitle 'DATABASE DATA FILES'
SPOOL datafile
BREAK ON tablespace_name SKIP 1 ON REPORT
COMPUTE SUM OF meg ON tablespace_name
COMPUTE SUM OF meg ON REPORT
SELECT
     tablespace_name,file_name,
     bytes/1048576 meg,
     status,autoextensible,
     maxbytes/1048576 maxmeg,
     increment_by
FROM
     dba_data_files
UNION
SELECT
     tablespace_name,file_name,
     bytes/1048576 meg,
     status,autoextensible,
     maxbytes/1048576 maxmeg,
     increment_by
FROM
     dba_temp_files
ORDER BY
     tablespace_name
/
SPOOL OFF
```

```
SET VERIFY ON FEEDBACK ON
TTITLE OFF
CLEAR COLUMNS
CLEAR COMPUTES
PAUSE Press Enter to continue
```

Here is a sample listing.

Tablespace	File Name	Megabytes	Status	AE?	Max Megabytes	Inc By
CWMLITE	/var/oracle/cwmlite01.dbf	20.00	AVAILABLE	YES	32,768	80
*************						
sum		20.00				
DBAUTIL_DATA	/opt/oracle/dbt1_dat1.dbf	10.00	AVAILABLE	NO	0	0
*************						
sum		10.00				
DBAUTIL_INDEX	/opt/oracle/dbt1_idx1.dbf	10.00	AVAILABLE	NO	0	0
*************						
sum		10.00				
DRSYS	/var/oracle/drsys01.dbf	20.00	AVAILABLE	YES	32,768	80
*************						
sum		20.00				
EXAMPLE	/var/oracle/example01.dbf	36.25	AVAILABLE	YES	32,768	80
*************						
sum		36.25				
INDX	/var/oracle/indx01.dbf	25.00	AVAILABLE	YES	32,768	160
*************						
sum		25.00				

Monitoring Tablespace Extent Mapping

The location of the freespace in a tablespace and the size of the fragments themselves is also handy to know. OEM and many third-party tools will provide a GUI-based map. The script in *mapper.sql* provides location and fragment data. The output from the script in is also shown below.

🖫 **mapper.sql**

```
--************************************************
--
--    Copyright © 2003 by Rampant TechPress Inc.
--
--    Free for non-commercial use.
--    For commercial licensing, e-mail info@rampant.cc
--
--    ************************************************

SET PAGES 47 LINES 132 VERIFY OFF FEEDBACK OFF
COLUMN file_id        HEADING 'File|id'
COLUMN value          NEW_VALUE dbblksiz NOPRINT
COLUMN meg            FORMAT 9,999.99 HEADING 'Meg'
COLUMN partition_name FORMAT a30      HEADING 'Partition|Name'
SELECT value FROM v$parameter WHERE name='db_block_size';
ttitle '&&ts Mapping Report'
SPOOL ts_map

SELECT
     'free space' owner, '        ' object,'Not Part.' partition
     file_id, block_id, blocks,
     (blocks*&dbblksiz)/(1024*1024) meg
FROM
     dba_free_space
WHERE
     tablespace_name=UPPER('&&ts')
UNION
SELECT
     SUBSTR(owner,1,20), SUBSTR(segment_name,
1,32),partition_name
     file_id, block_id, blocks,
     (blocks*&dbblksiz)/(1024*1024) meg
FROM
     dba_extents
WHERE
     tablespace_name = UPPER('&&ts')
ORDER BY 3,4;
SPOOL OFF
UNDEF ts
SET PAGES 22 LINES 80 VERIFY ON FEEDBACK ON
```

```
CLEAR COLUMNS
TTITLE OFF
```

Here is a sample listing.

```
                          File
OWNER      OBJECT           id  BLOCK_ID    BLOCKS      MEG
---------- ---------------  ---- ---------  -------   ------
TELE_DBA   LOAD_TEST         11         2   102655   401.00
TELE_DBA   LOAD_TEST         11    102657    25600   100.00
TELE_DBA   LOAD_TEST         11    128257    25600   100.00
SYSTEM     PARTITION_TEST    11    153857      260     1.02
SYSTEM     PARTITION_TEST    11    154117      260     1.02
SYSTEM     PARTITION_TEST    11    154377      260     1.02
free space                  11    154637    24564    95.95
```

Oracle10g Tablespace Renaming

In Oracle10g, you can simply rename a tablespace TBS01 to TBS02 by issuing the following command:

```
ALTER TABLESPACE tbs01 RENAME TO tbs02;
```

You must follow the rules when renaming a tablespace:

- You must set compatibility level to at least 10.0.1.

- You cannot rename the SYSTEM or SYSAUX tablespaces.

- You cannot rename an offline tablespace.

- You cannot rename a tablespace that contains offline datafiles.

- Rename a tablespace does not changes its tablespace identifier.

- Rename a tablespace does not change the name of its datafiles.

Tablespace Rename Benefits

Tablespace rename provides the following benefits:

- It simplifies the process of tablespace migration within a database.

- It simplifies the process of transport a tablespace between two databases.

Examples

Example 1: Rename a tablespace within a database

In Oracle9i or earlier releases, to rename a tablespace from OLD_TBS to NEW_TBS, you have to go through the following steps:

18. Create a new tablespace NEW_TBS.

19. Copy all objects from OLD_TBS to NEW_TBS.

20. Drop tablespace OLD_TBS.

In Oracle10g, you can accomplish the same thing in one step:

- Rename tablespace OLD_TBS to NEW_TBS.

```
ALTER TABLESPACE RENAME old_tbs to new_tbs;
```

Example 2: Transport a tablespace between two databases

In the example below (see figure 6.5), you cannot transport a tablespace TBS01 from database A to database B in the previous release of Oracle server because database B also has a tablespace called TBS01. In Oracle10g, you can simply rename TBS01 to TBS02 in database B before transporting tablespace TBS01.

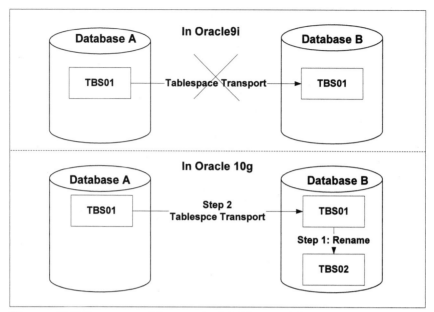

Figure 6.5 *Rename tablespace for Tablespace Transport*

Bigfile Tablespace

A *bigfile tablespace (BFT)* is a tablespace containing a single file that can have a very large size.

Bigfile Tablespace Overview

The traditional tablespace refers to as *smallfile tablespace (SFT)*. Smallfile tablespace contains multiple relatively small files. The bigfile tablespace has the following characteristics:

- An Oracle database can contain both bigfile and smallfile tablespaces.

- System default is to create the traditional smallfile tablespace.

- The SYSTEM and SYSAUX tablespaces are always created using the system default type.

- Bigfile tablespaces are supported only for locally managed tablespaces with automatic segment-space management.

  There are two exceptions that bigfile tablespace segments are manually managed:

  - Locally managed undo tablespace

  - Temporary tablespace

- Bigfile tablespace are intended to be used with Automated Storage Management (see chapter one) or other logical volume managers that support RAID.

Bigfile Tablespace Benefits

Bigfile tablespace has the following benefits:

- It simplifies large database tablespace management by reducing the number of datafiles needed.

- It simplifies datafile management with Oracle-managed files and Automated Storage Management (AMS) by eliminating the need for adding new datafiles and dealing with multiple files.

- It allows you to create bigfile tablespace up to 8 exabytes (8 million terabytes) in size, and significantly increase the storage capacity of an oracle database.

- It makes the concept that a tablespace and a datafile are logically equivalent.

Maximum Database Size

The BFT extended the maximum size of tablespace and database. Let us take a look at the two formulas that calculate the maximum size of data file and database.

The maximum data file size is calculated by:

Maximum datafile size = db_block_size * maximum number of blocks

The maximum amount of data in an Oracle database is calculated by:

Maximum database size = *maximum datafile size * maximum number of datafile*

The maximum number of datafiles in Oracle9i and Oracle10g database is **65,536**. However, the maximum number of blocks in a data file increase from **4,194,304** (4 million) blocks to **4,294,967,296** (4 billion) blocks.

The maximum amount of data for a 32K block size database is **eight Petabytes** (8,192 Terabytes) in Oracle9i (Table 6.1).

BLOCK SIZE	MAXIMUM DATA FILE SIZE	MAXIMUM DATABASE SIZE
32 K	128 GB	**8,388,608 GB**
16 K	64 GB	4,194,304 GB
8 K	32 GB	2,097,152 GB
4 K	16 GB	1,048,579 GB
2 K	8 GB	524,288 GB

Table 6.1 *Maximum Database Size in Oracle9i*

The maximum amount of data for a 32K block size database is **eight Exabytes** (8,388,608 Terabytes) in Oracle10g (Table 6.2).

BLOCK SIZE	MAXIMUM DATA FILE SIZE	MAXIMUM DATABASE SIZE
32 K	131,072 GB	**8,589,934,592 GB**
16 K	65,536 GB	4,294,967,296 GB
8 K	32,768 GB	2,147,483,648 GB
4 K	16,384 GB	1,073,741,824 GB
2 K	8,192 GB	536,870,912 GB

Table 6.2 *Maximum Database Size in Oracle10g*

As you can see that with BFT's new addressing scheme, Oracle10g can contain astronomical amount of data within a single database.

Oracle10g Data Dictionary View Enhancements

A new column is added to both DBA_TABLESPACES and *v$tablespace* views to indicate whether a particular tablespace is BIGFILE or SMALLFILE.

```
SQL> select name, bigfile
     from v$tablespace;

NAME                              BIGFILE
------------------------------    -------
SYSTEM                            NO
UNDOTBS01                         NO
SYSAUX                            NO
TEMP                              NO
EXAMPLE                           NO
USERS                             NO
BIG_TBS                           YES

SQL> select tablespace_name,bigfile
     from   dba_tablespaces;
```

```
TABLESPACE_NAME                      BIGFILE
-----------------------------        ---------
SYSTEM                               SMALLFILE
UNDOTBS01                            SMALLFILE
SYSAUX                               SMALLFILE
TEMP                                 SMALLFILE
EXAMPLE                              SMALLFILE
USERS                                SMALLFILE
BIG_TBS01                            BIGFILE
```

Another dictionary view *props$*, which contains different database properties, also specifies the default tablespace type for the database.

```
SQL> select name, values$, comment$
     from    props$;
NAME               VALUES$          COMMET$
----------         --------         --------------------
DBTIMEZONE         -07:00           DB time zone
DEFAULT_TBS_TYPE   SMALLFILE        Default tablespace type
NLS_LANGUAGE       AMERICAN         Language
NLS_TERRITORY      AMERICA          Territory
```

Bigfile Examples

Example 1: Create a database with default bigfile tablespace

```
CREATE DATABASE GRID
SET DEFAULT BIGFILE TABLESPACE
DATAFILE '/u02/oradata/grid/system01.dbf' SIZE 500 M,
SYSAUX DATA FILE '/u02/oradata/grid/sysaux01.dbf' SIZE 500 M
DEFAULT TEMPORARY TABLESPACE tbs01
TEMPFILE '/u02/oradata/grid/temp01.dbf' SIZE 1024 M
UNDO TABLESPACE undo01
DATAFILE '/u02/oradata/grid/undo01.dbf' SIZE 1024 M;
```

Example 2: Moving data between smallfile and bigfile tablespaces

```
ALTER TABLE employee MOVE TABLESPACE bigfile_tbs;
```

Example 3: Create a bigfile tablespace and change its size

```
CREATE BIGFILE TABLESPACE user_tbs
DATAFILE '/u02/oradata/grid/user_tbs01.dbf' SIZE 1024 M;

ALTER TABLESPACE user_tbs RESIZE 10G;
```

In previous release of Oracle server, K and M were used to specify storage size. Notice in this DDL statement, a user can specify size in gigabytes and terabytes using G and T respectively.

Example 4: Using DBVERIFY utility with bigfile

With smallfile tablespace, you can run multiple instances of DBVERIFY in parallel on multiple datafiles in order to speed up integrity checking for a tablespace. You can achieve integrity checking parallelism with BFTs by starting multiple instances of DBVERIFY on parts of the single big file.

```
$dbv FILE=bigfile01.dbf  START=1 END=10000
$dbv FILE=bigfile01.dbf  START=10001
```

Note: START = Start Block; END = End Block

Orackle10g Cross Platform Transportable Tablespaces

A transportable tablespace allows you to quickly move a subset of an Oracle database from one Oracle database to another. However, in previous release of Oracle server, you can only move a tablespace across Oracle databases within the same platform.

Oracle 10g is going one step further by allowing you to move tablespace across different platforms.

Benefit

For organization that hosts Oracle databases on different platforms, one of the major benefits now is that you can move data between databases quickly across different platforms. There is no need to use the traditional method of export and import.

Supported Platforms and New Data Dictionary Views

Oracle 10g Release 1 supports the eleven platforms for transportable tablespace. A new data dictionary view *v$transportable_platform* listed all eleven supported platforms along with platform id and endian format.

PLATFORM_ID	PLATFORM_NAME	ENDIAN_FORMAT
1	Solaris[tm] OE (32-bit)	Big
2	Solaris[tm] OE (64-bit)	Big
3	HP-UX (64-bit)	Big
4	HP-UX IA (64-bit)	Big
5	HP Tru64 UNIX	Little
6	AIX Systems (64-bit)	Big
7	Microsoft Windows NT	Little
10	Linux IA (32-bit)	Little
11	Linux IA (64-bit)	Little

Table 6.3 *Supported Platforms for Transportable Tablespaces*

The *v$database* data dictionary view also adds two columns: platform id, and platform name:

```
SQL> select name, platform_id,platform_name from v$database;

NAME      PLATFORM_ID    PLATFORM_NAME
-------   -----------    -----------------------
GRID            2        Solaris[tm] OE (64-bit)
```

The Oracle10g SYSAUX tablespace

The Oracle10g database was the first to release the SYSAUX tablespace. The SYSAUX tablespace allows for the specification of a tablespace that will provide storage of non-sys related tables and indexes that traditionally were placed in the SYSTEM tablespace.

An example would be the tables and indexes that were owned by the system user. Unfortunately Oracle still places the SCOTT schema and the other demonstration schemas in the SYSTEM tablespace. Go figure.

You specify the SYSAUX tablespace in the CREATE DATABASE command. This is demonstrated in the example database creation script:

🖫 **create_oracle10g.sql**

```
--********************************************
--
--    Copyright © 2003 by Rampant TechPress Inc.
--
--    Free for non-commercial use.
--    For commercial licensing, e-mail info@rampant.cc
--
--    ********************************************

CREATE DATABASE test
MAXINSTANCES 1
MAXLOGHISTORY 1
MAXLOGFILES 5
MAXLOGMEMBERS 3
MAXDATAFILES 100
DATAFILE
'/usr/oracle/OraHome1/oradata/aultdb1/test/system01.dbf' SIZE
300M REUSE AUTOEXTEND ON NEXT  10240K MAXSIZE UNLIMITED
EXTENT MANAGEMENT LOCAL
```

```
SYSAUX DATAFILE
'/usr/oracle/OraHome1/oradata/aultdb1/test/sysaux01.dbf' SIZE
120M REUSE AUTOEXTEND ON NEXT  10240K MAXSIZE UNLIMITED
DEFAULT TEMPORARY TABLESPACE TEMP TEMPFILE
'/usr/oracle/OraHome1/oradata/aultdb1/test/temp01.dbf' SIZE 20M
REUSE AUTOEXTEND ON NEXT  640K MAXSIZE UNLIMITED EXTENT
MANAGEMENT LOCAL
UNDO TABLESPACE "UNDOTBS1" DATAFILE
'/usr/oracle/OraHome1/oradata/aultdb1/test/undotbs01.dbf' SIZE
200M REUSE AUTOEXTEND ON NEXT  5120K MAXSIZE UNLIMITED
CHARACTER SET WE8ISO8859P1
NATIONAL CHARACTER SET AL16UTF16
LOGFILE GROUP 1
('/usr/oracle/OraHome1/oradata/aultdb1/test/redo01.log') SIZE
10240K,
GROUP 2 ('/usr/oracle/OraHome1/oradata/aultdb1/test/redo02.log')
SIZE 10240K,
GROUP 3 ('/usr/oracle/OraHome1/oradata/aultdb1/test/redo03.log')
SIZE 10240K
USER SYS IDENTIFIED BY "password" USER SYSTEM IDENTIFIED BY
"password";
```

With the new SYSAUX tablespace Oracle comes closer to providing all the needed tablespaces for a truly OFA compliant database right out of the box. In one CREATE DATABASE command we can specify the SYSTEM tablespace, the TEMPORARY tablespace, the AUXSYS tablespace, the default UNDO tablespace and the redo logs.

Of course using the Oracle Managed Files option you can create an entire database with a single command but the database created is not suitable for production use and is not OFA compliant.

The SYSAUX tablespace is required in all new Oracle10g databases. Only the SYSAUX tablespace datafile location is specified, Oracle specifies the remainder of the tablespace properties including:

- ONLINE
- PERMANENT

- READ WRITE

- EXTENT MANAGMENT LOCAL

- SEGMENT SPACE MANAGEMENT AUTO

If a datafile is specified for the SYSTEM tablespace then one must be specified for the SYSAUX tablespace. If one is not specified in this case then the CREATE DATABASE command will fail. The only exception is for an Oracle Managed File system.

During any update of a database to Oracle10g a SYSAUX tablespace must be created or the upgrade will fail. The SYSAUX tablespace has the same security profile as the SYSTEM tablespace. However, loss of the SYSAUX tablespace will not result in a database crash, just the functionalities of the schemas it contains.

Monitoring System IO

One aspect of monitoring tablespaces that is frequently overlooked is monitoring the tablespace IO profile. The tablespace IO profile consists of the number of IOs to each tablespace and datafile as well as the timing information (time per IO for both read and write operations.) The first script we will look at monitors the overall IO to the data files in an Oracle instance.

🖫 **io_sec.sql**

```
--*********************************************
--
--     Copyright © 2003 by Rampant TechPress Inc.
--
--     Free for non-commercial use.
--     For commercial licensing, e-mail info@rampant.cc
--
--     *********************************************
```

Monitoring System IO   **185**

```
set serveroutput on
declare
cursor get_io is select
        nvl(sum(a.phyrds+a.phywrts),0) sum_io1,to_number(null)
sum_io2
from sys.v_$filestat a
union
select
        to_number(null) sum_io1, nvl(sum(b.phyrds+b.phywrts),0)
sum_io2
from
        sys.v_$tempstat b;
now date;
elapsed_seconds number;
sum_io1 number;
sum_io2 number;
sum_io12 number;
sum_io22 number;
tot_io number;
tot_io_per_sec number;
fixed_io_per_sec number;
temp_io_per_sec number;
begin
open get_io;
for i in 1..2 loop
fetch get_io into sum_io1, sum_io2;
if i = 1 then sum_io12:=sum_io1;
else
sum_io22:=sum_io2;
end if;
end loop;
select sum_io12+sum_io22 into tot_io from dual;
select sysdate into now from dual;
select ceil((now-startup_time)*(60*60*24)) into elapsed_seconds
from v$instance;
fixed_io_per_sec:=sum_io12/elapsed_seconds;
temp_io_per_sec:=sum_io22/elapsed_seconds;
tot_io_per_sec:=tot_io/elapsed_seconds;
dbms_output.put_line('Elapsed Sec :'||to_char(elapsed_seconds,
'9,999,999.99'));
dbms_output.put_line('Fixed
IO/SEC:'||to_char(fixed_io_per_sec,'9,999,999.99'));
dbms_output.put_line('Temp IO/SEC :'||to_char(temp_io_per_sec,
'9,999,999.99'));
dbms_output.put_line('Total IO/SEC:'||to_char(tot_io_Per_Sec,
'9,999,999.99'));
end;
/
```

When executed the above PL/SQL generates the following type of report:

```
SQL> /
Elapsed Sec :    43,492.00
Fixed IO/SEC:       588.33
```

```
Temp IO/SEC :        95.01
Total IO/SEC:       683.34
```

The information in this report can then be used to determine if you have sufficient numbers of disks in your RAID stripe set, in the above output we need to ensure there are at least 7-8 disks servicing the database at all times (the usual IO rate for a single disk is around 100 IO/sec.)

But what if we want to see what datafiles are generating the most IO? The next script allows us to see a breakdown of IO by datafile.

🖫 file_io.sql

```
--*************************************************
--
--      Copyright © 2003 by Rampant TechPress Inc.
--
--      Free for non-commercial use.
--      For commercial licensing, e-mail info@rampant.cc
--
--  *************************************************

rem
rem NAME: fileio.sql
rem
rem FUNCTION: Reports on the file io status of all of the
rem FUNCTION: datafiles in the database.

rem HISTORY:
rem WHO             WHAT            WHEN
rem Mike Ault               Created       1/5/96
rem
column sum_io1 new_value st1 noprint
column sum_io2 new_value st2 noprint
column sum_io new_value divide_by noprint
column Percent format 999.999 heading 'Percent|Of IO'
column brratio format 999.99 heading 'Block|Read|Ratio'
column bwratio format 999.99 heading 'Block|Write|Ratio'
column phyrds heading 'Physical | Reads'
column phywrts heading 'Physical | Writes'
column phyblkrd heading 'Physical|Block|Reads'
column phyblkwrt heading 'Physical|Block|Writes'
column name format a45 heading 'File|Name'
column file# format 9999 heading 'File'
set feedback off verify off lines 132 pages 60 sqlbl on trims on
rem
```

```
select
    nvl(sum(a.phyrds+a.phywrts),0) sum_io1
from
    sys.v_$filestat a;
select nvl(sum(b.phyrds+b.phywrts),0) sum_io2
from
        sys.v_$tempstat b;
select &st1+&st2 sum_io from dual;
rem
ttitle 'File IO Statistics Report'
spool fileio
select
    a.file#,b.name, a.phyrds, a.phywrts,
    (100*(a.phyrds+a.phywrts)/&divide_by) Percent,
    a.phyblkrd, a.phyblkwrt, (a.phyblkrd/greatest(a.phyrds,1))
brratio,
    (a.phyblkwrt/greatest(a.phywrts,1)) bwratio
from
    sys.v_$filestat a, sys.v_$dbfile b
where
    a.file#=b.file#
union
select
    c.file#,d.name, c.phyrds, c.phywrts,
    (100*(c.phyrds+c.phywrts)/&divide_by) Percent,
    c.phyblkrd, c.phyblkwrt,(c.phyblkrd/greatest(c.phyrds,1))
brratio,
    (c.phyblkwrt/greatest(c.phywrts,1)) bwratio
from
    sys.v_$tempstat c, sys.v_$tempfile d
where
    c.file#=d.file#
order by
    1
/
spool off
pause Press enter to continue
set feedback on verify on lines 80 pages 22
clear columns
ttitle off
```

The output from this script resembles the following, what you should be watchin for is excessive I/O to one or more files indicating possible hot disk areas. In the following report notice that datafile 22 is receiving a whopping 71% of IO, obviously we need to look at that datafile with an eye towards spreading its contents.

File IO Statistics Report

File ID	File Name	Physical Reads	Physical Writes	Percent Of IO	Physical Block Reads	Physical Block Writes	Block Read Ratio	Block Write Ratio
1	/db01/oradata/example/system01.dbf	1051889	26896	.161	1995975	26896	1.90	1.00
2	/db01/oradata/example/tools01.dbf	1458	1306	.000	1689	1306	1.16	1.00
3	/db01/oradata/example/rep_adm.dbf	145611	4021	.022	256189	4021	1.76	1.00
4	/db01/oradata/example/rbs01.dbf	43497	9355179	1.403	43498	9355179	1.00	1.00
5	/db02/oradata/example/rbs02.dbf	30943	8652683	1.296	30943	8652683	1.00	1.00
6	/db03/oradata/example/temp01.dbf	1055370	535819	.238	2280477	2734983	2.16	5.10
7	/db01/oradata/example/users01.dbf	1303	1301	.000	1303	1301	1.00	1.00
8	/db01/oradata/example/sqllab_vision1.dbf	1313	1301	.000	1313	1301	1.00	1.00
9	/db01/oradata/example/data01.dbf	10041541	481795	1.571	12053842	498715	1.20	1.04
10	/db01/oradata/example/perfstat.dbf	190225	8350	.030	190521	8350	1.00	1.00
11	/db01/oradata/example/ad_data_part_01_idx_01.dbf	2146	11432	.002	2161	11432	1.01	1.00
12	/db03/oradata/example/ad_data_part_02_01.dbf	1645555	40299	.252	1990141	40299	1.21	1.00
13	/db01/oradata/example/ad_data_part_03_01.dbf	434576	129043	.084	446258	129043	1.03	1.00
14	/db01/oradata/example/ad_data_part_05_idx_01.dbf	2078	9541	.002	2078	9541	1.00	1.00
15	/db01/oradata/example/ad_misc_data_01.dbf	2131384	545375	.400	2914912	545483	1.37	1.00
16	/db01/oradata/example/dealer_data_idx_01.dbf	48065	29264	.012	49026	31244	1.02	1.07
17	/db01/oradata/example/phone_data_01.dbf	178876	7349	.028	390570	7349	2.18	1.00
18	/db01/oradata/example/photo_data_idx_01.dbf	846886	171977	.152	1059948	173472	1.25	1.01
19	/db02/oradata/example/ad_data_part_02_idx_01.dbf	1957	6062	.001	1959	6062	1.00	1.00
20	/db02/oradata/example/ad_data_part_03_idx_01.dbf	2236	12812	.002	2293	12812	1.03	1.00
21	/db02/oradata/example/ad_data_part_04_01.dbf	1686578	210410	.283	1738100	210410	1.03	1.00
22	/db02/oradata/example/customer_data_01.dbf	480388617	135342	71.739	1341213686	135342	2.79	1.00
23	/db02/oradata/example/phone_data_idx_01.dbf	365105	53291	.062	3490177	173921	9.56	3.26
24	/db02/oradata/example/ref_data_idx_01.dbf	48985	2814	.008	56376	2818	1.15	1.00
25	/db03/oradata/example/ad_data_part_04_idx_01.dbf	3468	20408	.004	3469	20408	1.00	1.00

Of course you also need to be concerned with the timing of your IO, the following script shows the timing per datafile for IO:

💾 **io_timing.sql**

```
--**********************************************
--
--    Copyright © 2003 by Rampant TechPress Inc.
--
--    Free for non-commercial use.
--    For commercial licensing, e-mail info@rampant.cc
--
--  **********************************************

col name format a58 heading 'Name'
col phywrts heading 'Phys. Writes'
col phyreads heading 'Phys. Reads'
col read_rat heading 'Avg. Read|Time'
col write_rat 'Avg. Write|Time'
set lines 132 pages 45
ttitle 'IO Timing Analysis'
spool io_time
select  f.FILE# ,d.name,
phyrds,phywrts,readtim/greatest(PHYRDS,1)

read_rat,
WRITETIM/greatest(PHYWRTS,1) write_rat
from v$filestat f, v$datafile d
where f.file#=d.file#
union
select  f.FILE# ,d.name,
PHYRDS,PHYWRTS,READTIM/greatest(PHYRDS,1)

read_rat,
WRITETIM/greatest(PHYWRTS,1) write_rat
from v$tempstat f, v$tempfile d
where f.file#=d.file#
order by 5 desc
/
spool off
ttitle off
clear columns
set lines 80 pages 22
```

An example report for the above script is shown below.

Sat Oct 11
page 1

                                    IO Timing Analysis

                                                                      Avg. Read   Avg. Write
FILE# Name   PHYRDS Phys. Writes   Time   Time
----- ---------------------------------------   ------ ------------   ----------   ----------
    4 D:\ORACLE\ORADATA\AULTDB1\EXAMPLE01.DBF   17   15   25.8823529   23.8
    6 D:\ORACLE\ORADATA\AULTDB1\ODM01.DBF   17   15   24.3529412   22.4666667
    5 D:\ORACLE\ORADATA\AULTDB1\INDX01.DBF   17   15   23   19.7333333
    1 D:\ORACLE\ORADATA\AULTDB1\TEMP02.DBF   3   0   20.3333333   0
    2 D:\ORACLE\ORADATA\AULTDB1\TEMP01.DBF   3   0   20.3333333   0
   10 D:\ORACLE\ORADATA\AULTDB1\OEM_REPOSITORY.DBF   17   15   20.2352941   17
    7 D:\ORACLE\ORADATA\AULTDB1\TOOLS01.DBF   17   15   18.6470588   15.6
    8 D:\ORACLE\ORADATA\AULTDB1\USERS01.DBF   17   15   17.3529412   13.8
    3 D:\ORACLE\ORADATA\AULTDB1\DRSYS01.DBF   17   15   13.0588235   9.6
   13 D:\ORACLE\ORADATA\AULTDB1\GRAPHICS_INDEX01.DBF 17   15   12   9.46666667
    9 D:\ORACLE\ORADATA\AULTDB1\XDB01.DBF   22   15   11.6818182   11.2666667
   12 D:\ORACLE\ORADATA\AULTDB1\GRAPHICS_DATA01.DBF   17   15   10.4117647   7.46666667
    2 D:\ORACLE\ORADATA\AULTDB1\UNDOTBS01.DBF   36   88   8.94444444   4.76136364
   11 D:\ORACLE\ORADATA\AULTDB1\LOB_DATA01.DBF   17   15   8.82352941   5.73333333
    1 D:\ORACLE\ORADATA\AULTDB1\SYSTEM01.DBF   1392   107   2.92385057   37.6074766

15 rows selected.

Most SCSI devices will do a single read in around 9 milliseconds, if your average IO timing is between 0 and 20 milliseconds you are usually ok.

Monitoring Rollback Segments

Rollback segments must also be monitored, as well as the new Oracle9i UNDO segments.

Rollback segment information in tablespaces is monitored through the freespace and extents reports shown in previous sections, but it is helpful to have a report just for rollback segments in one convenient location. Even in Oracle9i, information on UNDO usage is helpful for tuning the Oracle UNDO tablespace. The same views as with Oracle7, Oracle8, and Oracle8i are used to monitor UNDO segments in Oracle9i.

Monitoring Rollback Usage and Statistics

Unfortunately, the *dba_rollback_segs* view is just too large for a single report to cover all of the parameters. Therefore, two views and two reports are required to adequately cover the *dba_rollback_segs* view and the monitoring of rollback segments. The scripts in *rbs_view.sql* create two views, ROLLBACK1 and ROLLBACK2, both based on the *v$rollstat* and *v$rollname* views, which are very important for monitoring rollback activity. The *dba* view, *dba_rollback_segs*, is based on these two tables. In Oracle9i, a new V$ view was added to allow monitoring of the UNDO segment usage statistics; this new view is called *v$undostat*.

```
--*************************************************
--
--    Copyright © 2003 by Rampant TechPress Inc.
--
--    Free for non-commercial use.
--    For commercial licensing, e-mail info@rampant.cc
--
-- *************************************************

REM
REM FUNCTION: create views required for rbk1 and rbk2 reports.
REM
REM
CREATE OR REPLACE VIEW rollback1 AS
SELECT
     d.segment_name, extents, optsize, shrinks,
     aveshrink, aveactive, d.status
FROM
     v$rollname n,
     v$rollstat s,
     dba_rollback_segs d
WHERE
     d.segment_id=n.usn(+)
     AND d.segment_id=s.usn(+)
;

CREATE OR REPLACE VIEW rollback2 AS
SELECT
     d.segment_name,extents,xacts,hwmsize,
     rssize,waits,wraps,extends,d.status
FROM
     v$rollname n,
     v$rollstat s,
     dba_rollback_segs d
WHERE
     d.segment_id=n.usn(+)
     AND d.segment_id=s.usn(+);
```

Once the ROLLBACK1 and ROLLBACK2 views have been created, two simple SQL scripts are used to monitor rollback segments. These scripts are shown next; their output is shown below.

🖫 **all_rbk.sql**

```
--*************************************************
--
--    Copyright © 2003 by Rampant TechPress Inc.
--
```

```
--     Free for non-commercial use.
--     For commercial licensing, e-mail info@rampant.cc
--
-- **********************************************
```

```
REM NAME                 : RBK1.SQL
REM FUNCTION             : REPORT ON ROLLBACK SEGMENT STORAGE
REM FUNCTION             : USES THE ROLLBACK1 VIEW
REM USE                  : FROM SQLPLUS
REM Limitations          : None
REM
COLUMN hwmsize              FORMAT 9999999999    HEADING 'LARGEST
TRANS'
COLUMN tablespace_name      FORMAT a10           HEADING 'TABLESPACE'
COLUMN segment_name         FORMAT A10           HEADING 'ROLLBACK'
COLUMN optsize              FORMAT 9999999999    HEADING 'OPTL|SIZE'
COLUMN shrinks              FORMAT 9999            HEADING 'SHRINKS'
COLUMN aveshrink            FORMAT 9999999999    HEADING 'AVE|SHRINK'
COLUMN aveactive            FORMAT 9999999999    HEADING 'AVE|TRANS'
COLUMN waits                FORMAT 99999                HEADING
'WAITS'
COLUMN wraps                FORMAT 99999                HEADING
'WRAPS'
COLUMN extends              FORMAT 9999                 HEADING
'EXTENDS'
rem
BREAK ON REPORT
COMPUTE AVG OF AVESHRINK ON REPORT
COMPUTE AVG OF AVEACTIVE ON REPORT
COMPUTE AVG OF SHRINKS ON REPORT
COMPUTE AVG OF WAITS ON REPORT
COMPUTE AVG OF WRAPS ON REPORT
COMPUTE AVG OF EXTENDS ON REPORT
COMPUTE AVG OF HWMSIZE ON REPORT
SET FEEDBACK OFF VERIFY OFF LINES 132 PAGES 58
ttitle "ROLLBACK SEGMENT STORAGE"
SPOOL rbk1
rem
SELECT
   a.SEGMENT_NAME,a.OPTSIZE,a.SHRINKS,
   a.AVESHRINK,a.AVEACTIVE,b.HWMSIZE,
   b.WAITS,b.WRAPS,b.EXTENDS,A.STATUS
FROM rollback1 a, rollback2 b
WHERE A.SEGMENT_NAME=B.SEGMENT_NAME
ORDER BY segment_name;
SPOOL OFF
CLEAR COLUMNS
TTITLE OFF
SET FEEDBACK ON VERIFY ON LINES 80 PAGES 22
PAUSE Press enter to continue

REM
REM NAME        : RBK2.SQL
REM FUNCTION    : REPORT ON ROLLBACK SEGMENT STATISTICS
REM FUNCTION    : USES THE ROLLBACK2 VIEW
REM USE         : FROM SQLPLUS
REM Limitations : None
REM
```

```
COLUMN segment_name          FORMAT A8                    HEADING
'ROLLBACK'
COLUMN extents               FORMAT 99999                 HEADING
'EXTENTS'
COLUMN xacts                 FORMAT 9999         HEADING 'TRANS'
COLUMN hwmsize               FORMAT 9999999999   HEADING 'LARGEST
TRANS'
COLUMN rssize                FORMAT 9999999999   HEADING 'CUR SIZE'
COLUMN waits                 FORMAT 99999                 HEADING
'WAITS'
COLUMN wraps                 FORMAT 99999                 HEADING
'WRAPS'
COLUMN extends               FORMAT 9999                  HEADING
'EXTENDS'
rem
SET FEEDBACK OFF VERIFY OFF lines 132 pages 58
BREAK ON REPORT
COMPUTE AVG OF WAITS ON REPORT
COMPUTE AVG OF WRAPS ON REPORT
COMPUTE AVG OF EXTENDS ON REPORT
COMPUTE AVG OF HWMSIZE ON REPORT
rem
ttitle "ROLLBACK SEGMENT STATISTICS"
SPOOL rbk2
rem
SELECT * FROM rollback2 ORDER BY segment_name;
SPOOL OFF
SET LINES 80 PAGES 20 FEEDBACK ON VERIFY ON
TTITLE OFF
CLEAR COLUMNS
PAUSE Press enter to continue
REM
REM NAME                     : RBK3.SQL
REM FUNCTION                 : REPORT ON ROLLBACK SEGMENT HEALTH
REM FUNCTION                 : USES THE ROLLBACK1 and ROLLBACK2 VIEWs
REM USE                      : FROM SQLPLUS
REM Limitations              : None
REM
COLUMN hwmsize               FORMAT 9999999999   HEADING 'LARGEST
TRANS'
COLUMN tablespace_name FORMAT a10                HEADING 'TABLESPACE'
COLUMN segment_name    FORMAT A10                HEADING 'ROLLBACK'
COLUMN optsize         FORMAT 9999999999         HEADING 'OPTL|SIZE'
COLUMN shrinks         FORMAT 9999               HEADING 'SHRINKS'
COLUMN aveshrink       FORMAT 9999999999         HEADING 'AVE|SHRINK'
COLUMN aveactive       FORMAT 9999999999         HEADING 'AVE|TRANS'
COLUMN waits           FORMAT 99999                       HEADING
'WAITS'
COLUMN wraps           FORMAT 99999                       HEADING
'WRAPS'
COLUMN extends         FORMAT 9999                        HEADING
'EXTENDS'
rem
BREAK ON REPORT
COMPUTE AVG OF AVESHRINK ON REPORT
COMPUTE AVG OF AVEACTIVE ON REPORT
COMPUTE AVG OF SHRINKS ON REPORT
COMPUTE AVG OF WAITS ON REPORT
COMPUTE AVG OF WRAPS ON REPORT
```

```
COMPUTE AVG OF EXTENDS ON REPORT
COMPUTE AVG OF HWMSIZE ON REPORT

SET FEEDBACK OFF VERIFY OFF LINES 132 PAGES 47
ttitle "ROLLBACK SEGMENT HEALTH"
SPOOL rbk3
rem
SELECT c.tablespace_name, a.segment_name, a.optsize, a.shrinks,
a.aveshrink, a.aveactive,
        b.hwmsize, b.waits, b.wraps, b.extends
FROM rollback1 a, rollback2 b, dba_rollback_segs c
where a.segment_name=b.segment_name
and c.segment_name=a.segment_name
ORDER BY tablespace_name, segment_name;
SPOOL OFF
CLEAR COLUMNS
TTITLE OFF
SET FEEDBACK ON VERIFY ON LINES 80 PAGES 22
PAUSE Press enter to continue
```

Here is a sample listing.

ROLLBACK	OPTL SIZE	SHRINKS	AVE SHRINK	AVE TRANS	LARGEST TRANS	WAITS	WRAPS	EXTENDS	STATUS
SYSTEM		0	0	0	401408	0	0	0	ONLINE
_SYSSMU1$		0	0	6553	122880	0	1	0	ONLINE
_SYSSMU10$		0	0	0	122880	0	0	0	ONLINE
_SYSSMU2$		0	0	0	122880	0	0	0	ONLINE
_SYSSMU3$		0	0	0	122880	0	0	0	ONLINE
_SYSSMU4$		0	0	0	122880	0	0	0	ONLINE
_SYSSMU5$		0	0	6553	122880	0	1	0	ONLINE
_SYSSMU6$		0	0	6553	122880	0	1	0	ONLINE
_SYSSMU7$		0	0	6553	122880	0	1	0	ONLINE
_SYSSMU8$		0	0	0	122880	0	0	0	ONLINE
_SYSSMU9$		0	0	5734	122880	0	1	0	ONLINE
avg		0	0	2904	148201	0	0	0	

ROLLBACK	EXTENTS	TRANS	LARGEST TRANS	CUR SIZE	WAITS	WRAPS	EXTENDS
SYSTEM	5	0	401408	401408	0	0	0
_SYSSMU1$	2	0	122880	122880	0	1	0
_SYSSMU10$	2	0	122880	122880	0	0	0
_SYSSMU2$	2	0	122880	122880	0	0	0
_SYSSMU3$	2	0	122880	122880	0	0	0
_SYSSMU4$	2	0	122880	122880	0	1	0
_SYSSMU5$	2	0	122880	122880	0	0	0
_SYSSMU6$	2	0	122880	122880	0	1	0
_SYSSMU7$	2	0	122880	122880	0	1	0
_SYSSMU8$	2	0	122880	122880	0	0	0
_SYSSMU9$	2	0	122880	122880	0	1	0
avg			148201			0	0

TABLESPACE	ROLLBACK	OPTL SIZE	SHRINKS	AVE SHRINK	AVE TRANS	LARGEST TRANS	WAITS	WRAPS	EXTENDS
SYSTEM	SYSTEM		0	0	0	401408	0	0	0
UNDOTBS	_SYSSMU1$		0	0	6553	122880	0	1	0
UNDOTBS	_SYSSMU10$		0	0	0	122880	0	0	0
UNDOTBS	_SYSSMU2$		0	0	0	122880	0	0	0
UNDOTBS	_SYSSMU3$		0	0	0	122880	0	0	0
UNDOTBS	_SYSSMU4$		0	0	0	122880	0	1	0
UNDOTBS	_SYSSMU5$		0	0	6553	122880	0	1	0
UNDOTBS	_SYSSMU6$		0	0	6553	122880	0	1	0
UNDOTBS	_SYSSMU7$		0	0	6553	122880	0	1	0
UNDOTBS	_SYSSMU8$		0	0	0	122880	0	0	0
UNDOTBS	_SYSSMU9$		0	0	5734	122880	0	1	0
avg			0	0	2904	148201	0	0	0

The report above is from an Oracle9i database. Notice that the segments have system-generated names and all are in the UNDOTBS tablespace. In the reports shown, the parameters of concern to the DBA are location, status, and sizing data. The DBA needs to verify that no rollback segments have been created outside of the prescribed tablespaces. The DBA should also verify that all rollback segments that are supposed to be online are in fact online, and that those that are supposed to be offline are offline.

Excessive waits indicate the need for more rollback segments. Excessive extends indicate that larger extent sizes may be needed. Larger rollback segment extents are indicated if excessive shrinks are encountered while optimal is set. Usually, wraps aren't of concern, although excessive wraps may be indicative of a too-small rollback segment extent size. The reports are informational only if Oracle-managed UNDO is used. As far as I know the only method to increase the size of the individual automatically maintained undo segments in Oracle9i is to increase the size of the undo tablespace.

A report similar to *undo_list.sql* should be used to monitor undo usage. The *undo_retention* parameter should be based on the desired undo retention time. The retention time is in minutes, multiplied by the undo usage showed in this report. The output from the report is shown below.

```
--*********************************************
--
--   Copyright © 2003 by Rampant TechPress Inc.
--
--   Free for non-commercial use.
--   For commercial licensing, e-mail info@rampant.cc
--
-- *********************************************
REM undo_usage.sql
REM Function: reports undo usage for Oracle9i
REM
REM MRA 10/14/01 Initial Creation
REM
COLUMN undo_usage FORMAT 99,999,999.999 HEADING 'Undo
Usage|Blocks/Min'
COLUMN oer_old_errors FORMAT 99,999,999 HEADING 'Undo|Old
Errors'
COLUMN oer_space_errors FORMAT 9,999,999,999 HEADING 'Undo|Space
Errors'
SET FEEDBACK OFF
ttitle 'Undo Usage'
spool undo_usage
select
   sum(undoblks)/sum((end_time-begin_time)*24*60) undo_usage,
   sum(ssolderrcnt) OER_old_errors,
   sum(nospaceerrcnt) OER_space_errors
from
   v$undostat
where
   undoblks>0
/
spool off
SET FEEDBACK ON
TTITLE OFF
```

Here is a sample listing.

Undo Usage Blocks/Min	Undo Old Errors	Undo Space Errors
.123	0	0

Monitoring Rollback Current Usage

Run the script in *tx_rbs.sql* to identify which users are using which rollback segments. The report generated shows the Oracle Process ID, the System Process ID, and the rollback segment in use. An example of output from an active rollback report is also shown below.

💾 tx_rbs.sql

```
--***********************************************
--
--    Copyright © 2003 by Rampant TechPress Inc.
--
--    Free for non-commercial use.
--    For commercial licensing, e-mail info@rampant.cc
--
-- ***********************************************
COLUMN   name FORMAT a10          HEADING "Rollback|Segment"
COLUMN   pid  FORMAT 99999        HEADING "Oracle|PID"
COLUMN   spid FORMAT 99999        HEADING "Sys|PID"
COLUMN   curext FORMAT 999999     HEADING "Current|Extent"
COLUMN   curblk FORMAT 999999     HEADING "Current|Block"
COLUMN transaction FORMAT A15     Heading 'Transaction'
COLUMN program FORMAT a10 HEADING 'Program'

SET PAGES 56  LINES 80 VERIFY OFF FEEDBACK OFF
ttitle "Rollback Segments in Use"
SPOOL tx_rbs

SELECT
    r.name,
    l.Sid,
    p.spid,
    NVL(p.username, 'no transaction') "Transaction",
    p.program "Program",
    s.curext,s.curblk
FROM
    v$lock l,
    v$process p,
    v$rollname r,
     v$rollstat s
WHERE
    l.Sid = p.pid (+)
    AND
    TRUNC(l.id1(+) / 65536) = r.usn
    AND
     l.type(+) = 'TX'
    AND
    l.lmode(+) = 6
    AND
     r.usn=s.usn
    AND
     p.username is not null
ORDER BY r.name;

SPOOL OFF
SET PAGES 22  LINES 80 VERIFY ON FEEDBACK ON
CLEAR COLUMNS
TTITLE OFF
```

Here is a sample listing.

```
Rollback               Sys                          Current Current
Segment        SID PID     Transaction    Program     Extent  Block
----------  --------- ---------  -------------  ----------  ------- -------
_SYSSMU6$          7 157     oracle         oracle@tus       0       2
                                            cdiogenes (
                                            RECO)
```

Monitoring Rollback Transaction Size

Run some sample transactions through the script below to determine whether the rollback segments are properly sized. Simply place the SQL from the transaction or the call to the transaction into the script where indicated, and execute the script.

Note: Make sure that this transaction is the only one running when the test is done, or the results will be invalid.

🖫 **undo.sql**

```
--***********************************************
--
--    Copyright © 2003 by Rampant TechPress Inc.
--
--    Free for non-commercial use.
--    For commercial licensing, e-mail info@rampant.cc
--
--    ***********************************************
SET FEEDBACK OFF  TERMOUT OFF
COLUMN name FORMAT a40
DEFINE undo_overhead=54

DROP TABLE undo_data;
CREATE TABLE undo_data
    (
    tran_no number, start_writes number, end_writes number
    );
INSERT INTO undo_data
SELECT 1, SUM(writes),0 from v$rollstat;
SET FEEDBACK ON  TERMOUT ON
rem
```

```
rem    INSERT TRANSACTION HERE
rem
SET FEEDBACK OFF  TERMOUT OFF
UPDATE undo_data SET end_writes = SUM(writes) FROM v$rollstat;
 WHERE tran_no=1;
SET FEEDBACK ON  TERMOUT ON
SELECT  ((end-writes - start_writes) - &undo_overhead)
"Number of Rollback Bytes Generated"
FROM undo_data;
SET TERMOUT OFF FEEDBACK OFF
DROP TABLE undo_data;
```

If the DBA is concerned with the rollback usage in an individual transaction, the script above can be run with that transaction in the indicated spot in the script. The generated data will tell the DBA the exact amount of rollback usage for the transaction. This data can then be used to create a custom rollback segment that can be brought online and used during that transaction. Again, the script and test run of the transaction must be the only active transaction in the database when the test is run.

Monitoring Deferred Rollback Segments

If a rollback segment is taken offline, its transactions may be placed in a temporary segment in the rollback segment's tablespace. These temporary segments are referred to as deferred rollback segments. The following SQL code will list any deferred rollbacks in a 7.x, 8.x or 9.x database:

🖫 **deferred_rbs.sql**

```
--*************************************************
--
--   Copyright © 2003 by Rampant TechPress Inc.
--
--   Free for non-commercial use.
--   For commercial licensing, e-mail info@rampant.cc
--
--  *************************************************
```

```
SELECT
    segment_name,
    segment_type,
    tablespace_name
FROM
    sys.dba_segments
WHERE
    segment_type = 'DEFERRED ROLLBACK';
```

Example output from the preceding select statement:

```
SEGMENT_NAME    SEGMENT_TYPE       TABLESPACE_NAME
------------    ------------------ ----------------
RBK1            DEFERRED ROLLBACK  USERS
```

Under Oracle7, if a rollback segment is taken offline, its status will be changed to PENDING OFFLINE, and it will be taken offline as soon as it's pending transactions are complete. The preceding SELECT statement could be used to determine if any of these active transactions are in a deferred state. To determine if a rollback segment under Oracle7 has outstanding transactions, the following SELECT statement is used.

```
SELECT
    name,
    xacts 'ACTIVE TRANSACTIONS'
FROM
    v$rollname,
    v$rollstat
WHERE
    status = 'PENDING OFFLINE'
AND
    v$rollname.usn = v$rollstat.usn;
```

Be certain the database has a sufficient number of online rollback segments. If the ratio TRANSACTIONS/ TRANSACTIONS_PER_ROLLBACK is exceeded, the system automatically brings online any available public rollback segments. If the only available public rollback happens to be the maintenance segment in the system space, it will be brought online and could cause havoc in the system tablespace, as it extends to accommodate transactions.

Monitoring Redo Log Activity

The redo logs provide the information required to redo transactions on the database. For an Oracle8, Oracle8i, or Oracle9i database, redo logs are placed in log groups whose members consist of individual log files. For Oracle8, Oracle8i, or Oracle9i, there should be at least two mirrored groups of log files on separate drives to start up; three are highly recommended.

If activity is expected to be high, the use of five mirrored groups of 5 megabytes each will ensure that there is no log contention. Determining the number and size of redo logs is not an exact science; it must be done by trial and error. The alert log can be monitored for waits on log switches or checkpoints to help determine this.

Monitoring Redo Log Status

Redo log status should be monitored to determine which logs are in use and whether there are any odd status codes, such as stale log indications or indications of corrupt redo logs. The log files can have the following status values:

- **USED.** Indicates either that a log has just been added (never used), or that a RESETLOGS command has been issued.

- **CURRENT.** Indicates a valid log that is in use.

- **ACTIVE.** Indicates a valid log file that is not currently in use.

- **CLEARING.** Indicates a log is being re-created as an empty log due to DBA action.

- **CLEARING CURRENT.** Means that a current log is being cleared of a closed thread. If a log stays in this status, it could indicate there is some failure in the log switch.

- **INACTIVE.** Means that the log is no longer needed for instance recovery but may be needed for media recovery.

The *v$logfile* table has a status indicator that gives these additional codes:

- **INVALID.** File is inaccessible.

- **STALE.** File contents are incomplete (such as when an instance is shut down with SHUTDOWN ABORT or due to a system crash).

- **DELETED.** File is no longer used.

The script below provides some basic information on log status. The listing shows an example of output from the *log_stat.sql* script.

💾 **log_stat.sql**

```
--*********************************************
--
--    Copyright © 2003 by Rampant TechPress Inc.
--
--    Free for non-commercial use.
--    For commercial licensing, e-mail info@rampant.cc
--
--    *********************************************
COLUMN first_change#  FORMAT 99999999   HEADING Change#
COLUMN group#         FORMAT 9,999       HEADING Grp#
COLUMN thread#        FORMAT 999         HEADING Th#
COLUMN sequence#      FORMAT 999,999     HEADING Seq#
COLUMN members        FORMAT 999         HEADING Mem
COLUMN archived       FORMAT a4          HEADING Arc?
COLUMN first_time     FORMAT a21         HEADING 'Switch|Time'
```

Oracle Internals Monitoring & Tuning Scripts

```
BREAK ON thread#
SET PAGES 60 LINES 131 FEEDBACK OFF
ttitle 'Current Redo Log Status'
SPOOL log_stat

SELECT
   thread#,
   group#,
   sequence#,
   bytes,
   members,
   archived,
   status,
   first_change#,
   TO_CHAR(first_time, 'DD-MM-YYYY HH24:MI:SS') first_time
FROM
   sys.v_$log
ORDER BY
   thread#,
   group#;

SPOOL OFF
PAUSE Press Enter to continue
SET PAGES 22 LINES 80 FEEDBACK ON
CLEAR BREAKS
CLEAR COLUMNS
TTILE OFF
```

Here is a sample listing:

```
                                                Switch
Th# Grp#  Seq#      BYTES Mem Arc? STATUS   Change# Time
--- ----  -----    ------- -------- -------- ------- ------------------
  1    1 4,489    1048576    2 NO   INACTIVE  719114 15-JUN-97 16:54:23
       2 4,490    1048576    2 NO   INACTIVE  719117 15-JUN-97 16:56:10
       3 4,491    1048576    2 NO   CURRENT   719120 15-JUN-97 17:02:22
```

Monitoring Redo Log Switches

In addition to the alert logs, the frequency of log switches can also be monitored via the *v$log_history* and *v$archived_log* DPTs. A script using these DPTs for that purpose is shown in below. An example of output from an archive log switch script is also shown below.

```
--********************************************
--
--     Copyright © 2003 by Rampant TechPress Inc.
--
--     Free for non-commercial use.
--     For commercial licensing, e-mail info@rampant.cc
--
--  ********************************************

COLUMN thread#              FORMAT 999      HEADING 'Thrd#'
COLUMN sequence#            FORMAT 99999    HEADING 'Seq#'
COLUMN first_change#                        HEADING 'SCN Low#'
COLUMN next_change#                         HEADING 'SCN High#'
COLUMN archive_name         FORMAT a50      HEADING 'Log File'
COLUMN first_time           FORMAT a20      HEADING 'Switch Time'
COLUMN name                 FORMAT a30      HEADING 'Archive Log'

SET LINES 132 FEEDBACK OFF VERIFY OFF
ttitle "Log History Report"
SPOOL log_hist
REM

SELECT
   X.recid,
   a.thread#,
   a.sequence#,
   a.first_change#,
   a.switch_change#,
   TO_CHAR(a.first_time,'DD-MON-YYYY HH24:MI:SS') first_time,
   x.name
FROM
   v$loghist a,
   v$archived_log x
WHERE
   a.first_time>
   (SELECT b.first_time-1
   FROM v$loghist b WHERE b.switch_change# =
   (SELECT MAX(c.switch_change#) FROM v$loghist c)) AND
     x.recid(+)=a.sequence#;

SPOOL OFF
SET LINES 80 VERIFY ON FEEDBACK ON
CLEAR COLUMNS
TTITLE OFF
PAUSE Press Enter to continue
```

Here is a sample listing:

```
RECID Thrd#  Seq# SCN Low# SWITCH_CHANGE# Switch Time Archive Log
--------- ----- ----- -------- -------------- ----------- --------------------------
          1     8   375520         409741 05-SEP-2001 08:18:06
```

Monitoring Redo Statistics

There are no views in Oracle that allow the user to look directly at a log file's statistical data. It is necessary instead to derive statistics from redo log and log writer process statistics. These statistics can be found in the views *v$statname*, *v$session*, *v$process*, *v$sesstat*, *v$latch*, and *v$latchname*. An example of a report that uses these views is shown below. An example of the script's output is also shown.

🖫 **rdo_stat.sql**

```
-- *************************************************
--
--    Copyright © 2003 by Rampant TechPress Inc.
--
--    Free for non-commercial use.
--    For commercial licensing, e-mail info@rampant.cc
--
-- *************************************************

SET PAGES 56 LINES 78 VERIFY OFF FEEDBACK OFF
ttitle "Redo Latch Statistics"
SPOOL rdo_stat

COLUMN name        FORMAT a30       HEADING Name
COLUMN percent     FORMAT 999.999   HEADING Percent
COLUMN total                        HEADING Total

SELECT
   l2.name,
   immediate_gets+gets Total,
   immediate_gets "Immediates",
   misses+immediate_misses "Total Misses",
   DECODE (100.*(GREATEST(misses+immediate_misses,1)/
   GREATEST(immediate_gets+gets,1)),100,0) Percent
FROM
   v$latch l1,
   v$latchname l2
WHERE
   l2.name like '%redo%'
   and
   l1.latch#=l2.latch# ;

COLUMN name     FORMAT a30        HEADING 'Redo|Statistic|Name'
COLUMN value    FORMAT 999,999,999 HEADING 'Redo|Statistic|Value'
SET PAGES 80 LINES 60 FEEDBACK OFF VERIFY OFF
ttitle 'Redo Log Statistics'
```

Monitoring Rollback Segments **209**

```
SPOOL redo_stat

SELECT
   name,
   value
FROM
   v$sysstat
WHERE
   name LIKE '%redo%'
ORDER BY
   statistic#;

SPOOL OFF
SET LINES 24 FEEDBACK ON VERIFY ON
TTITLE OFF
CLEAR COLUMNS
CLEAR BREAKS
```

Here is a sample listing:

Name	Total	Immediates	Total Misses	Percent
redo allocation	172438	0	0	
redo copy	6259	6231	0	
redo writing	672470	0	0	

Press Enter to continue

Redo Statistic Name	Redo Statistic Value
redo synch writes	250
redo synch time	72
redo entries	6,231
redo size	1,569,816
redo buffer allocation retries	0
redo wastage	1,200,696
redo writer latching time	0
redo writes	3,635
redo blocks written	5,586
redo write time	151
redo log space requests	0
redo log space wait time	0
redo log switch interrupts	0
redo ordering marks	0

These numbers require a little interpretation. Let's look at what they mean and how they can be used. The first section of the report should be self-explanatory. The redo logs use two latches, REDO ALLOCATION and REDO COPY.

As a general rule, if the percent statistic (actually, the ratio of total misses to total gets) is greater than 10 percent, contention is occurring, and the way the redo logs are done should be examined (more about this in a second).

The initial latch granted for redo is the *redo_allocation* latch. The *redo_copy* latch is granted to a user when the size of the entry is greater than the *log_small_entry_max_size* parameter in the initialization file. If there is *redo_allocation* latch contention, decrease the value of *_log_small_entry_max_size*.

A system with a single CPU will show contention if there is more than one user that requires the *redo_copy* latch. The number of *redo_copy* latches is limited to twice the number of CPUs on the system. If there is only one CPU, only one latch is allowed. It is normal to see high contention for this latch on single-CPU systems, but there is nothing the DBA can do to increase the number of *redo_copy* latches.

However, even on single-CPU systems, Oracle can be forced to prebuild redo entries, thereby reducing the number of latches required. Raising the value of the *_log_entry_prebuild_threshold* entry in the initialization file does this. On multiple-CPU systems, increase the number of *redo_copy* latches to twice the number of CPUs.

Statistics from the caches that affect redo operations are shown in the second half of the report. Let's look at what these numbers tell us. The most important of the listed statistics are *redo blocks written, redo entries linearized, redo small copies,* and *redo writes.*

- *redo blocks written* is useful when two entries are compared for a specified time period. This will indicate how much redo is generated for the period between the two checks.

- *redo entries linearized*

- *redo small copies* tells how many times the entry was written on a redo allocation latch. This indicates that a redo copy latch was not required for this entry. This statistic should be compared with the redo entries parameter. If there is approximately a one-to-one relationship, then the system is making effective use of the redo allocation latch. If there is a large difference, then the *log_small_entry_max_size init.ora* parameter should be increased. If the *log_simultaneous_copies* parameter is 0, this value is ignored.

- *redo writes* is the total number of redo writes to the redo buffer. If this value is too large compared to the redo entries parameter value, then the DBA should tune the *init.ora* parameters mentioned in the previous sections to force prebuilding of the entries. If the entries are not prebuilt, it may require several writes to the buffer before it is fully entered. If it is prebuilt, it requires only one.

- *redo log space wait* tells whether users are having to wait for space in the redo buffer. If this value is nonzero, increase the size of the *log_buffer* in the initialization file.

- *redo buffer allocation retries* is the number of repeated attempts needed to allocate space in the redo buffer. If this value is high in comparison to redo entries, it indicates that the redo logs may be too small and should be increased in size. Normally, this value should be much less than the redo entries statistic. In the example, it has a value of 5 compared to the entry's value of 1044; this is satisfactory.

- *redo size* is the total number of redo bytes generated since the database was started. Comparison of two readings will give the amount generated over time. This value can then be used to determine if the log switch interval is set properly. Too many log switches over a small amount of time can impair performance.

Use the following formula to look at log switches over time:

```
(X / (dN / dt)) / interval of concern
```

Where:

- **X** is the value of the *log_checkpoint_interval* or the size of the redo log in system blocks.

- **dN** is the change in the redo size over the time interval.

- **dt** is the time differential for the period (usually minutes).

Once the number of log switches is known, the number determines the size of redo logs based on system I/O requirements. If the number of log switches needs to be reduced, increase the redo log size. Of course, this may impact system availability, since it takes longer to write out a large redo log buffer than a small one to disk. A balance must be struck between redo logs that are too small, affecting database performance, and logs that are too large, affecting I/O performance.

Directory and Library Internals

Oracle8 introduced two new internal database structures, directories and libraries. Libraries point to external sharable libraries of 3GL routines. They can be called via the external procedures call option, also new to Oracle8. Directories point to external directories, where BFILE and other LOB data objects can be stored outside the database.

Monitoring Directories

Directory information is available from the *dba_directories* view. This view has three columns. A simple report will show everything the database knows about directories:

🖫 **dir_rep.sql**

```
--***************************************************
--
--    Copyright © 2003 by Rampant TechPress Inc.
--
--    Free for non-commercial use.
--    For commercial licensing, e-mail info@rampant.cc
--
-- ***************************************************
COLUMN owner              FORMAT a10 HEADING 'Owner'
COLUMN directory_name     FORMAT a15 HEADING 'Directory'
COLUMN directory_path     FORMAT a45 HEADING 'Full Path'
SET VERIFY OFF PAGES 58 LINES 78 FEEDBACK OFF
ttitle 'Database Directories Report'
SPOOL dir_rep.lis

SELECT
   owner,
   directory_name,
   directory_path
FROM
   dba_directories
ORDER BY
```

```
      owner;
SPOOL OFF
SET VERIFY ON FEEDBACK ON
TTITLE OFF
CLEAR COLUMNS
```

A sample of the output is shown below. Remember, directories aren't verified for existence until access is attempted.

```
Owner      Directory         Full Path
---------- ---------------   -----------------------------------------
SYS        MEDIA_DIR         /project/linux/install/d2/pse/cus/901/demo/sc
                             hema/product_media/

SYS        LOG_FILE_DIR      /project/linux/install/d2/pse/cus/901/admin/s
                             tp1/create/

SYS        DATA_FILE_DIR     /project/linux/install/d2/pse/cus/901/demo/sc
                             hema/sales_history/

SYS        SQL_DIR           /home/oracle/sql_scripts
```

Monitoring Libraries

The *dba_libraries* view contains five fields that are monitored through the *dba_libraries* view. A monitor report is shown below. The output from the library report script follows.

🖫 **lib_rep.sql**

```
--*************************************************
--
--     Copyright © 2003 by Rampant TechPress Inc.
--
--     Free for non-commercial use.
--     For commercial licensing, e-mail info@rampant.cc
--
-- *************************************************
COLUMN owner           FORMAT a8    HEADING 'Library|Owner'
COLUMN library_name    FORMAT a15   HEADING 'Library|Name'
COLUMN file_spec       FORMAT a30   HEADING 'File|Specification'
COLUMN dynamic         FORMAT a7    HEADING 'Dynamic'
COLUMN stauts          FORMAT a10   HEADING 'Status'
BREAK ON owner
SET FEEDBACK OFF VERIFY OFF LINES 78 PAGES 58
ttitle 'Database External Libraries Report'
SPOOL lib_rep.lis
SELECT
```

```
      owner,
      library_name,
      file_spec,
      dynamic,
      status
FROM
   dba_libraries
ORDER BY
   owner;

SPOOL OFF
SET VERIFY ON FEEDBACK ON
TTITLE OFF
CLEAR COLUMNS
CLEAR BREAKS
```

Here is a sample listing:

```
Library  Library            File
Owner    Name               Specification                  Dynamic STATUS
-------- ---------------    ----------------------------    ------- ---
CTXSYS   DR$LIB                                             N       VALID
         DR$LIBX            /var/oracle/OraHome2/ctx/lib/l  Y       VALID
                            ibctxx9.so

LBACSYS  LBAC$CACHE_LIBT                                    N       VALID
         LBAC$COMPS_LIBT                                    N       VALID
         LBAC$EVENT_LIBT                                    N       VALID
         LBAC$LABEL_LIBT                                    N       VALID
         LBAC$LABLT_LIBT                                    N       VALID
         LBAC$PRIVS_LIBT                                    N       VALID
         LBAC$RLS_LIBT                                      N       VALID
         LBAC$STD_LIBT                                      N       VALID
         LBAC$TYPE_LIBT                                     N       VALID
         LBAC$USER_LIBT                                     N       VALID
```

Remember, as with directories, the existence of the actual libraries isn't tested until they are called by an external procedure.

Conclusion

This chapter has discussed several issues involved in monitoring and managing tablespaces. The next chapter is concerned with some additional table issues to be aware of since the advent of Oracle8.

Storage and Object Internal Scripting

Prior to Oracle8, the DBA was concerned with four major table issues: Who owns them? Where were they created? Are they clustered? What is their space utilization? With newer versions, the DBA must also ask: Is the table an object or relational table? Does the table contain REFs, VARRAYS, or NESTED TABLES? Is the table (if relational) partitioned? This section offers scripts and techniques to answer these questions.

The Schema Manager

The Schema Manager, found in the Oracle Administrator toolbar, allows GUI-based management of database schema objects. The screen for Oracle version 7.3 of this product is shown in Figure 7.1. The Oracle Administrator is fine for viewing database objects, but it lacks suitable report capabilities. Thus, the ability to monitor database objects via scripts is still critical. We will examine a few simple reports. First, take a look at Figure 7.2, which shows the cluster of *dba_* views used to monitor tables.

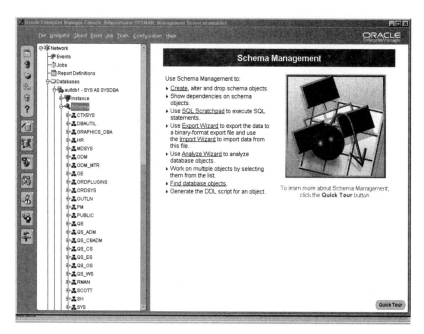

Figure 7.1 *Oracle Enterprise Manager schema screen*

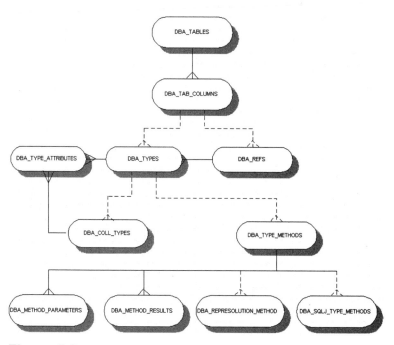

Figure 7.2 *dba_tables view cluster*

Oracle Internals Monitoring & Tuning Scripts

Monitoring Ownership, Placement, and Clustering

Table ownership, creation information, and whether they are clustered can be shown in a single report. This report is shown in *tab_rep.sql*. It is important to monitor tables soon after creation to make sure they are properly sized and their storage parameters are appropriate. This can be accomplished through the use of the script in *tab_rep.sql* , which documents how a table was created. The Enterprise Manager application provides this data in a very user-friendly format.

🖫 tab_rep.sql

```
--***************************************************
--
--    Copyright © 2003 by Rampant TechPress Inc.
--
--    Free for non-commercial use.
--    For commercial licensing, e-mail info@rampant.cc
--
--  ***************************************************

REM
REM NAME        : TABLE.SQL
REM FUNCTION    : GENERATE TABLE REPORT
REM Limitations : None
clear COLUMNs
COLUMN owner             FORMAT a15      HEADING 'Table | Owner'
COLUMN table_name        FORMAT a18      HEADING Table
COLUMN tablespace_name   FORMAT A13      HEADING Tablespace
COLUMN pct_increase                      HEADING 'Pct|Increase'
COLUMN init                              HEADING 'Initial|Extent'
COLUMN next                              HEADING 'Next|Extent'
COLUMN partitioned       FORMAT a4       HEADING 'Par?'
COLUMN iot_type          FORMAT a4       HEADING 'Iot?'
COLUMN nested            FORMAT a5       HEADING 'Nest?'
COLUMN temporary         FORMAT a5       HEADING 'Temp?'
COLUMN extern            FORMAT a8       Heading 'External?'
BREAK ON owner ON tablespace_name
SET PAGES 48 LINES 132
TTITLE "ORACLE TABLE REPORT"
SPOOL tab_rep
SELECT
     owner,
     tablespace_name,
```

```
      table_name,
      initial_extent Init,
      next_extent Next,
      pct_increase,
      partitioned,
      DECODE(iot_type,NULL,'No','Yes') iot_type,
      nested,
      DECODE(temporary,'N','No','Yes') temporary,
         DECODE(initial_extent, null,
              DECODE(iot_type,null,
              DECODE(temporary,'N','Yes')),'No') extern
FROM
      sys.dba_tables
WHERE
      owner NOT IN   (
'SYSTEM','SYS','DBSNMP','AURORA$JIS$UTILITY$',
'AURORA$ORB$UNAUTHENTICATED','SCOTT','OSE$HTTP$ADMIN',
'OUTLN','LBACSYS','OE','QS','QS_CS','QS_CB','QS_CBADM',
'QS_OS','QS_ES','QS_WS','QS_ADM','SH','HR','WKSYS','ORDSYS',
'ORDPLUGINS','CTXSYS','MDSYS','PM')
ORDER BY
      owner,
      tablespace_name,
      table_name;
SPOOL OFF
CLEAR COLUMNS
PAUSE Press enter to continue
SET PAGES 22 LINES 80
TTITLE OFF
CLEAR COLUMNS
CLEAR BREAKS
```

Here is a sample listing:

Table Owner	Tablespace	Table	Initial Extent	Next Extent	Pct Inc	Par?	Iot?	Nest?	Temp?	External
DBAUTIL	DBAUTIL_DATA	DBAUTIL_KEPT_OBJ	16384	204800	0	NO	No	NO	No	
		DBAUTIL_UPD_TABS	57344	204800	0	NO	No	NO	No	
		DBA_RUNNING_STATS	1048576	204800	0	NO	No	NO	No	
		DBA_TEMP	16384	204800	0	NO	No	NO	No	
		HIT_RATIOS	16384	204800	0	NO	No	NO	No	
		TEMP_SIZE_TABLE	16384	204800	0	NO	No	NO	No	
	SYSTEM	SQL_SCRIPTS				NO	No	NO	No	Yes
		SQL_SCRIPTS2				NO	No	NO	No	Yes
QS	EXAMPLE	AQ$_AQ$_MEM_MC_S	65536			NO	No	NO	No	
		AQ$_MEM_MC	65536			NO	No	NO	No	
		QS_ORDERS_PR_MQTAB	65536			NO	No	NO	No	
		QS_ORDERS_SQTAB	65536			NO	No	NO	No	
		SYS_IOT_OVER_31044	65536			NO	Yes	NO	No	
		SYS_IOT_OVER_31065	65536			NO	Yes	NO	No	
		AQ$_AQ$_MEM_MC_H				NO	Yes	NO	No	
		AQ$_AQ$_MEM_MC_I				NO	Yes	NO	No	
		AQ$_AQ$_MEM_MC_NR				NO	Yes	NO	No	
		AQ$_AQ$_MEM_MC_T				NO	Yes	NO	No	

Notice that the script only includes tables not owned by SYSTEM, SYS, and other Oracle provided schemas. Oracle9*i* has added a plethora of new user names to the list of Oracle-provided users. It seems there must be a new user for each new feature. Since a good DBA rarely employs these users unless absolutely required, no extraneous tables should be created after product loads; therefore, the data won't change.

For the purposes of this report, we are more concerned with new tables. (That said, astute readers should note that the QS user is included so other examples can be shown in the report.) For Oracle8*i* and earlier, remove the union clause and the extern column; for Oracle8, remove the temporary column select; for Oracle7, remove the temporary, IOT, nested, and partitioned columns. The items to look for in the output report are shown below:

- Tables that should belong to a specific application, but belong to a specific user rather than the assigned application owner.

- Excessive use of clusters.

- Tables that appear in the SYSTEM tablespace or in tablespaces other than where they belong.

Note that this report gives no sizing information. This is covered in the next section. Determining whether the table size is correct is one of the important tasks of the DBA.

Monitoring Size of Tables

There are a couple of methods to determine whether the default storage size is correct for a tablespace. The first is to monitor the extents for each of the tables that reside in the tablespace. Another method is to monitor the used space against the available space for each table. Scripts to perform these functions are shown in *extents.sql* and *act_size.sql*. The output from the script is shown below also. Note: In early Oracle extent limitation was a holy grail for DBAs and many rules of thumb as to how many were bad were stated. Now, only if they become excessive (i.e. 4000 or so) do you really need to worry about them except if you do large updates, truncates or drops of tables with a large number of extents.

🖫 **extents.sql**

```
--****************************************************
--
--    Copyright © 2003 by Rampant TechPress Inc.
--
--    Free for non-commercial use.
--    For commercial licensing, e-mail info@rampant.cc
--
-- ****************************************************

REM
REM NAME                : EXTENTS.SQL
REM FUNCTION            : GENERATE EXTENTS REPORT
REM USE                 : FROM SQLPLUS OR OTHER FRONT END
REM LIMITATIONS         : NONE
REM
CLEAR COLUMNS
COLUMN segment_name      HEADING 'Segment'     FORMAT A15
COLUMN tablespace_name HEADING 'Tablespace'  FORMAT A10
COLUMN owner             HEADING 'Owner'       FORMAT A10
COLUMN segment_type      HEADING 'Type'        FORMAT A10
COLUMN size              HEADING 'Size'          FORMAT 999,999,999
COLUMN extents           HEADING 'Current|Extents'
COLUMN max_extents .     HEADING 'Max|Extents'
COLUMN bytes             HEADING 'Size|(Bytes)'
SET PAGESIZE 58 NEWPAGE 0 LINESIZE 130 FEEDBACK OFF
SET ECHO OFF VERIFY OFF
```

```
ACCEPT extents PROMPT 'Enter max number of extents: '
BREAK ON tablespace_name SKIP PAGE ON owner
TTITLE "Extents Report"
DEFINE output = extent
SPOOL &output
SELECT  tablespace_name,
     segment_name,
     extents,
     max_extents,
     bytes,
     owner "owner",
     segment_type
FROM    dba_segments
WHERE extents >= &extents AND owner LIKE UPPER('%&owner%')
ORDER BY tablespace_name,owner,segment_type,segment_name;
SPOOL OFF
CLEAR COLUMNS
CLEAR BREAKS
SET TERMOUT ON FEEDBACK ON VERIFY ON
UNDEF extents
UNDEF owner
TTITLE OFF
UNDEF OUTPUT
PAUSE Press enter to continue
```

Here is a sample listing:

Tablespace	Segment	Current Extents	Max Extents	Size (Bytes)	Owner	Type
SYSTEM	C_OBJ#	10	249	1323008	SYS	CLUSTER
	C_TOID_VERSION#	7	249	352256		CLUSTER
	I_ARGUMENT1	6	249	229376		INDEX
	I_COL1	8	249	565248		INDEX
	I_COL2	6	249	258048		INDEX
	I_COL3	5	249	176128		INDEX
	I_DEPENDENCY1	5	249	147456		INDEX
	I_DEPENDENCY2	5	249	147456		INDEX
	I_OBJ2	5	249	147456		INDEX
	I_Source1	11	249	1765376		INDEX
	SYSTEM	16	249	983040		ROLLBACK
	ACCESS$	6	249	229376		TABLE
	ARGUMENT$	6	249	229376		TABLE
	COM$	5	249	147456		TABLE
	DEPENDENCY$	5	249	147456		TABLE
	IDL_CHAR$	5	249	147456		TABLE
	IDL_SB4$	6	249	229376		TABLE
	IDL_UB1$	9	249	802816		TABLE
	IDL_UB2$	10	249	1191936		TABLE
	OBJ$	6	249	229376		TABLE
	Source$	13	249	3915776		TABLE
	VIEW$	9	249	802816		TABLE

```
--*************************************************
--
--   Copyright © 2003 by Rampant TechPress Inc.
--
--   Free for non-commercial use.
--   For commercial licensing, e-mail info@rampant.cc
--
-- *************************************************

rem
****************************************************************
rem
rem  NAME: ACT_SIZE.sql
rem
rem
****************************************************************
ACCEPT owner PROMPT 'Enter table owner name: '
SET HEADING OFF FEEDBACK OFF VERIFY OFF ECHO OFF RECSEP OFF
PAGES 0
COLUMN db_block_size NEW_VALUE blocksize NOPRINT
TTITLE OFF
DEFINE cr='chr(10)'
DEFINE qt='chr(39)'
TRUNCATE TABLE temp_size_table;
SELECT value db_block_size FROM v$parameter WHERE
name='db_block_size';
SPOOL fill_sz.sql
SELECT
 'INSERT INTO temp_size_table'||&&cr||
 'SELECT '||&&qt||segment_name||&&qt||&&cr||
 ',COUNT(DISTINCT(dbms_rowid.rowid_block_number(rowid)))
blocks'||&&cr||
 'FROM &&owner..'||segment_name, ';'
FROM
  dba_segments
WHERE
  segment_type ='TABLE'
  AND owner = UPPER('&owner');
SPOOL OFF
SPOOL index_sz.sql
SELECT
    'CREATE TABLE stat_temp AS SELECT * FROM
index_stats;'||&&cr||
    'TRUNCATE TABLE stat_temp;'
FROM
    dual;
SELECT
'ANALYZE INDEX '||owner||'.'||index_name||' VALIDATE
STRUCTURE;'||&&cr||
'INSERT INTO stat_temp SELECT * FROM index_stats;'||&&cr||
'COMMIT;'
FROM
   dba_indexes
WHERE
   owner=UPPER('&owner');
```

```
SPOOL OFF
SET FEEDBACK ON TERMOUT ON LINES 132
START index_sz.sql
INSERT INTO temp_size_table SELECT
name,trunc(used_space/&&blocksize)
FROM stat_temp;
DROP TABLE stat_temp;
DEFINE temp_var = &&qt;
START fill_sz
HOST rm fill_size_table.sql
DEFINE bs = '&&blocksize K'
COLUMN t_date        NOPRINT NEW_VALUE t_date
COLUMN user_id       NOPRINT NEW_VALUE user_id
COLUMN segment_name      FORMAT A25          HEADING
"SEGMENT|NAME"
COLUMN segment_type      FORMAT A7           HEADING
"SEGMENT|TYPE"
COLUMN extents           FORMAT 999          HEADING "EXTENTS"
COLUMN kbytes            FORMAT 999,999,999  HEADING "KILOBYTES"
COLUMN blocks            FORMAT 9,999,999    HEADING
"ALLOC.|&&bs|BLOCKS"
COLUMN act_blocks        FORMAT 9,999,990    HEADING
"USED|&&bs|BLOCKS"
COLUMN pct_block         FORMAT 999.99       HEADING
"PCT|BLOCKS|USED"
ttitle "Actual Size Report for &owner"
SET PAGES 55
BREAK ON REPORT ON segment_type SKIP 1
COMPUTE SUM OF kbytes ON segment_type REPORT
SPOOL &owner
SELECT
    segment_name,
    segment_type,
    SUM(extents) extents,
    SUM(bytes)/1024 kbytes,
    SUM(a.blocks) blocks,
    NVL(MAX(b.blocks),0) act_blocks,
   (MAX(b.blocks)/SUM(a.blocks))*100 pct_block
 FROM
    sys.dba_segments a,
    temp_size_table b
 WHERE
    segment_name = UPPER( b.table_name )
 GROUP BY
    segment_name,
    segment_type
 ORDER BY
    segment_type,
    segment_name;
SPOOL OFF
TRUNCATE TABLE temp_size_table;
SET TERMOUT ON FEEDBACK 15 VERIFY ON PAGESIZE 20 LINESIZE 80
SPACE 1
UNDEF qt
UNDEF cr
TTITLE OFF
CLEAR COLUMNS
CLEAR COMPUTES
PAUSE press enter to continue
```

Monitoring Size of Tables

The script to calculate the actual size of a table or index uses the *temp_size_table*, which is created with the script shown in *temp_size_table.sql*. As shown, the *act_size.sql* script will work only with Oracle8 and Oracle8*i*. To use *act_size.sql* with Oracle7, replace the call to the *dbms_rowid.rowid_block_number* procedure with substr(rowid,1,8).

The *act_size.sql* report cannot resolve index-only overflow tables or complex objects involving nested tables. Output from the *act_size* report is shown below.

🖫 **temp_size_table.sql**

```
-- ************************************************
--
--      Copyright © 2003 by Rampant TechPress Inc.
--
--      Free for non-commercial use.
--      For commercial licensing, e-mail info@rampant.cc
--
-- ************************************************
rem
rem Create temp_size_table for use by actsize.sql
rem
CREATE TABLE temp_size_table (
     table_name VARCHAR2(64),
     blocks NUMBER);
```

Here is a sample listing:

ALLOC. SEGMENT NAME	USED SEGMENT TYPE	PCT	EXTENTS	KILOBYTES	4096 K BLOCKS	4096 K BLOCKS	BLOCKS USED
FK_ACCOUNT_EXECS_1	INDEX		1	12	3	0	.00
FK_ADDRESSES_1			1	10,240	2,560	0	.00
FK_ADDRESSES_2			1	51,200	12,800	2,480	19.38
FK_ADDRESSES_3			1	12,800	2,560	2,967	23.18
FK_FRANCHISE_CODES_1			1	10,240	2,560	461	18.01
FK_SIC_CODES_1			1	51,200	12,800	3,893	30.41
FK_USERS_1			1	102,400	25,600	0	.00
LI_LOAD_TEST			1	40,960	10,240	5,536	54.06
OID_CLIENTSV8			1	20	5	0	.00
OID_EARNINGS_INFO_NMBRS			1	20	5	0	.00
...							
PK_ADDRESSES			1	102,400	25,600	5,203	20.32
PK_CLIENTS			1	102,400	25,600	3,212	12.55
PK_EARNINGS_INFO_NMBRS			1	102,400	25,600	2,780	10.86
PK_FRANCHISE_CODES			1	51,200	12,800	573	4.48
PK_SIC_CODES			1	51,200	12,800	4,863	37.99
UI_EARNINGS_INFO_NMBRS_ID			1	51,200	12,800	4,466	34.89
UK_CLIENTS			1	51,200	12,800	4,292	33.53
UK_LOAD_TEST			1	51,200	12,800	4,650	36.33
******* sum				1,116,564			
ACCOUNT_EXECS	TABLE		1	12	3	0	.00
ADDRESSES			1	204,800	51,200	32,827	64.12
ADDRESS_TEST			1	20	5	1	20.00
CLIENTS			2	307,200	76,800	61,587	80.19
...							
EARNINGS_INFO_NMBRS			1	204,800	51,200	28,485	55.63
EARNINGS_INFO_NUMBERSV8			1	20,480	5,120	0	.00
EMPLOYEES			1	20	5	0	.00
FRANCHISE_CODES			1	76,800	19,200	803	4.18
INTERACTION_LOG_ACTIVITY			3	12	3	0	.00
LOAD_TEST			1	615,420	153,855	140,441	91.28
LOOKUPS			1	12	3	0	.00
SIC_CODES			1	102,400	25,600	16,765	65.49
USERS			1	204,800	51,200	1	.00
******* sum				2,036,056			
sum				3,152,620			

Each of the reports columns above gives specific information. In the report above if a table shows more than 1,000 extents, the DBA should review its size usage via the size columns and if it exceeds 4000 extents (generally speaking) rebuild the table with better storage parameters. In the columns for sizes if a table shows that it is using less space than has been allocated, and history indicates it won't grow into the space, it should be re-created accordingly.

Table Statistics Scripts

The *dba_tables* view has several additional columns that are populated once a table has been analyzed using the *analyze table* command, or by the *dbms_utility* or *dbms_stats* analysis procedures. These columns include table-specific data, such as the number of rows, the number of allocated blocks, the number of empty blocks, the average percentage of free space in a table, the number of chained rows, and the average row length. In Oracle8*i,* the view also includes the *avg_space_freelist_blocks* and *num_freelist_blocks* columns. The dependencies column was added in Oracle9*i.*

These columns provide a more detailed view of database tables than ever before. It is clear that a new report is needed to document this data in hard-copy format, in order to easily track a table's growth, space usage, and chaining. The sample script in *tab_stat.sql* shows such a report. Example output from the report is shown below.

🖫 tab_stat.sql

```
--*************************************************
--
--    Copyright © 2003 by Rampant TechPress Inc.
--
--    Free for non-commercial use.
--    For commercial licensing, e-mail info@rampant.cc
--
-- *************************************************

rem
rem  NAME: tab_stat.sql
rem
rem  FUNCTION:  Show table statistics for user's tables or all
tables.
rem  10/08/01 Updated for 9i Mike Ault
rem
 SET PAGES 56 LINES 132 NEWPAGE 0 VERIFY OFF ECHO OFF FEEDBACK
OFF
rem
COLUMN owner              FORMAT a12            HEADING "Table
Owner"
COLUMN table_name         FORMAT a20            HEADING "Table"
COLUMN tablespace_name    FORMAT a20            HEADING
"Tablespace"
COLUMN num_rows           FORMAT 999,999,999    HEADING "Rows"
COLUMN blocks             FORMAT 999,999        HEADING "Blocks"
COLUMN empty_blocks       FORMAT 999,999        HEADING "Empties"
COLUMN space_full         FORMAT 999.99         HEADING "% Full"
COLUMN chain_cnt          FORMAT 999,999        HEADING "Chains"
COLUMN avg_row_len        FORMAT 99,999,999 HEADING "Avg
Length|(Bytes)"
rem
ttitle "Table Statistics Report"
DEFINE OUTPUT = 'rep_out\&db\tab_stat..lis'
SPOOL &output
rem
BREAK ON OWNER SKIP 2 ON TABLESPACE_NAME SKIP 1;
SELECT owner, table_name, tablespace_name, num_rows, blocks,
     empty_blocks,
     100*((num_rows *
     avg_row_len)/((GREATEST(blocks,1)+empty_blocks)*value))
     space_full,
     chain_cnt, avg_row_len
FROM dba_tables, v$parameter
WHERE OWNER NOT IN ('SYS','SYSTEM')
and num_rows>0
and name='db_block_size'
ORDER BY owner, tablespace_name;
SPOOL OFF
PAUSE Press enter to continue
SET PAGES 22 LINES 80 NEWPAGE 1 VERIFY ON FEEDBACK ON
CLEAR COLUMNS
CLEAR BREAKS
TTITLE OFF
```

Table Statistics Scripts   **229**

Here is a sample listing:

```
Avg Length
Table Owner  Table       Tablespace     Rows  Blocks  Empties % Full  Chains (Bytes)
------------ ----------  -------------  -----  ------- ------- -------------  ---
DBAUTIL      DBA_TEMP    DBAUTIL_DATA    50      1       23    .74        0   29
HR           REGIONS     EXAMPLE          4      1        6    .12        0   17
             LOCATIONS                   23      1        0  13.76        0   49
             DEPARTMENTS                 27      1        0   6.59        0   20
             EMPLOYEES                  107      2        0  44.41        0   68
             JOB_HISTORY                 10      1        0   3.78        0   31
             JOBS                        19      1        0   7.65        0
```

The tables should be rebuilt if the actual space report, or if the report above shows improper space utilization or excessive chaining. These statistics will only be as accuratre as your last analysis run allows. Oddly, the report above shows the Empties columns for many of the HR schema tables at the value of 0, yet the used space calculations (% Full) show there should be some empty blocks. Analyzing the REGIONS table in this example caused them to appear. Oracle has apparently used the *dbms_stats* package to load statistics into the data dictionary for their example tables.

The selection of the *db_block_size* will only work in 9*i* if the tablespace in which the table resides is using the default blocksize. If the new capability of Oracle9*i* to use multiple blocksizes in the same database will be used, change the query to use the *block_size* column in the *dba_tablespaces* view instead.

Note: This script has been left generic so it can be used with older releases of Oracle.

One method of rebuilding a table is as follows:

1. Using a SQL script, unload the table into a flat file.

2. Drop the table and re-create it with a more representative storage clause.

3. Use SQLLOADER to reload the table data.

A second method is:

1. Using the CREATE TABLE. . .AS SELECT. . .FROM command, build a second table that is a mirror image of the first table (SELECT * FROM first table) with a storage clause that specifies a larger initial extent.

2. Delete the first table.

3. Use the RENAME command to rename the second table with the first table's name.

The easiest method (since version 7.3) is to use the Oracle ALTER TABLE...MOVE command, without specifying a new tablespace (unless the table is being moved to a new tablespace). This allows the DBA to re-create the table in place, changing the desired storage characteristics.

Table Type Internals

Numerous new columns were added to the *dba_tables* view in later versions of Oracle. These rows indicate whether a table is nested or partitioned, whether it is an index-only or overflow table, and its logging status. A simple report such as the one shown in *tab_rep.sql* provides a convenient format for managing this data.

```
--*********************************************
--
--    Copyright © 2003 by Rampant TechPress Inc.
--
--    Free for non-commercial use.
--    For commercial licensing, e-mail info@rampant.cc
--
-- *********************************************

REM
REM     Name:       tab_rep.sql
REM     FUNCTION:   Document table extended parameters
REM     Use:        From SQLPLUS
REM      MRA 6/13/97 Created for ORACLE8
REM   MRA 5/08/99 Updated for ORACLE8i
REM  MRA 10/08/01 Updated for Oracle9i
REM
COLUMN owner              FORMAT a10 HEADING 'Owner'
COLUMN table_name         FORMAT a15 HEADING 'Table'
COLUMN tablespace_name    FORMAT a13 HEADING 'Tablespace'
COLUMN table_type_owner   FORMAT a10 HEADING 'Type|Owner'
COLUMN table_type         FORMAT a13 HEADING 'Type'
COLUMN iot_name           FORMAT a10 HEADING 'IOT|Overflow'
COLUMN iot_type           FORMAT a12 HEADING 'IOT or|Overflow'
COLUMN nested             FORMAT a6  HEADING 'Nested'
COLUMN extern             FORMAT a3  HEADING 'Ext'
UNDEF owner
SET LINES 130 VERIFY OFF FEEDBACK OFF PAGES 58
ttitle 'Extended Table Report'
SPOOL ext_tab.lis
SELECT
    owner,
    table_name,
    tablespace_name,
    iot_name,
    logging,
    partitioned,
    iot_type,
    'N/A' table_type_owner,
    'N/A' table_type,
    DECODE(temporary,'N','No',temporary),
    nested,
    'N/A' extern
FROM
    dba_tables
WHERE
    owner LIKE UPPER('%&&owner%')
UNION
SELECT
    owner,
    table_name,
    tablespace_name,
    iot_name,
    logging,
    partitioned,
```

```
        iot_type,
        table_type_owner,
        table_type,
        DECODE(temporary,'N','No',temporary),
        nested,
         'N/A' extern
FROM
        dba_object_tables
WHERE
        owner LIKE UPPER('%&&owner%')
UNION
SELECT
        Owner,
        'None' tablespace_name,
         'N/A' Iot_name,
         'N/A' logging,
         'N/A' partitioned,
         'N/A' Iot_type,
        type_owner table_type_owner,
        type_name table_type,
         'N/A' temporary,
         'N/A' nested,
         'Yes' extern
FROM
        Dba_external_tables
WHERE
        Owner LIKE UPPER('%&&owner%');
SPOOL OFF
SET VERIFY ON LINES 80 PAGES 22 FEEDBACK ON
TTITLE OFF
UNDEF OWNER
CLEAR COLUMNS
```

The output from the report on extended table parameters is shown below. This is about the only place to find documentation on index-only tables without going back to the XX$ table level.

Notice the UNION command. The table name can be changed to *dba_tables* after removing the first half. The *dba_object_tables* view and the type-related columns were also added in Oracle8*i*.

Here is a sample listing:

Owner	Table	Tablespace	IOT Ovf	LOG	PAR	IOT or Type Ovf	Owner	Type	Tmp	Nest	Ext
DBAUTIL	DBAUTIL_KEPT_OB	DBAUTIL_DATA		YES	NO		N/A	N/A	No	NO	N/A
DBAUTIL	DBAUTIL_UPD_TAB	DBAUTIL_DATA		YES	NO		N/A	N/A	No	NO	N/A
DBAUTIL	DBA_RUNNING_STA	DBAUTIL_DATA		YES	NO		N/A	N/A	No	NO	N/A
DBAUTIL	DBA_TEMP	DBAUTIL_DATA		YES	NO		N/A	N/A	No	NO	N/A
DBAUTIL	HIT_RATIOS	DBAUTIL_DATA		YES	NO		N/A	N/A	No	NO	N/A
DBAUTIL	SQL_SCRIPTS	None	N/A	N/A	N/A	N/A	SYS	ORACLE_L	N/A	N/A	Yes
DBAUTIL	SQL_SCRIPTS	SYSTEM		YES	NO		N/A	N/A	No	NO	N/A
DBAUTIL	SQL_SCRIPTS2	None	N/A	N/A	N/A	N/A	SYS	ORACLE_L	N/A	N/A	Yes
DBAUTIL	SQL_SCRIPTS2	SYSTEM		YES	NO		N/A	N/A	No	NO	N/A
DBAUTIL	STAT_TEMP	DBAUTIL_DATA		YES	NO		N/A	N/A	No	NO	N/A
DBAUTIL	TEMP_SIZE_TABLE	DBAUTIL_DATA		YES	NO		N/A	N/A	No	NO	N/A

The report output in the listing above shows the following information for Oracle8, Oracle8*i*, and oracle9*i* tables. (Note: For Oracle8 and Oracle8*i* tables, remove sections that don't have counterparts to Oracle9*i*'s new features, such as the UNION to *dba_external_tables*.)

- **Owner.** The owner of the table.

- **Table.** The table name.

- **Tablespace.** The tablespace name.

- **IOT Overflow.** Gives the name of the IOT tables overflow table.

- **LOG.** Does this table use redo logging?

- **PAR.** Is this table partitioned?

- **IOT or Overflow.** Is this table an IOT or overflow table?

- **Type Owner.** The owner of the type used to build this table.

- **Type.** The main type used to build this table.

- **Tmp.** Is this a temporary table?

- **Nest.** Is this a nested table store table?

- **Ext.** Is this an external table (9*i* only)?

Note that there are entries for the external tables stored in both the *dba_tables* and *dba_external_tables* views. In the *dba_tables* views, the tablespace for all external tables is SYSTEM, and the initial extent, next extent, and pctincrease will be null.

The relative statistics of a table will be shown in the *dba_tables* or *dba_object_tables* views, as long as it has been analyzed. The code below shows an example of a report for monitoring the statistics of analyzed tables. These statistics bear close attention since they are gathered by the analyzer and used by the optimizer to tune the queries (when Choose mode is set). If rule-based optimization is being used, there should be no statistics present for the tables in the application. The output from the *tab_stat.sql* report is shown following.

🖫 tab_stat.sql

```
--*************************************************
--
--      Copyright © 2003 by Rampant TechPress Inc.
--
--      Free for non-commercial use.
--      For commercial licensing, e-mail info@rampant.cc
--
--      *************************************************

rem
rem   NAME: tab_stat.sql
rem
rem   FUNCTION:Show table statistics for a user's tables or all
tables.
rem
 set pages 56 lines 130 newpage 0 verify off echo off feedback
off
rem
COLUMN owner            FORMAT a12          HEADING "Table
Owner"
COLUMN table_name       FORMAT a17          HEADING "Table"
COLUMN tablespace_name  FORMAT a13          HEADING
"Tablespace"
COLUMN num_rows         FORMAT 99,999,999   HEADING "Rows"
COLUMN blocks           FORMAT 99,999       HEADING "Blocks"
COLUMN empty_blocks     FORMAT 99,999       HEADING "Empties"
```

```
COLUMN space_full          FORMAT 999.99           HEADING "% Full"
COLUMN chain_cnt           FORMAT 99,999           HEADING "Chains"
COLUMN avg_row_len         FORMAT 9,999,999 HEADING
"Avg|Length|(Bytes)"
COLUMN num_freelist_blocks FORMAT 99,999 HEADING
"Num|Freelist|Blocks"
COLUMN avg_space_freelist_blocks FORMAT 99,999 HEADING
"Avg|Space|Freelist Blocks"
rem
ttitle "Table Statistics Report"
DEFINE OUTPUT = 'rep_out\&db\tab_stat..lis'
SPOOL &output
rem
BREAK ON OWNER SKIP 2 ON TABLESPACE_NAME SKIP 1;
SELECT
   owner, table_name, tablespace_name,
   num_rows, blocks,empty_blocks,
   100*((num_rows * avg_row_len)/((GREATEST(blocks,1) +
empty_blocks)
   * 2048)) space_full,
   chain_cnt, avg_row_len,avg_space_freelist_blocks,
   num_freelist_blocks
FROM
   dba_tables
WHERE
  owner NOT IN ('SYS','SYSTEM')
UNION
SELECT
   owner, table_name, tablespace_name,
   num_rows, blocks,empty_blocks,
   100*((num_rows * avg_row_len)/((GREATEST(blocks,1) +
empty_blocks)
   * 2048)) space_full,
   chain_cnt, avg_row_len,avg_space_freelist_blocks,
   num_freelist_blocks
FROM
   dba_object_tables
WHERE
  owner NOT IN ('SYS','SYSTEM')
ORDER BY
   owner, tablespace_name;
SPOOL OFF
PAUSE Press enter to continue
SET PAGES 22 LINES 80 NEWPAGE 1 VERIFY ON FEEDBACK ON
CLEAR COLUMNS
CLEAR BREAKS
TTITLE OFF
```

Here is a sample listing:

Table Owner	Table	Tablespace	Rows	Blocks	Empties	% Full	Chains	Avg Length (Bytes)	Space Blocks	Num FL Blocks
GRAPHICS_DBA	BASIC_LOB_TABLE	GRAPHICS_DATA	0	0	0	.00	0	0	0	0
	GRAPHICS_TABLE		32	1	259	.31	0	52	2,276	1
	INTERNAL_GRAPHICS		32	2	257	.93	1	154	2,212	1
MIGRATE	FET$	SYSTEM	5,482	55	0	175.21	0	36	3,768	13
	TS$		24	55	0	2.22	0	104	3,768	13
OUTLN	OL$	SYSTEM	4	1	1	16.80	0	172	3,308	1
	OL$HINTS		175	5	0	90.58	0	53	3,168	3
TELE_DBA	ADDRESSESV8i	GRAPHICS_DATA	0	0	4	.00	0	0	0	0
	CIRCUITSV8i		0	0	4	.00	0	0	0	0
	CLIENTSV8i		0	0	5,119	.00	0	0	0	0
	CONTRACTSV8i		0	0	4	.00	0	0	0	0
	DEPT		1	1	3	.52	0	43	3,959	1
	EMP		1	1	3	.40	0	33	3,971	1

Table Columns Internals

The general table reports are completed with a report on the columns within a table. The script below generates this report.

💾 **tab_col.sql**

```
--*********************************************
--
--    Copyright © 2003 by Rampant TechPress Inc.
--
--    Free for non-commercial use.
--    For commercial licensing, e-mail info@rampant.cc
--
--  *********************************************

rem
rem tab_col.sql
rem
rem FUNCTION: Report on Table and View Column Definitions
rem
rem MRA 9/18/96
rem MRA 6/14/97 Added table level selectivity
rem
COLUMN owner               FORMAT a10      HEADING Owner
COLUMN table_name          FORMAT a30      HEADING "Table or View
Name"
COLUMN COLUMN_name         FORMAT a32      HEADING "Table or
View|Attribute"
COLUMN data_type           FORMAT a15      HEADING "Data|Type"
COLUMN data_type_owner     FORMAT a13      HEADING "Type|Owner"
COLUMN data_length                         HEADING Length
COLUMN nullable            FORMAT a5       HEADING Null
BREAK ON owner ON table_name SKIP 1
SET LINES 132 PAGES 48 FEEDBACK OFF VERIFY OFF
ttitle "Table Columns Report"
SPOOL tab_col
SELECT
        a.owner,
        table_name||' '||object_type table_name,
        column_name,
        data_type,
        data_type_owner,
        data_length,
        DECODE(nullable,'N','NO','YES') nullable
FROM
        dba_tab_columns a, dba_objects b
WHERE
        a.owner=UPPER('&owner') AND
        a.owner=b.owner AND
        a.table_name LIKE UPPER('%&table%') AND
```

```
        a.table_name=b.object_name AND
        object_type IN ('TABLE','VIEW','CLUSTER')
ORDER BY
        owner,
        object_type,
        table_name,
        column_id
/
SPOOL OFF
TTITLE OFF
SET LINES 80 PAGES 22 FEEDBACK ON VERIFY ON
```

The script above specifies the table columns to be viewed for a specific owner. If a naming convention that includes prefix or suffix designations is used for naming tables, then the prefix or suffix can be specified to pull the values for a specific type of table. The output from the script is shown in below.

Here is a sample listing:

Owner	Table or View Name	Type	Table or View Attribute	Data Type	Type Owner	Length	Null
TELE_DBA	CLIENTS_INFO_NUMBERS	V8i TABLE	CLIENTS_INFO_NMBRS_ID	NUMBER		22	NO
			CLIENTS_ID_R	CLIENT_T	TELE_DBA	50	YES
			LISTED_NAME	VARCHAR2		100	YES
			EARNING_NUMBER	CHAR		13	YES
			SERVICE_CLASS	VARCHAR2		5	YES
			NO_OF_LINES	NUMBER		22	YES
			DISCONNECT_DATE	DATE		7	YES
			DISCONNECT_REASON	CHAR		2	YES
			BILLING_NAME	VARCHAR2		40	YES
			PHONE	VARCHAR2		10	YES
			BTN	CHAR		13	YES
			OLD_CLIENTS_NUMBER	CHAR		13	YES
			SERVICE_ADDRESS	VARCHAR2		100	YES
			CON_CTRL_NUMBER	CHAR		15	YES
			TERM_AGREEMENT	CHAR		13	YES
			SHARED_TENANT_SVCS	VARCHAR2		10	YES
			INSTALLATION_DATE	DATE		7	YES
			CONTRACTS	CONTRACT_LIST	TELE_DBA	16	YES
			CIRCUITS	CIRCUIT_LIST	TELE_DBA	16	YES

Table Column Statistics Internals

The *dba_tab_columns* view provides column-level statistics. Several of the statistics, such as average length, number of null values, and so on, are useful to the DBA. The table must be analyzed for the column statistics to be populated. A report script for these table column statistics is shown below. The output from the script follows the report script.

🖫 **tab_sol_stats.sql**

```
--*********************************************
--
--    Copyright © 2003 by Rampant TechPress Inc.
--
--    Free for non-commercial use.
--    For commercial licensing, e-mail info@rampant.cc
--
-- *********************************************

rem
rem tab_col_stat.sql
rem
rem FUNCTION: Report on Table and View Column Definitions
rem
rem MRA 9/18/96
rem MRA 6/14/97 Added table level selectivity
rem MRA 5/8/99 Converted to do stats
rem
COLUMN owner           FORMAT a12      HEADING Owner
COLUMN table_name      FORMAT a20      HEADING "Table Name"
COLUMN COLUMN_name     FORMAT a13      HEADING
"Table|Attribute"
COLUMN data_type       FORMAT a10      HEADING "Data|Type"
COLUMN avg_col_len     FORMAT 99,999   HEADING "Aver|Length"
COLUMN density         FORMAT 9.9999   HEADING "Density"
COLUMN last_analyzed                   Heading "Analyzed"
COLUMN num_distinct                    HEADING
"Distinct|Values"
COLUMN num_nulls                       HEADING "Num.|Nulls"
COLUMN sample_size                     HEADING "Sample|Size"
BREAK ON owner ON table_name SKIP 1
SET LINES 132 PAGES 48 FEEDBACK OFF VERIFY OFF
ttitle "Table Column Stats Report"
SPOOL tab_col
SELECT
    owner,table_name,column_name,data_type,
    num_distinct,density,num_nulls,
    TO_CHAR(last_analyzed,'dd-mon-yyyy hh24:mi') last_analyzed,
```

```
   sample_size, avg_col_len
FROM
   dba_tab_columns
WHERE
   owner LIKE UPPER('%&owner%')
   and table_name LIKE UPPER('%&tabname%')
/
SPOOL OFF
TTITLE OFF
SET LINES 80 PAGES 22 FEEDBACK ON VERIFY ON
```

Here is a sample listing:

Enter value for owner: graphics_dba
Enter value for tabname:

Owner	Table Name	Table Attribute	Data Type	Distinct Values	Density	Num. Nulls	Analyzed	Sample Size	Aver Length
GRAPHICS_DBA	BASIC_LOB_TABLE	X	VARCHAR2	0	.0000	0	09-may-1999 10:44		0
		B	BLOB						
		C	CLOB						
	GRAPHICS_TABLE	BFILE_ID	NUMBER	32	.0313	0	09-may-1999 10:44	32	2
		BFILE_DESC	VARCHAR2	0	.0313	32	09-may-1999 10:44		0
		BFILE_LOC	BFILE	30	.0333	0	09-may-1999 10:44	32	40
		BFILE_TYPE	VARCHAR2	2	.5000	0	09-may-1999 10:44	32	1
	INTERNAL_GRAPHICS	GRAPHIC_ID	NUMBER	32	.0313	0	09-may-1999 10:45	32	2
		GRAPHIC_DESC	VARCHAR2	31	.0323	0	09-may-1999 10:45	32	18
		GRAPHIC_BLOB	BLOB						
		GRAPHIC_TYPE	VARCHAR2	2	.5000	0	09-may-1999 10:45	32	1

Table Key Internals

Each table is required to have a unique identifier consisting of one or more of the table's columns, as mandated by the Third Normal Form. As an alternative, a derived key consisting of a number pulled from an Oracle sequence can be used, but this method should be employed only if the key would be excessively long (over three columns). This is called the *primary key* of the table, and it should be identified using a constraint clause when the table is created. A second type of key, called a *foreign key*, is also present in most tables. The foreign key is used to enforce relationships between two or more tables. The foreign key consists of the primary key from the related table. The foreign key, too, should be identified by a constraint clause when the table is created.

The two types of keys can be readily monitored via the *pk_fk_rpt.sql* script. An example of this script's output is also shown below.

💾 **pk_fk_rep.sql**

```
--*********************************************
--
--      Copyright © 2003 by Rampant TechPress Inc.
--
--      Free for non-commercial use.
--      For commercial licensing, e-mail info@rampant.cc
--
--  *******************************************

REM          FUNCTION: SCRIPT FOR DOCUMENTING DATABASE
CONSTRAINTS
REM
REM FUNCTION: Running this script will document the primary key
- foreign key
REM FUNCTION: constraints in the database
REM
```

```
REM
REM

set arraysize 1
set verify off
rem set feedback off
rem set termout off
rem set echo off
set pagesize 0
set long 4000
set termout on
select 'Creating constraint build script...' from dual;
rem set termout off

create table cons_temp (owner varchar2(30),
                    constraint_name varchar2(30),
                    constraint_type varchar2(11),
                    search_condition varchar2(2000),
                    table_name varchar2(30),
                    referenced_owner varchar2(30),
                    referenced_constraint varchar2(30),
                    delete_rule varchar2(9),
                    constraint_columns varchar2(2000),
                    con_number number);
truncate table cons_temp;

DECLARE

   CURSOR cons_cursor IS select    owner,
                         constraint_name,
   decode(constraint_type,'P','Primary Key',
                    'R','Foreign Key',
                    'U','Unique',
                    'C','Check',
                    'D','Default'),
                         search_condition,
                         table_name,
                         r_owner,
                         r_constraint_name,
                         delete_rule
   from user_constraints
   where owner not in ('SYS','SYSTEM')
   order by owner;

   cursor cons_col (cons_name in varchar2) is
   select
           owner,
           constraint_name,
           column_name
   from user_cons_columns
   where owner not in ('SYS','SYSTEM') and
   constraint_name = upper(cons_name)
   order by owner, constraint_name,
                         position;

   cursor get_cons (tab_nam in varchar2) is
   select distinct
           OWNER,TABLE_NAME,CONSTRAINT_NAME,CONSTRAINT_TYPE
   from cons_temp
```

```
         where table_name=tab_nam
         and constraint_type='Foreign Key'
         order by owner,table_name,constraint_name;

         cursor get_tab_nam is
         select distinct table_name
         from cons_temp
         where constraint_type='Foreign Key'
         order by table_name;

         tab_nam         user_constraints.table_name%TYPE;
         cons_owner      user_constraints.owner%TYPE;
         cons_name       user_constraints.constraint_name%TYPE;
         cons_type       varchar2(11);
         cons_sc         user_constraints.search_condition%TYPE;
         cons_tname      user_constraints.table_name%TYPE;
         cons_rowner     user_constraints.r_owner%TYPE;
         cons_rcons      user_constraints.r_constraint_name%TYPE;
         cons_dr         user_constraints.delete_rule%TYPE;
         cons_col_own    user_cons_columns.owner%TYPE;
         cons_col_nam    user_cons_columns.constraint_name%TYPE;
         cons_column     user_cons_columns.column_name%TYPE;
         cons_tcol_name  user_cons_columns.table_name%TYPE;
         all_columns     varchar2(2000);
         counter         integer:=0;
         cons_nbr        integer;

BEGIN
   OPEN cons_cursor;
   LOOP
      FETCH cons_cursor INTO         cons_owner,
                                     cons_name,
                                     cons_type,
                                     cons_sc,
                                     cons_tname,
                                     cons_rowner,
                              cons_rcons,
                                     cons_dr;
      EXIT WHEN cons_cursor%NOTFOUND;
      all_columns :='';
      counter := 0;
      open cons_col (cons_name);
      loop
            fetch cons_col  into
                                     cons_col_own,
                                     cons_col_nam,
                                     cons_column;
      exit when cons_col%NOTFOUND;
            if cons_owner = cons_col_own and
cons_name=cons_col_nam
            then
                    counter := counter+1;
                    if counter = 1 then
                    all_columns := all_columns||cons_column;
                    else
                    all_columns := all_columns||',
'||cons_column;
                    end if;
            end if;
```

```
        end loop;
      close cons_col;
      insert into cons_temp values (cons_owner,
                                    cons_name,
                                    cons_type,
                                    cons_sc,
                                    cons_tname,
                                    cons_rowner,
                                    cons_rcons,
                                    cons_dr,
                             all_columns,
                             0);
    commit;
    END LOOP;
    CLOSE cons_cursor;
    commit;
begin
 open get_tab_nam;
loop
  fetch get_tab_nam into tab_nam;
  exit when get_tab_nam%NOTFOUND;
/*sys.dbms_output.put_line(tab_nam);*/
  open get_cons (tab_nam);
  cons_nbr:=0;
  loop
    fetch get_cons into cons_owner,
                     cons_tname,
                     cons_name,
                     cons_type;
    exit when get_cons%NOTFOUND;
    cons_nbr:=cons_nbr+1;
/*    sys.dbms_output.put_line('cons_nbr='||cons_nbr);*/
/*sys.dbms_output.put_line(cons_owner||'.'||cons_name||'
'||cons_type);*/
    update cons_temp set con_number=cons_nbr where
    constraint_name=cons_name and
    constraint_type=cons_type and
    owner=cons_owner;
  end loop;
  close get_cons;
  commit;
end loop;
close get_tab_nam;
commit;
end;
END;
/
create index pk_cons_temp on cons_temp(constraint_name);
create index lk_cons_temp2 on cons_temp(referenced_constraint);
set feedback off pages 0 termout off echo off
set verify off
set pages 48 lines 132
column pri_own format a15 heading 'Pri Table|Owner'
column for_own format a15 heading 'For Table|Owner'
column pri_tab format a15 heading 'Pri Table|Name'
column for_tab format a15 heading 'For Table|Name'
column pri_col format a30 heading 'Pri Key|Columns' word_wrapped
column for_col format a30 heading 'For Key|Columns' word_wrapped
ttitle 'Primary Key - Foreign Key Report'
```

```
spool pk_fk
break on a.owner on a.table_name on b.owner on b.table_name
select
    b.owner pri_own,
    b.table_name pri_tab,
    rtrim(b.constraint_columns) pri_col,
    a.owner for_own,
    a.table_name for_tab,
    rtrim(a.constraint_columns) for_col
from
    cons_temp a,
    cons_temp b
where
    a.referenced_constraint(+)=b.constraint_name
order by
    1,2,4,5;
spool off
drop table cons_temp;
set verify on
set feedback on
set termout on
set echo on
set pagesize 22 lines 80
clear columns
clear breaks
ttitle off
```

Here is a sample listing:

Pri Table Owner	Pri Table Name	Pri Key COLUMNs	For Table Owner	For Table Name	For Key COLUMNs
TELE_DBA	BBS_DUNS_PROFILE	SITE_ID	TELE_DBA	BBS_FRANCHISE_CODES	SITE_ID
		SITE_ID		BBS_SIC_CODES	SITE_ID
	BBS_EARNINGS_INFO	EARNING_NO_DOCID	TELE_DBA	BBS_AUDIT_RECORD	EARNING_NO_DOCID
		EARNING_NO_DOCID		BBS_CIRCUIT_ID_INFO	EARNING_NO_DOCID
		EARNING_NO_DOCID		STI_ADDRESS	EARNING_NO_DOCID
	CUSTOMER_SITES	SITE_ID	TELE_DBA	BBS_DUNS_PROFILE	SITE_ID
		SITE_ID		BBS_EARNINGS_INFO	SITE_ID
TEMP_USER	DEPT	DEPTNO	TEMP_USER	EMP	DEPTNO

Finding Tables with Chained Rows

As data is added to an existing record, row chaining occurs. When there is insufficient room for new data, the row is chained to another block and added. Block chaining occurs when a row is too long to fit into a single block (such as with long raw or LOB columns or when a row has more than 255 columns). Frequent chaining can lead to significant performance degradation, because multiple blocks must be read to retrieve a single record. An example of a script to monitor a single table for chained rows is shown below.

🖫 chaining.sql

```
--*********************************************
--
--    Copyright © 2003 by Rampant TechPress Inc.
--
--    Free for non-commercial use.
--    For commercial licensing, e-mail info@rampant.cc
--
--  *******************************************
rem
***********************************************************************
rem
rem  NAME: CHAINING.sql
rem
rem  FUNCTION: Report on the number of CHAINED rows within a
named table
rem
rem  NOTES:  Requires DBA priviledges.
rem            The target table must have a column that is the
leading portion
rem            of an index and is defined as not null.
rem            Uses the V$SESSTAT table where USERNAME is the
current user.
rem            A problem if > 1 session active with that
USERID.
rem            The statistics in V$SESSTAT may change between
releases and
rem            platforms.  Make sure that 'table fetch
continued row' is
rem            a valid statistic.
```

```
rem              This routine can be run by AUTO_CHN.sql by
remarking the two
rem              accepts and un-remarking the two defines.
rem
rem  INPUTS: obj_own = the owner of the table.
rem          obj_nam = the name of the table.
rem
rem
****************************************************************

rem accept obj_own prompt 'Enter the table owner''s name: '
rem accept obj_nam prompt 'Enter the name of the table: '

define obj_own = &1
define obj_nam = &2

set termout off feedback off verify off echo off heading off
embedded on

rem  Find out what statistic we want
column statistic# new_value stat_no
select statistic#
  from v$statname n
 where n.name = 'table fetch continued row'
/

rem  Find out who we are in terms of sid
column sid new_value user_sid
select distinct sid from v$session
 where audsid = userenv('SESSIONID')
/

rem  Find the last col of the table and a not null indexed
column
column column_name new_value last_col
column name new_value indexed_column
column value new_value before_count
select column_name
  from dba_tab_columns
 where table_name = upper('&&obj_nam')
   and owner      = upper('&&obj_own')
 order by column_id
/
select c.name
  from sys.col$ c, sys.obj$ idx, sys.obj$ base, sys.icol$ ic
 where base.obj#   = c.obj#
   and ic.bo#      = base.obj#
   and ic.col#     = c.col#
   and base.owner# = (select user# from sys.user$
                      where name = upper('&&obj_own'))
   and ic.obj#     = idx.obj#
   and base.name   = upper('&&obj_nam')
   and ic.pos#     = 1
   and c.null$     > 0
/
select value
  from v$sesstat
 where v$sesstat.sid = &user_sid
   and v$sesstat.statistic# = &stat_no
```

Finding Tables with Chained Rows   **251**

```
/
rem  Select every row from the target table
select &last_col xx
  from &obj_own..&obj_nam
 where &indexed_column <= (select max(&indexed_column)
                           from &obj_own..&obj_nam)
/

column value new_value after_count
select value
  from v$sesstat
 where v$sesstat.sid = &user_sid
   and v$sesstat.statistic# = &stat_no
/

set termout on

select 'Table '||upper('&obj_own')||'.'||upper('&obj_nam')||'
contains '||
       (to_number(&after_count) - to_number(&before_count))||
       ' chained row'||
       decode(to_number(&after_count) -
to_number(&before_count),1,'.','s.')
  from dual
 where rtrim('&indexed_column') is not null
/

rem If we don't have an indexed column this won't work so say so
select 'Table '||
       upper('&obj_own')||'.'||upper('&obj_nam')||
       ' has no indexed, not null columns.'
  from dual
 where rtrim('&indexed_column') is null
/

set termout on feedback 15 verify on pagesize 20 linesize 80
space 1 heading on
undef obj_nam
undef obj_own
undef before_count
undef after_count
undef indexed_column
undef last_col
undef stat_no
undef user_sid
clear columns
clear computes
```

Note that this script will only work if the table has a
primary or unique key defined. With a companion script,
all tables in an application can be checked with this
script. As an alternative, analyze the tables of concern

and use the table statistics report, described in the following subsection.

Using the ANALYZE Command

Chained-row information can be placed into the *dba_tables* view with the ANALYZE command. Actual chained-row rowids can be listed in a separate table if desired. The general format of this command is:

```
ANALYZE TABLE_or_CLUSTER [schema.]table_or_cluster
LIST CHAINED ROWS INTO [schema.]table;
```

A script called *utlchain.sql* will build the chained row table in Oracle8, Oracle8*i*, and Oracle9*i*. The script below will perform a chain analysis of a table for an owner. A second script will analyze all tables for a specified owner for chains, with the first script altered as annotated. The listing that follows shows the results of this automated chain analysis for an owner's tables.

🖫 Chaining2.sql

```
--*******************************************
--
--    Copyright © 2003 by Rampant TechPress Inc.
--
--    Free for non-commercial use.
--    For commercial licensing, e-mail info@rampant.cc
--
--    *******************************************
rem
****************************************************************
rem
rem  NAME:      CHAINING2.sql
rem
rem  FUNCTION: Report number of CHAINED rows within a named
table
rem
rem  NOTES:  Requires DBA priviledges.
rem        Target table must have column that is the leading
portion
rem        of an index and is defined as not null.
```

```
rem         Uses the V$SESSTAT table. USERNAME is the current
user.
rem         A problem if > 1 session active with that USERID.
rem         V$SESSTAT may change between releases and
rem         platforms.  Make sure that 'table fetch continued
row' is
rem         a valid statistic.
rem         This routine can be run by AUTO_CHN.sql by remarking
the
rem         two accepts and un-remarking the two defines.
rem
rem   INPUTS: obj_own = the owner of the table.
rem           obj_nam = the name of the table.
rem
rem
********************************************************************
***
ACCEPT obj_own PROMPT 'Enter the table owner''s name: '
ACCEPT obj_nam PROMPT 'Enter the name of the table: '

rem DEFINE obj_own = &1    fl Remove comment to use with
auto_chain
rem DEFINE obj_nam = &2    fl Remove comment to use with
auto_chain

SET TERMOUT OFF FEEDBACK OFF VERIFY OFF ECHO OFF HEADING OFF
SET EMBEDDED ON
COLUMN statistic# NEW_VALUE stat_no NOPRINT
SELECT
     statistic#
FROM
     v$statname

WHERE
     n.name = 'table fetch continued row'
/
rem  Find out who we are in terms of sid
COLUMN sid NEW_VALUE user_sid
SELECT
     distinct sid
FROM
     v$session
WHERE
     audsid = USERENV('SESSIONID')
/

rem  Find the last col of the table and a not null indexed
column
COLUMN column_name      NEW_VALUE last_col
COLUMN name      NEW_VALUE indexed_column
COLUMN value      NEW_VALUE before_count
SELECT
     column_name
  FROM
     dba_tab_columns
  WHERE
     table_name = upper('&&obj_nam')
        and owner = upper('&&obj_own')
 ORDER BY
```

```
        column_id
/
SELECT
     c.name
  FROM
     sys.col$ c,
     sys.obj$ idx,
     sys.obj$ base,
     sys.icol$ ic
 WHERE
     base.obj#      = c.obj#
        and ic.bo#      = base.obj#
        and ic.col#     = c.col#
        and base.owner# = (SELECT user# FROM sys.user$
                 WHERE name = UPPER('&&obj_own'))
        and ic.obj#     = idx.obj#
        and base.name   = UPPER('&&obj_nam')
        and ic.pos#     = 1
        and c.null$     > 0
/
SELECT value
  FROM v$sesstat
 WHERE v$sesstat.sid = &user_sid
   AND v$sesstat.statistic# = &stat_no
/
rem  Select every row from the target table
SELECT &last_col xx
  FROM &obj_own..&obj_nam
 WHERE &indexed_column <= (SELECT MAX(&indexed_column)
                 FROM &obj_own..&obj_nam)
/
COLUMN value NEW_VALUE after_count
SELECT value
  FROM v$sesstat
 WHERE v$sesstat.sid = &user_sid
   AND v$sesstat.statistic# = &stat_no
/
SET TERMOUT ON

SELECT
'Table '||UPPER('&obj_own')||'.'||UPPER('&obj_nam')||' contains
'||
       (TO_NUMBER(&after_count) - TO_NUMBER(&before_count))||
       ' chained row'||
       DECODE(to_NUMBER(&after_count) -
TO_NUMBER(&before_count),1,'.','s.')
  FROM dual
 WHERE RTRIM('&indexed_column') IS NOT NULL
/

rem If we don't have an indexed column this won't work so say so
SELECT 'Table '||
       UPPER('&obj_own')||'.'||UPPER('&obj_nam')||
       ' has no indexed, not null columns.'
  FROM dual
 WHERE RTRIM('&indexed_column') IS NULL
/
```

Finding Tables with Chained Rows   **255**

```
SET TERMOUT ON FEEDBACK 15 VERIFY ON PAGESIZE 20 LINESIZE 80
SPACE 1
SET HEADING ON
UNDEF obj_nam
UNDEF obj_own
UNDEF before_count
UNDEF after_count
UNDEF indexed_column
UNDEF last_col
UNDEF stat_no
UNDEF user_sid
CLEAR COLUMNS
CLEAR COMPUTES
```

💾 auto_chn.sql

```
--*****************************************************
--
--     Copyright © 2003 by Rampant TechPress Inc.
--
--     Free for non-commercial use.
--     For commercial licensing, e-mail info@rampant.cc
--
-- *****************************************************

ACCEPT tabown PROMPT 'Enter table owner: '
rem
SET TERMOUT OFF FEEDBACK OFF VERIFY OFF ECHO OFF HEADING OFF
PAGES 999
SET EMBEDDED ON
COLUMN name NEW_VALUE db NOPRINT
SELECT name FROM v$database;
SPOOL rep_out\auto_chn.gql
rem
SELECT 'start chaining &tabown '||table_name
  FROM dba_tables
 WHERE owner = UPPER('&tabown')
/

SPOOL OFF
SPOOL rep_out\&db\chaining
START rep_out\auto_chn.gql
SPOOL OFF
UNDEF tabown
SET TERMOUT ON FEEDBACK 15 VERIFY ON PAGESIZE 20 LINESIZE 80
SPACE 1
SET EMBEDDED OFF
HO del rep_out\auto_chn.gql
PAUSE Press enter to continue
```

Here is a sample listing.

```
Table SYSTEM.CGS_REFLINE contains 0 chained rows.
Table SYSTEM.CGS_WKSTATION contains 0 chained rows.
Table SYSTEM.CGS_WSATTRIBUTES contains 0 chained rows.
Table SYSTEM.CGS_WSCOLORS contains 0 chained rows.
Table SYSTEM.CGS_WSFONTS contains 0 chained rows.
Table SYSTEM.CGS_WSLNSTYLES contains 0 chained rows.
Table SYSTEM.CGS_WSPATTERNS contains 0 chained rows.
Table SYSTEM.DBA_TEMP has no indexed, not null columns.
Table SYSTEM.DEF$_CALL contains 0 chained rows.
Table SYSTEM.DEF$_CALLDEST contains 0 chained rows.
Table SYSTEM.DEF$_DEFAULTDEST contains 0 chained rows.
```

A column showing chained rows for a specific table is also provided in the *dba_tables* view. If the table has been analyzed, a simple query against this view will indicate whether any chaining is occurring. This is useful if there is no need to know which rows are chained. An example script to generate a list of tables with chained rows from a system that has been analyzed is shown below.

🖫 Chained_tab.sql

```
--*************************************************
--
--    Copyright © 2003 by Rampant TechPress Inc.
--
--    Free for non-commercial use.
--    For commercial licensing, e-mail info@rampant.cc
--
-- *************************************************

rem chained_tab.sql
rem FUNCTION: Reports chained tables
rem MRA
rem
col tablespace_name format a15
col owner format a10
col table_name format a32
set lines 132 pages 47
ttitle 'Tables With Chained Rows'
spool chained_tab
select
owner,table_name,chain_cnt,num_rows,chain_cnt/num_rows*100
chn_pct,tablespace_name from dba_tables where chain_cnt>0
order by 1,4
/
spool off
ttitle off
```

Partitioned Table Internals

Oracle8 introduced partitioned tables and indexes. In Oracle8*i*, their functionality has been expanded to include sub-partitions and the ability to hash partitions. These new types of tables need to be monitored. Essentially, the DBA needs to know which tables are partitioned, the ranges for each partition, and the table fraction locations for each partition. In Oracle9i the ability to perform LIST partitioning was added to the table partitioning arsenal.

Let's examine a couple of reports that provide this level of information. The first script gives information on partition names, partitioning value, partition tablespace location, and whether the partition is logging or not. The script is shown below.

📇 **tab_part.sql**

```
--*************************************************
--
--    Copyright © 2003 by Rampant TechPress Inc.
--
--    Free for non-commercial use.
--    For commercial licensing, e-mail info@rampant.cc
--
--    *********************************************

rem
rem Name: tab_part.sql
rem Function : Report on partitioned table structure
rem History: MRA 6/13/97 Created
rem
COLUMN table_owner        FORMAT a10 HEADING 'Owner'
COLUMN table_name         FORMAT a15 HEADING 'Table'
COLUMN partition_name     FORMAT a15 HEADING 'Partition'
COLUMN tablespace_name    FORMAT a15 HEADING 'Tablespace'
COLUMN high_value         FORMAT a10 HEADING 'Partition|Value'
COLUMN sub-partition_count FORMAT 9,999 HEADING 'Sub-Partitions'
SET LINES 130
ttitle 'Table Partition Files'
BREAK ON table_owner ON table_name
SPOOL tab_part.lis
```

```
SELECT
    table_owner,
    table_name,
    partition_name,
    sub_partition_count,
    high_value,
    tablespace_name,
    logging
FROM sys.dba_tab_partitions
ORDER BY table_owner,table_name
/
SPOOL OFF
```

The output from the script is below. Bear in mind that the partition value must be less than the column value.

Owner	Table	Partition	Partition Value	Tablespace	LOGGING	Sub Partitions
SYSTEM	TEST5	Q1_1997	TO_DATE(' 1997-04-01 00:00:00' , 'SYYYY-M M-DD HH24: MI:SS', 'N LS_CALENDA R=GREGORIA	USER_DATA	NONE	5
		Q2_1997	TO_DATE(' 1997-07-01 00:00:00' , 'SYYYY-M M-DD HH24: MI:SS', 'N LS_CALENDA R=GREGORIA	USER_DATA	NONE	4
		Q3_1997	TO_DATE(' 1997-10-01 00:00:00' , 'SYYYY-M M-DD HH24: MI:SS', 'N LS_CALENDA R=GREGORIA	USER_DATA	NONE	2
		Q4_1997	TO_DATE(' 1998-01-01 00:00:00' , 'SYYYY-M M-DD HH24: MI:SS', 'N LS_CALENDA R=GREGORIA	USER_DATA	NONE	8
		Q1_1998	TO_DATE(' 1998-04-01 00:00:00' , 'SYYYY-M M-DD HH24: MI:SS', 'N LS_CALENDA R=GREGORIA	USER_DATA	NONE	4

The storage characteristics of a partition structure are also of interest to a DBA. The report below shows an example of a report with this type of information. An example of output follows the script.

🖫 tab_pstor.sql

```
--*************************************************
--
--    Copyright © 2003 by Rampant TechPress Inc.
--
--    Free for non-commercial use.
--    For commercial licensing, e-mail info@rampant.cc
--
-- *************************************************

rem
rem NAME:     Tab_pstor.sql
rem FUNCTION: Provide data on part. table stor. charcacteristics
rem HISTORY: MRA 6/13/97 Created
rem

COLUMN table_owner       FORMAT a6        HEADING 'Owner'
COLUMN table_name        FORMAT a14       HEADING 'Table'
COLUMN partition_name    FORMAT a9        HEADING 'Partition'
COLUMN tablespace_name   FORMAT a11       HEADING 'Tablespace'
COLUMN pct_free          FORMAT 9999      HEADING '%|Free'
COLUMN pct_used          FORMAT 999       HEADING '%|Use'
COLUMN ini_trans         FORMAT 9999      HEADING 'Init|Tran'
COLUMN max_trans         FORMAT 9999      HEADING 'Max|Tran'
COLUMN initial_extent    FORMAT 9999999   HEADING 'Init|Extent'
COLUMN next_extent       FORMAT 9999999   HEADING 'Next|Extent'
COLUMN max_extent                         HEADING 'Max|Extents'
COLUMN pct_increase      FORMAT 999       HEADING '%|Inc'
COLUMN partition_position FORMAT 9999     HEADING 'Part|Nmbr'

SET LINES 130
ttitle 'Table Partition File Storage'
BREAK ON table_owner on table_name
SPOOL tab_pstor.lis

SELECT
   table_owner,
   table_name,
   tablespace_name,
   partition_name,
   partition_position,
   pct_free,
   pct_used,
   ini_trans,
   max_trans,
   initial_extent,
   next_extent,
   max_extent,
```

```
      pct_increase
FROM
      sys.dba_tab_partitions
ORDER BY
      table_owner,table_name
/
SPOOL OFF
```

Here is a sample listing.

```
                                    Part  %    %   Init Max  Init    Next
Max       %
Owner Table        Tablespace Partition Nmbr Free Use Tran Tran Extent  Extent
Extents Inc
----- ----------- ---------- --------- ---- ---- --- ---- ---- ------- ------ ---
SYSTEM PART_TEST   RAW_DATA   TEST_P1 1 10   90   1   255  1048576 1048576 249   0
                   RAW_DATA   TEST_P2 2 10   90   1   255  1048576 1048576 249   0
                   RAW_DATA   TEST_P3 3 10   90   1   255  1048576 1048576 249   0
```

In general, the storage characteristics of the partitions should be similar, if not identical, for a given table. However, only you know your data – if you are partitioning a sales table by month, and your business is seasonal, then the partitions for some months would be different from others.

Monitoring Partition Statistics

Oracle8, Oracle8*i*, and Oracle9*i* partitions store their analysis results in the *dba_tab_partitions* view. Partitions and sub-partitions need to be monitored just as chained rows and extents do. The script below provides an example of how to retrieve the statistics data in *dba_tab_partitions*. The report generated by the table partition statistic script also follows.

💾 **tab_part_stat.sql**

```
--*****************************************************
--
--     Copyright © 2003 by Rampant TechPress Inc.
--
--     Free for non-commercial use.
--     For commercial licensing, e-mail info@rampant.cc
```

```
--
-- *************************************************
rem
rem Name: tab_part_stat.sql
rem Function : Report on partitioned table statistics
rem History: MRA 6/13/97 Created
rem

COLUMN table_name          FORMAT a15   HEADING 'Table'
COLUMN partition_name      FORMAT a15   HEADING 'Partition'
COLUMN num_rows                         HEADING 'Num|Rows'
COLUMN blocks                           HEADING 'Blocks'
COLUMN avg_space                        HEADING 'Avg|Space'
COLUMN chain_cnt                        HEADING 'Chain|Count'
COLUMN avg_row_len                      HEADING 'Avg|Row|Length'
COLUMN last_analyzed                    HEADING 'Analyzed'

ACCEPT owner1 PROMPT 'Which Owner to report on?:'
SET LINES 130
ttitle 'Table Partition Statistics For &owner1'
BREAK ON table_owner ON table_name ON partition_name
SPOOL tab_part_stat.lis

SELECT
    table_name,
    partition_name,
    num_rows,
    blocks,
    avg_space,
    chain_cnt,
    avg_row_len,
    to_char(last_analyzed,'dd-mon-yyyy hh24:mi') last_analyzed
FROM
    sys.dba_tab_partitions
WHERE
    table_owner LIKE UPPER('%&&owner1%')
ORDER BY
    table_owner,table_name
/
SPOOL OFF
CLEAR BREAKS
CLEAR COLUMNS
TTITLE OFF
UNDEF owner1
```

Here is a sample listing.

```
Avg
                        Num                    Avg      Chain      Row
Table     Partition     Rows       Blocks      Space    Count      Length Analyzed
--------  ------------  ---------  ----------  -------- ---------- -------------------
TEST5     Q1_1997       0          0           0        0          0 09-may-1999 16:40
          Q2_1997       0          0           0        0          0 09-may-1999 16:40
          Q3_1997       0          0           0        0          0 09-may-1999 16:40
          Q4_1997       0          0           0        0          0 09-may-1999 16:40
          Q1_1998       0          0           0        0          0 09-may-1999 16:40
```

Pay special attention to the chain count. If this column starts showing a 5 to 10 percent ratio against the num rows column, the partition needs to be rebuilt. If any partition is out of balance (excessive rows when filled in comparison to other partitions), then perhaps that partition needs to be split.

Table Sub-partition Internals

Sub-partitions became available in Oracle8*i*. The name of the sub-partition is necessary to execute many of the commands, such as ALTER. Usually, Oracle8*i* automatically names the partitions created as sub-partitions, unless a sub-partition is specifically added to an existing set of partitions and sub-partitions. The report below demonstrates how to extricate the sub-partition information from the database data dictionary. An example of a report generated by the script follows the script.

🖫 **tab_subpart.sql**

```
--*********************************************
--
--    Copyright © 2003 by Rampant TechPress Inc.
--
--    Free for non-commercial use.
--    For commercial licensing, e-mail info@rampant.cc
--
--    *********************************************

rem
rem Name: tab_subpart.sql
rem Function : Report on partitioned table structure
rem History: MRA 6/13/97 Created
rem
COLUMN table_owner NEW_VALUE owner1 NOPRINT
COLUMN table_name       FORMAT a15    HEADING 'Table'
COLUMN partition_name   FORMAT a15    HEADING 'Partition'
COLUMN tablespace_name  FORMAT a15    HEADING 'Tablespace'
COLUMN initial_extent   FORMAT 9,999  HEADING 'Initial|Extent
(K)'
COLUMN next_extent      FORMAT 9,999  HEADING 'Next|Extent (K)'
```

```
COLUMN pct_increase     FORMAT 999   HEADING 'PCT|Increase'
SET LINES 130
ttitle 'Table Sub-Partition Files For &owner1'
BREAK ON table_owner ON table_name ON partition_name
SPOOL tab_subpart.lis
SELECT
    table_owner,
    table_name,
    partition_name,
        sub-partition_name,
    tablespace_name,
    logging,
        initial_extent/1024 initial_extent,
        next_extent/1024 next_extent,
        pct_increase
FROM sys.dba_tab_sub-partitions
ORDER BY table_owner,table_name,partition_name
/
SPOOL OFF
```

Here is a sample listing.

```
Initial    Next    PCT
Table      Partition  SUB-PARTITION_NAME Tablespace  LOG Extent (K) Extent (K)
Increase
---------------  ------------  -------------------- ------------ --- ------ --- ------ ---
TEST5   Q1_1997  SYS_SUBP1       DATA_TBS1   YES   40      40      0
                 SYS_SUBP2       DATA_TBS2   YES   40      40      0
                 SYS_SUBP4       DATA_TBS4   YES   40      40      0
                 SYS_SUBP3       DATA_TBS3   YES   40      40      0
                 WEEK1           DATA_TBS1   YES   40      40      0
        Q1_1998  SYS_SUBP17      DATA_TBS1   YES   40      40      0
                 SYS_SUBP18      DATA_TBS2   YES   40      40      0
                 SYS_SUBP19      DATA_TBS3   YES   40      40      0
                 SYS_SUBP20      DATA_TBS4   YES   40      40      0
        Q2_1997  SYS_SUBP5       DATA_TBS1   YES   40      40      0
                 SYS_SUBP8       DATA_TBS4   YES   40      40      0
                 SYS_SUBP7       DATA_TBS3   YES   40      40      0
                 SYS_SUBP6       DATA_TBS2   YES   40      40      0
        Q3_1997  Q3_1997_S1      DATA_TBS1   YES   40      40      0
                 Q3_1997_S2      DATA_TBS2   YES   40      40      0
        Q4_1997  SYS_SUBP9       Q4_TBS1     YES   40      40      0
                 SYS_SUBP10      Q4_TBS2     YES   40      40      0
                 SYS_SUBP11      Q4_TBS3     YES   40      40      0
                 SYS_SUBP12      Q4_TBS4     YES   40      40      0
                 SYS_SUBP13      Q4_TBS5     YES   40      40      0
                 SYS_SUBP14      Q4_TBS6     YES   40      40      0
                 SYS_SUBP15      Q4_TBS7     YES   40      40      0
                 SYS_SUBP16      Q4_TBS8     YES   40      40      0
```

Monitoring Sub-partition Statistics

Statistics are gathered at the sub-partition level, just as for tables and partitions. The *dba_tab_sub-partitions* view contains the statistics for all analyzed sub-partitions. A sample report on sub-partition statistics in Oracle8*i* and Oracle9*i* is shown below.

```
--*************************************************
--
--    Copyright © 2003 by Rampant TechPress Inc.
--
--    Free for non-commercial use.
--    For commercial licensing, e-mail info@rampant.cc
--
-- *************************************************

rem
rem Name: tab_subpart_stat.sql
rem Function : Report on partitioned table structure
rem History: MRA 6/13/97 Created
rem
COLUMN table_name            FORMAT a15   HEADING 'Table'
COLUMN partition_name        FORMAT a15   HEADING 'Partition'
COLUMN sub-partition_name    FORMAT a15   HEADING 'Sub|Partition'
COLUMN num_rows                           HEADING 'Num|Rows'
COLUMN blocks                             HEADING 'Blocks'
COLUMN avg_space                          HEADING 'Avg|Space'
COLUMN chain_cnt                          HEADING 'Chain|Count'
COLUMN avg_row_len                        HEADING 'Avg|Row|Length'
COLUMN last_analyzed                      HEADING 'Analyzed'
ACCEPT owner1 PROMPT 'Owner to Report On?: '
SET LINES 130
START ttitle 'Table Sub-Partition Statistics For &owner1'
BREAK ON table_owner ON table_name ON partition_name
SPOOL tab_subpart_stat.lis
SELECT
     table_owner,
     table_name,
     partition_name,
     sub-partition_name,
     num_rows,
     blocks,
     avg_space,
     chain_cnt,
     avg_row_len,
     to_char(last_analyzed,'dd-mon-yyyy hh24:mi') last_analyzed
FROM
     sys.dba_tab_sub-partitions
WHERE
     Table_owner LIKE UPPER('%&&owner1%')
ORDER BY
     table_owner,table_name,partition_name
/
SPOOL OFF
CLEAR COLUMNS
TTITLE OFF
UNDEF owner1
```

The output from the report above is shown below. This example isn't highly complex, because the sub-partitions are not loaded with data. Nevertheless, the value of this report is readily seen.

Table	Partition	Sub Partition	Rows	Num Blocks	Avg Space	Chain Count	Row Length	Analyzed
TEST5	Q1_1997	SYS_SUBP1	0	0	0	0	0	09-may-1999 16:40
		SYS_SUBP2	0	0	0	0	0	09-may-1999 16:40
		SYS_SUBP3	0	0	0	0	0	09-may-1999 16:40
		SYS_SUBP4	0	0	0	0	0	09-may-1999 16:40
		WEEK1	0	0	0	0	0	09-may-1999 16:40
	Q1_1998	SYS_SUBP17	0	0	0	0	0	09-may-1999 16:40
		SYS_SUBP18	0	0	0	0	0	09-may-1999 16:40
		SYS_SUBP20	0	0	0	0	0	09-may-1999 16:40
		SYS_SUBP19	0	0	0	0	0	09-may-1999 16:40
	Q2_1997	SYS_SUBP5	0	0	0	0	0	09-may-1999 16:40
		SYS_SUBP6	0	0	0	0	0	09-may-1999 16:40
		SYS_SUBP7	0	0	0	0	0	09-may-1999 16:40
		SYS_SUBP8	0	0	0	0	0	09-may-1999 16:40
	Q3_1997	Q3_1997_S1	0	0	0	0	0	09-may-1999 16:40
		Q3_1997_S2	0	0	0	0	0	09-may-1999 16:40
	Q4_1997	SYS_SUBP9	0	0	0	0	0	09-may-1999 16:40
		SYS_SUBP10	0	0	0	0	0	09-may-1999 16:40
		SYS_SUBP11	0	0	0	0	0	09-may-1999 16:40
		SYS_SUBP12	0	0	0	0	0	09-may-1999 16:40
		SYS_SUBP13	0	0	0	0	0	09-may-1999 16:40
		SYS_SUBP14	0	0	0	0	0	09-may-1999 16:40
		SYS_SUBP15	0	0	0	0	0	09-may-1999 16:40
		SYS_SUBP16	0	0	0	0	0	09-may-1999 16:40

Again, pay attention to the chain count, for if this column starts showing a 5 to 10 percent ratio against the rows column, the sub-partition needs to be rebuilt. If any sub-partition shows that it is out of balance (excessive rows when filled in comparison to other sub-partitions), then perhaps the main partition needs to be re-split using more sub-partitions.

Nested Table Internals

Oracle8 introduced another new table type, the *nested table*. Defined as a table referenced by another table, whose reference value appears as a column. Refer back to the table columns report, and note the columns named "xxxx_list". Each is an example of a nested table reference column.

You may find it convenient to impose a similar convention to recognize a nested table column. , Each of these "xxxx_list" columns contains a pointer value that points to a nested table. The *dba_nested_tables* view provides a convenient place to monitor nested tables. An example of a report run against the *dba_nested_tables* view is shown below.

⊟ tab_nest.sql

```
--**************************************************
--
--    Copyright © 2003 by Rampant TechPress Inc.
--
--    Free for non-commercial use.
--    For commercial licensing, e-mail info@rampant.cc
--
-- **************************************************

rem
rem NAME: tab_nest.sql
rem PURPOSE: Report on Nested Tables
rem HISTORY: MRA 6/14/97 Created
rem Updated 5//8/99 to Oracle8i
rem
COLUMN owner                  FORMAT a10 HEADING 'Owner'
COLUMN table_name             FORMAT a15 HEADING 'Store Table'
COLUMN table_type_owner       FORMAT a10 HEADING 'Type|Owner'
COLUMN table_type_name        FORMAT a15 HEADING 'Type|Name'
COLUMN parent_table_name      FORMAT a25 HEADING 'Parent|Table'
COLUMN parent_table_column    FORMAT a12 HEADING 'Parent|Column'
COLUMN storage_spec           FORMAT a15 HEADING 'Storage|Spec'
COLUMN return_type            FORMAT a7  HEADING 'Return|Type'
COLUMN element_substitutable FORMAT a14 HEADING 'Substitutable'
SET PAGES 58 LINES 132 VERIFY OFF FEEDBACK OFF
ttitle 'Nested Tables'
BREAK ON owner
SPOOL tab_nest.lis

SELECT
     owner,
     table_name,
     table_type_owner,
     table_type_name,
     parent_table_name,
     parent_table_column,
     LTRIM(storage_spec) storage_spec,
     LTRIM(return_type) return_type,
     LTRIM(element_substitutable) element_substitutable
FROM
     sys.dba_nested_tables
```

```
ORDER BY
    owner;
SPOOL OFF
```

Note the use of LTRIM on the *storage_spec* and *return_type* fields. For some reason, Oracle8*i*, version 8.1.3, stores these columns left-padded. If developers under Oracle8 do not adhere to a proper naming discipline, it is impossible to track down various components. The output from the script is shown below.

It is imperative to emphasize how important a good naming convention is for using the new table types, object types, and various new structures in Oracle8, 9i and 9i. For this reason, several other table-monitoring scripts are included in the script zip file in the code depot, specifically for monitoring bound tables and tables that can't get their next extent.

Here is the sample listing.

Nested Tables

Owner	Store Table	Substitutable	Type Owner	Type Name	Parent Table	Parent Column	Storage Spec	Return Type
SYSTEM	GALLERIES_NTAB	N	SYSTEM	PICTURE_NT	GALLERIES	CONTENTS	USER_SPECIFIED	LOCATOR
TELE_DBA	ADDRESSESV8i	N	TELE_DBA	ADDRESS_LIST	CLIENTSV8i	ADDRESSES	DEFAULT	VALUE
	CONTRACTSV8i	N	TELE_DBA	CONTRACT_LIST	CLIENTS_INFO_NUMBERSV8i	CONTRACTS	DEFAULT	VALUE
	CIRCUITSV8i	N	TELE_DBA	CIRCUIT_LIST	CLIENTS_INFO_NUMBERSV8i	CIRCUITS	DEFAULT	VALUE

Nested Table Internals

269

External Table Internals

External tables were introduced in Oracle9*i*. These external tables allow data to be accessed outside the *Oracle9i* database files, as if it were an unindexed normal database table, by combining aspects of an Oracle table, SQLLOADER, and a BFILE.

These new external tables are monitored using the *dba_external_tables* and *dba_external_locations* views. A sample external tables report script is shown below. Sample output follows the script.

💾 **ext_tab.sql**

```
--******************************************
--
--     Copyright © 2003 by Rampant TechPress Inc.
--
--     Free for non-commercial use.
--     For commercial licensing, e-mail info@rampant.cc
--
--  *****************************************
REM EXT_TAB.SQL
REM MRA 10/08/01 Initial Creation
REM Script to monitor external tables
REM

COLUMN owner FORMAT a8 HEADING 'Owner'
COLUMN table_name FORMAT a15 Heading 'Table'
COLUMN type_owner FORMAT a8 HEADING 'Type|Owner'
COLUMN type_name FORMAT a13 HEADING 'Type|Name'
COLUMN default_directory_owner FORMAT a10 HEADING 'Dir|Owner'
COLUMN default_directory_name FORMAT a10 HEADING 'Dir|Name'
COLUMN reject_limit FORMAT a9 HEADING 'Reject|Limit'
COLUMN access_type FORMAT a6 HEADING 'Access|Type'
COLUMN access_parameters FORMAT a35 WORD_WRAPPED HEADING 'Access
Parameters'

SET LINES 132 PAGES 55
ttitle 'External Tables'
SPOOL ext_tab
SELECT
    owner,
    table_name,
```

```
    type_owner,
    type_name,
    default_directory_owner,
    default_directory_name,
    reject_limit,
    access_type,
    access_parameters
from
    dba_external_tables
/
SPOOL OFF
SET lines 80 Pages 22
```

Here is a sample listing.

Owner	Table	Type Owner	Type Name	Dir Owner	Dir Name	Reject Limit	Access Type	Access Parameters
SYSTEM	SQL_SCRIPTS	SYS	ORACLE_LOADER	SYS	SQL_DIR	0	CLOB	fields terminated by ';' optionally enclosed by "'" (permissions, filetype,owner,group_name,size_in_b ytes, date edited DATE(19) "Mon dd 2001 hh24:mi", script_name)
DBAUTIL	SQL_SCRIPTS	SYS	ORACLE_LOADER	SYS	SQL_DIR	0	CLOB	fields terminated by ';' optionally enclosed by "'" (permissions, filetype,owner,group_name,size_in_b ytes, date edited DATE(19) "Mon dd 2001 hh24:mi", script_name)
DBAUTIL	SQL_SCRIPTS2	SYS	ORACLE_LOADER	SYS	SQL_DIR	0	CLOB	fields terminated by ';' optionally enclosed by "'" (permissions, filetype,owner,group_name,size_in_b ytes, date edited DATE(19) "Mon dd 2001 hh24:mi", script_name)
SH	SALES_TRANSACTI ONS_EXT	SYS	ORACLE_LOADER	SYS	DATA_FILE_ DIR	UNLIMITED	CLOB	RECORDS DELIMITED BY NEWLINE CHARACTERSET US7ASCII BADFILE log_file_dir:'sh_sales_ext.bad' LOGFILE log_file_dir:'sh_sales_ext.log' FIELDS TERMINATED BY "|" LDRTRIM

Cluster Table Internals

Clusters can be indexed or hashed in Oracle8, Oracle8*i*, or Oracle9*i*. Using the various views and tables available to the DBA, such as *dba_clusters*, *dba_clu_columns*, *dba_cluster_hash_functions*, and *dba_table*, clusters can be readily monitored.

A single table cluster has the ability to store key values in physically contiguous blocks. This makes access by cluster key very fast, and became available with Oracle8*i*. Clusters didn't change in Oracle9*i*. The relationships between the views that monitor clusters are shown in Figure 7.3 below. A script for generating a cluster report is shown, and the sample report is shown under that.

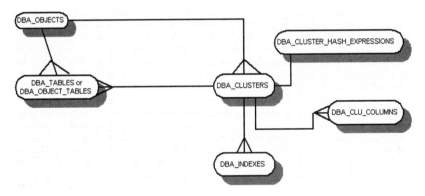

Figure 7.3 *dba_clusters view cluster*

🖫 **clu_rep.sql**

```
--*************************************************
--
--    Copyright © 2003 by Rampant TechPress Inc.
--
--    Free for non-commercial use.
--    For commercial licensing, e-mail info@rampant.cc
--
--    *************************************************
```

```
rem File:       CLU_REP.SQL
rem Purpose:    Document Cluster Data
rem Use:        From user with access to DBA_ views
rem
rem When        Who         What
rem ----        --------    --------------------
rem 5/27/93     Mike Ault   Initial Creation
rem 6/15/97     Mike Ault   Verified against Oracle8
rem 10/11/01    Mike Ault   Verified against oracle9i
rem
COLUMN owner               FORMAT a10
COLUMN cluster_name        FORMAT a15 HEADING "Cluster"
COLUMN tablespace_name     FORMAT a20 HEADING "Tablespace"
COLUMN table_name          FORMAT a20 HEADING "Table"
COLUMN tab_column_name     FORMAT a20 HEADING "Table Column"
COLUMN clu_column_name     FORMAT a20 HEADING "Cluster Column"
SET PAGES 56 LINES 130 FEEDBACK OFF
ttitle "Cluster Report"
BREAK ON owner SKIP 1 ON cluster ON tablespace
SPOOL cluster
SELECT
    a.owner,a.cluster_name,tablespace_name,
    table_name,tab_column_name,clu_column_name
FROM
    dba_clusters a,dba_clu_columns b
WHERE
    a.owner = b.owner and
    a.cluster_name=b.cluster_name
ORDER BY 1,2,3,4
/
SPOOL OFF
```

Here is a sample listing.

OWNER Column	Tablespace	Cluster	Table	Table Column	Cluster
SYS	SYSTEM	C_COBJ#	CCOL$	OBJ#	OBJ#
			CDEF$	OBJ#	OBJ#
		C_FILE#_BLOCK#	SEG$	FILE#	SEGFILE#
				BLOCK#	SEGBLOCK#
				TS#	TS#
			UET$	TS#	TS#
				SEGBLOCK#	SEGBLOCK#
				SEGFILE#	SEGFILE#
		C_MLOG#	MLOG$	MOWNER	MOWNER
				MASTER	MASTER
			SLOG$	MASTER	MASTER
				MOWNER	MOWNER
		C_OBJ#	ATTRCOL$	OBJ#	OBJ#
			CLU$	OBJ#	OBJ#
			COL$	OBJ#	OBJ#

Monitoring Table Cluster Storage Statistics

Many DBAs are interested in the storage statistics used to create each cluster. This data is found in the *dba_clusters* view. The script below is an example of this type of report. An example of the script's output follows.

🖫 **clus_size.sql**

```
--*************************************************
--
--    Copyright © 2003 by Rampant TechPress Inc.
--
--    Free for non-commercial use.
--    For commercial licensing, e-mail info@rampant.cc
--
-- *************************************************

rem Name: clus_siz.sql
rem
rem FUNCTION: Generate a cluster sizing report
rem
COLUMN owner            FORMAT a10
COLUMN cluster_name     FORMAT a15            HEADING "Cluster"
COLUMN tablespace_name  FORMAT a15            HEADING
"Tablespace"
COLUMN pct_free         FORMAT 999            HEADING "%|Fre"
COLUMN pct_used         FORMAT 999            HEADING "%|Use"
COLUMN key_size         FORMAT 999999         HEADING "Key Size"
COLUMN ini_trans        FORMAT 999            HEADING "Ini|Trn"
COLUMN max_trans        FORMAT 999            HEADING "Max|Trn"
COLUMN initial_extent   FORMAT 999999999      HEADING "Init Ext"
COLUMN next_extent      FORMAT 999999999      HEADING "Next Ext"
COLUMN min_extents      FORMAT 999            HEADING "Min|Ext"
COLUMN max_extents      FORMAT 999            HEADING "Max|Ext"
COLUMN pct_increase     FORMAT 999            HEADING "%|Inc"

SET PAGES 56 LINES 130 FEEDBACK OFF
START ttitle "Cluster Sizing Report"
BREAK ON owner ON tablespace_name
SPOOL cls_sze

SELECT
    owner,
    tablespace_name,
    cluster_name,
    pct_free,
    pct_used,
    key_size,
    ini_trans,
    max_trans,
    initial_extent,
    next_extent,
    min_extents,
    max_extents,
    pct_increase
FROM
```

```
      dba_clusters
ORDER BY
     1,2,3
/
SPOOL OFF
CLEAR COLUMNS
CLEAR BREAKS
SET PAGES 22 LINES 80 FEEDBACK ON
PAUSE Press enter to continue
```

Here is a sample listing.

```
Schema                     %   %         Int Max                   Min Max %
Owner Tblespace Cluster    Fre Use Key Sze Trn Trn Init Ext Nxt Ext Ext Ext Inc
----- --------- --------------- --- --- --- --- --- --- ---- --- --- ----- --- --- ---
SYS   SYSTEM    C_COBJ#         10  50  300  2 255   51200     83968  1 121  50
                C_FILE#_BLOCK#  10  40  225  2 255   20480    190464  1 121  50
                C_MLOG#         10  40       2 255   10240     10240  1 121  50
                C_OBJ#           5  40  800  2 255  122880    430080  1 121  50
                C_RG#           10  40       2 255   10240     10240  1 121  50
                C_TS#           10  40       2 255   10240     16384  1 121  50
                C_USER#         10  40  315  2 255   10240     10240  1 121  50
                HIST$            5  40  200  2 255   10240     10240  1 121  50
```

The reports above provide information on cluster keys, cluster columns, cluster tables, and columns and cluster sizing. Combined with the actual size and extent reports shown previously, the DBA can have a complete overview of the clusters in the database.

Monitoring Cluster Statistics

Since Oracle8, the *dba_clusters* view has several additional columns. These include the *avg_blocks_per_key*, *cluster_type*, *function*, and *hashkeys*. These additional columns provide a more detailed glimpse of cluster status. The report script shown below can be modified to include these columns (132 is about the maximum, and not a good choice) or a new report can be created. An example of the output follows the script.

```
--*************************************************
--
--     Copyright © 2003 by Rampant TechPress Inc.
--
--     Free for non-commercial use.
--     For commercial licensing, e-mail info@rampant.cc
--
-- *************************************************

rem Name          : clu_stat.sql
rem Purpose       : Report on new DBA_CLUSTER columns
rem Use           : From an account that accesses DBA_ views
rem
COLUMN owner                    FORMAT a10      HEADING "Owner"
COLUMN cluster_name             FORMAT a15      HEADING "Cluster"
COLUMN tablespace_name          FORMAT a10      HEADING
"Tablespace"
COLUMN avg_blocks_per_key       FORMAT 999999   HEADING "Blocks
per Key"
COLUMN cluster_type             FORMAT a8       HEADING "Type"
COLUMN function                 FORMAT 999999   HEADING
"Function"
COLUMN hashkeys                 FORMAT 99999    HEADING "# of
Keys"
SET PAGES 56 LINES 79 FEEDBACK OFF
 ttitle "Cluster Statistics Report"
SPOOL clu_type
SELECT
   owner,
   cluster_name,
   tablespace_name,
   avg_blocks_per_key,
   cluster_type,
   function,
   hashkeys
FROM
   dba_clusters
ORDER BY 2
GROUP BY  owner, tablespace, type
/
SPOOL OFF
SET PAGES 22 LINES 80 FEEDBACK ON
CLEAR COLUMNS
TTITLE OFF
```

Here is a sample listing.

```
                              Blocks
                              per                        # of
Owner   Cluster         Tablespace Key     Type     Function         Keys
------  --------------  ---------- -------  --------  ---------------  -
SYS     C_COBJ#         SYSTEM              INDEX
        C_FILE#_BLOCK#
        C_MLOG#
        C_OBJ#
        C_RG#
        C_TS#
        C_USER#
        HIST$
        C_RG#
```

Monitoring Cluster Hash Expressions

Hash expressions can be specified for a hash cluster beginning with the later versions of Oracle7. These hash expressions can be viewed for a specific cluster by querying the *dba_cluster_hash_expression* view. The *dba_cluster_hash_expression* view has three columns: *owner*, *cluster_name*, and *hash_expression*. When querying *hash_expression*, allow for extra-length character strings by using the *word_wrapped* parameter on a COLUMN command, since *hash_expression* is a LONG.

Later in this chapter, you will learn how to monitor DIMENSIONS, a new Oracle8*i* feature used with materialized views to provide query rewrite.

Monitoring LOB Storage

In Oracle8 and all subsequent releases Oracle provides the capability to use large objects (LOBs). These LOBs can be of type BLOB, CLOB or NCLOB (binary, character or National Character) and can either be stored inline with other data if less than 4000 bytes in length or in a special form of storage known as LOB storage if greater than 4000 bytes in length. In most operating systems LOBs can be up to 4 gigabytes in length if stored out-of-line using LOB storage.

However, in order to ensure that proper parameters have been used to set up the LOBs and LOB storage in your database you must use two basic DBA views:

DBA_SEGMENTS - Information on lob segments used in the database
DBA_LOBS - Information on lob storage areas.

An example report to show all lob segments not owned by SYS or SYSTEM and several other default Oracle users is shown below. You need to monitor LOB segments to be sure that:

1. The aren't collocated with base tables
2. They don't have excessive extents

These two items will prevent excessive IO causing hot blocking in your base tablespace. Poor (read:default) settings for LOB storage clauses will lead to bad LOB performance, always tune LOB storage. Always provide a LOB storage clause for any table using lobs in case the lob size exceeds 4000 bytes.

🖫 **Lob_seg.sql**

```
--*********************************************
--
--   Copyright © 2003 by Rampant TechPress Inc.
--
--   Free for non-commercial use.
--   For commercial licensing, e-mail info@rampant.cc
--
--   *********************************************
rem NAME lob_seg.sql
rem FUNCTION : Create a report of lob segments for a
rem all non-oracle provided users
rem HISTORY: MRA 1/21/03 Created
rem
```

```
col owner format a10 heading 'Owner'
col segment_name format a27 heading 'Segment|Name'
col tablespace_name format a15 heading 'Tablespace'
column extents format 9,999 heading 'Extents'
column bytes format 99,999 heading 'Meg'
col segment_type format a10 heading 'Segment|Type'
start title80 'Lob Segments'
set lines 90
spool rep_out\&db\lob_seg
select
owner,segment_name,segment_type,tablespace_name,extents,bytes/(1
024*1024) bytes
from dba_segments
where owner not in
('SYS','SYSTEM','PRECISE','MAULT','PATROL','QDBA','OUTLN','XDB',
'WMSYS','MDSYS','CTXSYS','ODM','SYSMAN') and segment_type like
'LOB%'
/
spool off
ttitle off
```

Here is an example listing from the above script.

```
Date: 01/21/03                                                    Page:   1
Time: 04:19 PM                       Lob Segments                 PERFSTAT
                                     Example database

            Segment                 Segment
Owner       Name                    Type       Tablespace      Extents    Meg
---------   -------------------     ---------  ---------------  -------  ------
VSA_ADMIN   SYS_IL0000027902C00002$$ LOBINDEX  VSA_ADMIN_DATA        1      0
MERCURY     SYS_IL0000029473C00007$$ LOBINDEX  MERCURY_DATA          1      4
MERCURY     SYS_IL0000012038C00004$$ LOBINDEX  MERCURY_DATA          3     12
MERCURY     SYS_IL0000012255C00014$$ LOBINDEX  MERCURY_DATA          1      4
DDEWITT     SYS_IL0000042781C00004$$ LOBINDEX  DDEWITT
DDEWITT     SYS_IL0000042775C00004$$ LOBINDEX  DDEWITT
MERCURY     SYS_IL0000042516C00006$$ LOBINDEX  MERCURY_DATA          1      4
VSA_ADMIN   SYS_LOB0000027902C00002$$ LOBSEGMENT VSA_ADMIN_DATA      1      0
MERCURY     SYS_LOB0000029473C00007$$ LOBSEGMENT MERCURY_DATA        1      4
MERCURY     SYS_LOB0000012038C00004$$ LOBSEGMENT MERCURY_DATA    5,108 19,953
MERCURY     SYS_LOB0000012255C00014$$ LOBSEGMENT MERCURY_DATA        1      4
MERCURY     SYS_LOB0000042516C00006$$ LOBSEGMENT MERCURY_DATA        5     20
```

The next LOB report shows the tablespace where the
LOB is located and other storage related parameters.

🖫 Lob_seg_size.sql

```
--*************************************************
--
--      Copyright © 2003 by Rampant TechPress Inc.
--
--      Free for non-commercial use.
--      For commercial licensing, e-mail info@rampant.cc
--
--  *************************************************
```

```
rem NAME lob_seg_size.sql
rem FUNCTION : Create a report of lob segment sizes for a
rem all non-oracle provided users
rem HISTORY: MRA 1/21/03 Created
rem
col owner format a10 heading 'Owner'
col segment_name format a25 heading 'Segment|Name'
col tablespace_name format a15 heading 'Tablespace|Name'
col extents format 999,999,999 heading 'Extents'
col bytes format 999,999,999,999 heading 'Bytes'
set lines 132 pages 50 verify off feedback off
start title132 'Lob Segment Sizes'
spool rep_out\&db\lob_seg_size
select
owner,segment_name,segment_type,tablespace_name,extents,bytes
from dba_segments
where owner not in
('SYS','SYSTEM','PRECISE','MAULT','PATROL','QDBA','OUTLN','XDB',
'WMSYS','MDSYS','CTXSYS','ODM','SYSMAN')and segment_type LIKE
'LOB%'
/
spool off
set lines 80 pages 22 feedback on
ttitle off
```

And here is an example listing:

```
Date: 01/21/03                                                      Page:   1
Time: 04:20 PM                    Lob Segment Sizes                  PERFSTAT
                                  Example database

           Segment                    Segment   Tablespace
Owner      Name                        Type      Name           Extents         Bytes
---------- -------------------------- --------- -------------- ------- --------------
VSA_ADMIN  SYS_IL0000027902C00002$$   LOBINDEX  VSA_ADMIN_DATA       1        516,096
MERCURY    SYS_IL0000029473C00007$$   LOBINDEX  MERCURY_DATA         1      4,096,000
MERCURY    SYS_IL0000012038C00004$$   LOBINDEX  MERCURY_DATA         3     12,288,000
MERCURY    SYS_IL0000012255C00014$$   LOBINDEX  MERCURY_DATA         1      4,096,000
MERCURY    SYS_IL0000042516C00006$$   LOBINDEX  MERCURY_DATA         1      4,096,000
VSA_ADMIN  SYS_LOB0000027902C00002$$  LOBSEGMENT VSA_ADMIN_DATA      1        516,096
MERCURY    SYS_LOB0000029473C00007$$  LOBSEGMENT MERCURY_DATA        1      4,096,000
MERCURY    SYS_LOB0000012038C00004$$  LOBSEGMENT MERCURY_DATA    5,108 20,922,368,000
MERCURY    SYS_LOB0000012255C00014$$  LOBSEGMENT MERCURY_DATA        1      4,096,000
MERCURY    SYS_LOB0000042516C00006$$  LOBSEGMENT MERCURY_DATA        5     20,480,000
```

The final LOB report shows the tables that contain lobs and their lobs.

🖫 Tab_lobs.sql

```
--*********************************************************
--
--     Copyright © 2003 by Rampant TechPress Inc.
--
--     Free for non-commercial use.
--     For commercial licensing, e-mail info@rampant.cc
```

```
--
-- *************************************************
rem NAME tab_lobs.sql
rem FUNCTION : Create a report of lob segments
rem and their tables for all
rem non-oracle provided users
rem HISTORY: MRA 1/21/03 Created
rem
col column_name format a15 heading 'Column|Name'
col segment_name format a26 heading 'Segment|Name'
col index_name format a26 heading 'Index|Name'
col owner format a10 heading 'Owner'
col table_name format a15 heading 'Table|Name'
col in_row format a3 heading 'In|Row'
set lines 132 pages 50
start title132 'Database Lob Column Data'
spool rep_out\&db\lob_col
select
owner,table_name,column_name,segment_name,index_name,in_row from
dba_lobs
where owner not in
('SYS','SYSTEM','PRECISE','MAULT','PATROL','QDBA','OUTLN','XDB',
'WMSYS','MDSYS','CTXSYS','ODM','SYSMAN')
/
spool off
set lines 80 pages 22
ttitle off
```

And here is an example listing:

Date: 08/25/03
Time: 12:19 AM

Database Lob Column Data
Example database

Page: 1
SYSTEM

Owner	Table Name	Column Name	Segment Name	Index Name	In Row
OE	CUSTOMERS	"CUST_GEO_LOCAT ION"."SDO_ELEM_ INFO"	SYS_LOB0000028585C00022$$	SYS_IL0000028585C00022$$	YES
OE	CUSTOMERS	"CUST_GEO_LOCAT ION"."SDO_ORDIN ATES"	SYS_LOB0000028585C00023$$	SYS_IL0000028585C00023$$	YES
OE	WAREHOUSES	"WH_GEO_LOCATIO N"."SDO_ELEM_IN FO"	SYS_LOB0000028591C00012$$	SYS_IL0000028591C00012$$	YES
OE	WAREHOUSES	"WH_GEO_LOCATIO N"."SDO_ORDINAT ES"	SYS_LOB0000028591C00013$$	SYS_IL0000028591C00013$$	YES
OE	WAREHOUSES	SYS_NC00003$	SYS_LOB0000028591C00003$$	SYS_IL0000028591C00003$$	YES
PM	ONLINE_MEDIA	PRODUCT_TEXT	SYS_LOB0000028684C00069$$	SYS_IL0000028684C00069$$	YES
PM	ONLINE_MEDIA	"PRODUCT_TESTIM ONIALS"."SOURCE "."LOCALDATA"	SYS_LOB0000028684C00071$$	SYS_IL0000028684C00071$$	YES
PM	ONLINE_MEDIA	"PRODUCT_TESTIM ONIALS"."COMMEN TS"	SYS_LOB0000028684C00080$$	SYS_IL0000028684C00080$$	YES
PM	ONLINE_MEDIA	"PRODUCT_PHOTO_ SIGNATURE"."SIG NATURE"	SYS_LOB0000028684C00017$$	SYS_IL0000028684C00017$$	YES
PM	ONLINE_MEDIA	"PRODUCT_THUMBN AIL"."SOURCE"." LOCALDATA"	SYS_LOB0000028684C00019$$	SYS_IL0000028684C00019$$	YES
PM	ONLINE_MEDIA	"PRODUCT_VIDEO" ."SOURCE"."LOCA LDATA"	SYS_LOB0000028684C00034$$	SYS_IL0000028684C00034$$	YES
PM	ONLINE_MEDIA	"PRODUCT_VIDEO" ."COMMENTS"	SYS_LOB0000028684C00042$$	SYS_IL0000028684C00042$$	YES
PM	ONLINE_MEDIA	"PRODUCT_AUDIO" ."SOURCE"."LOCA	SYS_LOB0000028684C00054$$	SYS_IL0000028684C00054$$	YES

Monitoring Oracle8 Types, Collections, Methods, and Operators

Oracle added an entirely new set of objects to monitor in Oracle8. They have been variously called collections, types, user-defined types, ADTs, and others. The all-inclusive terms, such as types, collections, and methods are preferred. *Types* allow the grouping of related data sets to form more complex objects. For example, a table object might consist of standard columns, a user-defined type, a nested table (built from a type), and a collection (called a VARRAY), which is in itself a type. In order to declare a table as an object and have its OIDs implicitly defined, it must be created as an object type from a defined type.

As previously explained, there can be named types that have no other attributes. These are called *incomplete types* and are used where circular references may need to be defined. Of course, these incomplete types must be completed before an object is built from them.

The major types view is *dba_types*. The cluster of views associated with types is shown in Figure 7.4.

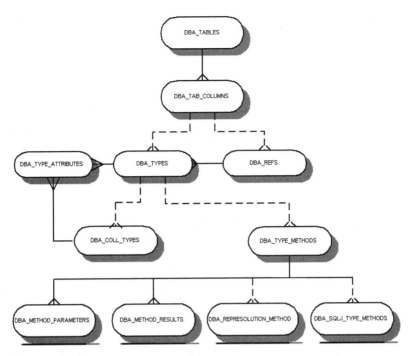

Figure 7.4 *dba_types view cluster*

Monitoring Types

The script below creates a simple report that provides some basic information about the types stored in the database. The report uses the *dba_types* view. To get detailed information on the attributes for each type, join with the *dba_type_attrs* view. The script produces a report similar to the one above. The only columns not reported are *type_oid* and *typeid raw*.

⊞ **types.sql**

```
--*************************************************
--
--    Copyright © 2003 by Rampant TechPress Inc.
--
--    Free for non-commercial use.
--    For commercial licensing, e-mail info@rampant.cc
--
```

```
-- *************************************************
rem
rem NAME: types.sql
rem FUNCTION: Provide basic report of all database types
rem for a specific owner or all owners
rem HISTORY : MRA 6/15/97 Created
rem
COLUMN owner              FORMAT a10     HEADING 'Type|Owner'
COLUMN type_name          FORMAT a15     HEADING 'Type|Name'
COLUMN typecode           FORMAT a11     HEADING 'Type|Code'
COLUMN predefined         FORMAT a3      HEADING Pre?
COLUMN incomplete         FORMAT a3      HEADING Inc?
COLUMN methods            FORMAT 9999    HEADING '#|Methods'
COLUMN attributes         FORMAT 9999    HEADING '#|Attrib'
COLUMN final              FORMAT A5      HEADING 'Final'
COLUMN instantiable       FORMAT A5      HEADING 'Inst.'
COLUMN supertype_owner    FORMAT a10     HEADING 'SuperType|Owner'
COLUMN supertype_name     FORMAT a15     HEADING 'SuperType|Name'
COLUMN local_attributes   FORMAT 99999   HEADING 'Local|Attri'
COLUMN local_methods      FORMAT 99999   HEADING 'Local|Meth'
SET LINES 130 PAGES 58 VERIFY OFF FEEDBACK OFF
BREAK ON owner
ttitle 'Database Types Report'
SPOOL types.lis
SELECT
     DECODE(owner, null,'SYS-GEN',owner) owner,
     type_name,
     typecode,
     attributes,
     methods,
     predefined,
     incomplete,
     final,
     Instantiable,
     Supertype_owner,
     Supertype_name,
     local_attributes,
     local_methods
FROM dba_types
WHERE owner LIKE '%&owner%'
ORDER BY owner, type_name;
SPOOL OFF
TTITLE OFF
SET VERIFY ON FEEDBACK ON LINES 80 PAGES 22
CLEAR COLUMNS
CLEAR BREAKS
```

Here is a sample listing.

Type Owner	Type Name	Type Code	# Attrib	# Methods	Pre	Inc	Final	Inst	Super Owner	Super Name	Local Attri
SYSTEM	ADDRESS_T	OBJECT	9	0	NO	NO	NO	YES			
	EMPLOYEE_T	OBJECT	9	0	NO	NO	YES	YES	SYSTEM	PERSON_T	
	GALLERY_T	OBJECT	4	0	NO	NO	YES	YES			
	PERSON_T	OBJECT	6	0	NO	NO	NO	YES			
	PICTURE_NT	COLLECTION	0	0	NO	NO	YES	YES			
	PICTURE_T	OBJECT	6	0	NO	NO	YES	YES			
	ROOM_T	OBJECT	2	1	NO	NO	YES	YES			

There are many kinds of types. Many types (those labeled SYSGEN) are system-generated at system build; others, such as OBJECT and COLLECTION, are user-defined. The collection types are further documented in the *dba_coll_types* view.

Monitoring Type Collections

Another kind of type is a collection (such as a VARRAY). The script shown below generates a simple report that documents the important columns from *dba_coll_types*. If other data is needed (for simple scalar collections), then by all means add them to the script. To determine the attributes that map into each collection, join to the *dba_type_attrs* view.

🖫 **coll_type.sql**

```
--*********************************************************
--
--      Copyright © 2003 by Rampant TechPress Inc.
--
--      Free for non-commercial use.
--      For commercial licensing, e-mail info@rampant.cc
--
-- *********************************************************

rem
rem NAME: coll_type.sql
rem FUNCTION: Document the collection types in the database
rem for a specified user or all users
rem HISTORY: MRA 6/15/97 Created
rem          MRA 10/10/01 Updated to 9i
rem
COL owner           FORMAT a10 HEADING 'Collec.|Owner'
COL type_name       FORMAT a16 HEADING 'Type|Name'
COL coll_type       FORMAT a15 HEADING 'Collec.|Type'
COL upper_bound                HEADING 'VARRAY|Limit'
COL elem_type_owner FORMAT a10 HEADING 'Elementary|Type|Owner'
COL elem_type_name  FORMAT a11 HEADING 'Elementary|Type|Name'
SET PAGES 58 LINES 130 VERIFY OFF FEEDBACK OFF
ttitle 'Collection Type Report'
SPOOL col_type.lis
select
```

```
      owner,
      type_name,
      coll_type,
      upper_bound,
      elem_type_mod,
      elem_type_owner,
      elem_type_name,
      length,
      precision,
      scale,
      elem_storage,
      nulls_stored
FROM dba_coll_types
WHERE owner LIKE '%&owner%'
/
SPOOL OFF
CLEAR COLUMNS
CLEAR BREAKS
TTILTE OFF
SET VERIFY ON FEEDBACK ON
```

Here is a sample listing.

```
                              diogenes1 database

                                        Element  Element
Collec.  Type                 Collec.  VARRAY  Type     Type
Owner    Name                 Type     Limit   Owner    Name        Length  Prec Scale
Nulls
-------- -------------------- -------  ------- -------  ---------   ------- ---- -----
SYS      AQ$_SUBSCRIBERS      VARRAY    1024   SYS      AQ$_AGENT                 YES
SYS      DBMS_DEBUG_VC2COLL   TABLE                     VARCHAR2    1000          YES
SYS      ODCIRIDLIST          VARRAY   32767            VARCHAR2    5072          YES
SYS      ODCIGRANULELIST      VARRAY   65535            NUMBER                    YES
WKSYS    VARCHAR2_TABLE_100   TABLE                     VARCHAR2     100          YES
WKSYS    VARCHAR2_TABLE_200   TABLE                     VARCHAR2     200          YES
WKSYS    VARCHAR2_TABLE_300   TABLE                     VARCHAR2     300          YES
WKSYS    VARCHAR2_TABLE_400   TABLE                     VARCHAR2     400          YES
SYSTEM   PICTURE_NT           TABLE            SYSTEM   PICTURE_T                 YES
```

Monitoring Type Methods

Types can also have methods associated with them. A *type method* is a procedure or function that is intrinsic to the type and is generally defined when the type is created. Look closely at the output report for the script below as it only shows types with defined methods.

The methods are documented in *dba_type_methods*. Additional information is located in the *dba_method_params* and *dba_method_results* views. A simple report showing the types with methods in the database is given below, with the output results following.

🖫 typ_meth.sql

```
--***********************************************
--
--   Copyright © 2003 by Rampant TechPress Inc.
--
--   Free for non-commercial use.
--   For commercial licensing, e-mail info@rampant.cc
--
-- ***********************************************

rem NAME typ_meth.sql
rem FUNCTION : Create a report of type methods for a
rem specific user or all users
rem HISTORY: MRA 6/16/97 Created
rem         MRA 10/10/01 Updated to 9i
rem
COLUMN owner          FORMAT a10      HEADING 'Owner'
COLUMN type_name      FORMAT a25      HEADING 'Type|Name'
COLUMN method_name    FORMAT a25      HEADING 'Method|Name'
COLUMN method_type                    HEADING 'Method|Type'
COLUMN parameters     FORMAT 99999    HEADING '#|Param'
COLUMN results        FORMAT 99999    HEADING '#|Results'
COLUMN method_no      FORMAT 99999    HEADING 'Meth.|Number'
COLUMN final          FORMAT A5       HEADING 'Final'
COLUMN Instantiable   FORMAT A6       HEADING 'Instan'
COLUMN overriding     FORMAT A6       HEADING 'ORide?'
COLUMN Inherited      FORMAT A9       HEADING 'Inherited'

BREAK ON owner ON type_name
SET LINES 132 PAGES 58 VERIFY OFF FEEDBACK OFF
START ttitle 'Type Methods Report'
SPOOL typ_meth.lis

SELECT
    owner,
    type_name,
    method_name,
    method_no,
    method_type,
    parameters,
    results,
    final,
    Instantiable,
    Overriding,
    Inherited
FROM
    dba_type_methods
WHERE
    owner LIKE UPPER('%&owner%')
ORDER BY
    owner,
```

```
    type_name;

SPOOL OFF
CLEAR COLUMNS
CLEAR BREAKS
SET VERIFY ON FEEDBACK ON LINES 80 pages 22
TTITLE OFF
```

Here is a sample listing.

Owner	Type Name	Method Name	Meth. Number	Method Type	# Param	# Results	Final	Instan	ORide?	Inherited
SYS	DBURITYPE	GETCLOB	7	PUBLIC	1	1	YES	YES	NO	
		GETURL	3	PUBLIC	1	1	YES	NO		
	FTPURITYPE	GETCLOB	1	PUBLIC	1	1	NO	NO	YES	
		CREATEFTPURI	9	PUBLIC	1	1	YES	NO	NO	
		GETBLOB	4	PUBLIC	1	1	NO	NO	YES	
		GETEXTERNALU	5	PUBLIC	1	1	YES	YES	NO	
		GETURL	6	PUBLIC	1	1	YES	YES	NO	
		GETBLOB	8	PUBLIC	1	1	YES	YES	NO	
		GETCLOB	7	PUBLIC	1	1	YES	YES	YES	
		GETURL	3	PUBLIC	1	1	YES	NO	YES	
		GETEXTERNALU	2	PUBLIC	1	1	YES	NO	YES	
	HTTPURITYPE	GETCLOB	1	PUBLIC	1	1	NO	NO	NO	
		GETBLOB	4	PUBLIC	1	1	YES	YES	NO	
		GETEXTERNALU	5	PUBLIC	1	1	YES	YES	YES	
		GETCLOB	7	PUBLIC	1	1	YES	NO	NO	
		CREATEURI	9	PUBLIC	1	1	YES	NO	NO	
		GETBLOB	8	PUBLIC	1	1	YES	NO	NO	
		GETURL	6	PUBLIC	1	1	YES	YES	NO	
		GETEXTERNALU	2	PUBLIC	1	1	YES	YES	YES	
		GETURL	3	PUBLIC	1	1	YES	NO	YES	

Monitoring Type REFs

A REF internalizes the foreign key relationship between a child and parent table. It provides the only object-oriented method of relating two object tables after Oracle8. A REF always goes between child and parent, since a REF can only reference one column. The *dba_refs* view provides documentation on existing REFs in the database.

The script below shows how a report can be generated to show the REFs in the database. Refer back to Figure 7.4, which shows the relationships between views used to document REFs in the database. An example of a report from the script follows.

🖫 tab_ref.sql

```
--*********************************************
--
--    Copyright © 2003 by Rampant TechPress Inc.
--
--    Free for non-commercial use.
--    For commercial licensing, e-mail info@rampant.cc
--
-- *********************************************

rem
rem NAME: tab_ref.sql
rem FUNCTION: Generate a lit of all REF columns in the database
rem  for a specific user or all users
rem HISTORY: MRA 6/16/97 Created
rem
COLUMN owner              FORMAT a8   HEADING 'Owner'
COLUMN table_name         FORMAT a23  HEADING 'Table|Name'
COLUMN column_name        FORMAT a15  HEADING 'Column|Name'
COLUMN with_rowid         FORMAT a5   HEADING 'With|Rowid'
COLUMN is_scoped          FORMAT a6   HEADING 'Scoped'
COLUMN scope_table_owner  FORMAT a8   HEADING 'Scope|Table|Owner'
COLUMN scope_table_name   FORMAT a15  HEADING 'Scope|Table|Name'
BREAK ON owner
SET PAGES 58 LINES 130 FEEDBACK OFF VERIFY OFF
START ttitle 'Database REF Report'
SPOOL tab_ref.lis
SELECT
```

```
    owner,
    table_name,
    column_name,
    with_rowid,
    is_scoped,
    scope_table_owner,
    scope_table_name
FROM
    dba_refs
WHERE
    Owner LIKE UPPER('%&owner%')
ORDER BY
    owner;

SPOOL OFF
SET FEEDBACK ON VERIFY ON
CLEAR COLUMNS
CLEAR BREAKS
TTITLE OFF
```

Here is a sample listing.

```
                                                     Scope     Scope
              Table             Column      With     Table     Table
Owner         Name              Name        Rowid Scoped Owner  Name
--------      -------------     -----------  ----- ------ -------- ---------
TELE_DBA EARNINGS_INFO CLIENTS_ID_R YES     YES    TELE_DBA CLIENTSV8
```

Monitoring Operators

Oracle8*i* introduced operators. They enable extensibility of Oracle by allowing users to add operators (operators are similar to: +, -, AND, OR, BETWEEN) to the database. Operators are also a key component of the Oracle8*i* INDEXTYPE (domain indexes).

The views used to monitor operators are *dba_operators*, *dba_oparguments*, *dba_opancillary*, and *dba_opbindings*. The operators' series of views are diagrammed in Figure 7.5, along with the *dimension* and *outline* views. The script below shows an example of an operator report. An example of the output follows the script.

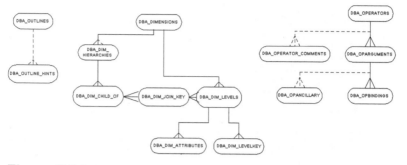

Figure 7.5 *Miscellaneous dba_ view clusters*

💾 **operator.sql**

```
-- ************************************************
--
--    Copyright © 2003 by Rampant TechPress Inc.
--
--    Free for non-commercial use.
--    For commercial licensing, e-mail info@rampant.cc
--
-- ************************************************


rem
rem NAME: operator.sql
rem FUNCTION: Generate a lit of all OPERATORS in the database
rem for a specific user or all users
rem HISTORY: MRA 5/12/98 Created
COLUMN owner              FORMAT a8    HEADING 'Owner'
COLUMN operator_name      FORMAT a10   HEADING 'Operator|Name'
COLUMN number_of_binds    FORMAT 9999  HEADING 'Binds'
COLUMN position                        HEADING 'Position'
COLUMN argument_type      FORMAT A20   HEADING 'Argument|Type'
COLUMN function_name      FORMAT A20   HEADING 'Binding|Argument'
COLUMN return_schema      FORMAT A10   HEADING 'Return|Schema'
COLUMN return_type        FORMAT A20   HEADING 'Return|Type'

BREAK ON owner ON operator_name ON number_of_binds
SET PAGES 58 LINES 130 FEEDBACK OFF VERIFY OFF
ttitle 'Database OPERATOR Report'
SPOOL operator.lis

SELECT
   a.owner,
   a.operator_name,
   a.number_of_bindings,
   b.position,
   b.argument_type,
   c.function_name,
   DECODE(c.return_schema,NULL,'Internal',c.return_schema)
return_schema,
   c.return_type
```

```
FROM
    dba_operators a,
    dba_oparguments b,
    dba_opbindings c
WHERE
    Owner LIKE '%&owner%'
AND
    a.owner=b.owner
AND
    a.operator_name=b.operator_name
AND
    a.owner=c.owner
AND
    a.operator_name=c.operator_name
AND
    b.binding#=c.binding#;

SPOOL OFF
CLEAR BREAKS
CLEAR COLUMNS
TTITLE OFF
SET FEEDBACK ON VERIFY ON
```

Here is a sample listing.

```
        Operator           Argument Bound                   Return   Return
Owner   Name    Binds Position Type  Function                Schema   Type
------- ------- ----- -------- -------- -------------------- -------- --------
SYSTEM  CONCAT    1        1 VARCHAR2 "CON"."CONCAT_STRING" Internal VARCHAR2
                           2 VARCHAR2 "CON"."CONCAT_STRING" Internal VARCHAR2
```

The operator report should be reviewed to ensure that
the operator bindings are properly ascribed and of the
correct type. Also, make sure that the function for the
operator is properly assigned and that input and output
types are properly defined.

Monitoring Dimensions

Dimensions, new in Oracle8*i*, are usually used in data
warehouse applications to allow Oracle to efficiently
remap queries against summaries (materialized views).
Dimensions describe the relationships in a large de-
normalized table or a set of quasi-normalized tables,
such as would be found in a star or snowflake design

DSS or data warehouse application. The views used to monitor dimensions are shown in Figure 7.6.

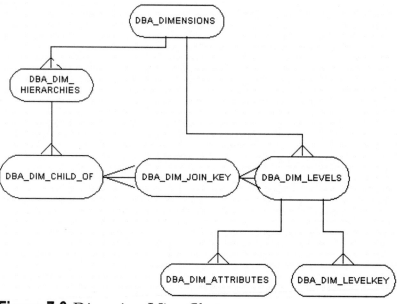

Figure 7.6 *Dimensions View Cluster*

Dimensions contain levels and hierarchies that are linked using join keys. A report showing some of these aspects of dimensions is shown below. An example of the output from the script is shown below that.

🖫 dim_level.sql

```
--*************************************************
--
--    Copyright © 2003 by Rampant TechPress Inc.
--
--    Free for non-commercial use.
--    For commercial licensing, e-mail info@rampant.cc
--
--    *************************************************
rem NAME: dim_level.sql
rem FUNCTION: Generate a lit of all Dimensions and levels in the
rem database for a specific user or all users
```

```
rem HISTORY: MRA 5/12/98 Created
rem

COLUMN owner            FORMAT a8    HEADING 'Owner'
COLUMN dimension_name   FORMAT a10   HEADING 'Dimension|Name'
COLUMN level_name       FORMAT a10 HEADING 'Level|Name'
COLUMN column_name      FORMAT a20 HEADING 'Column|Name'
COLUMN key_position     FORMAT 9999 HEADING 'Key|Position'

BREAK ON owner ON operator_name ON number_of_binds
SET PAGES 58 LINES 130 FEEDBACK OFF VERIFY OFF
ttitle 'Database Dimension Levels Report'
SPOOL dim_level.lis

SELECT
   a.owner,
   a.dimension_name,
   b.level_name,
   c.column_name,
   c.key_position
FROM
   dba_dimensions a,
   dba_dim_levels b,
   dba_dim_level_key c
WHERE
   a.Owner LIKE '%&owner%'
AND
   a.owner=b.owner
AND
   a.dimension_name=b.dimension_name
AND
   a.owner=c.owner
AND
   a.dimension_name=c.dimension_name
AND
   b.level_name=c.level_name
ORDER BY
   a.owner,
   a.dimension_name,
    b.level_name;

SPOOL OFF
CLEAR BREAKS
CLEAR COLUMNS
TTITLE OFF
SET FEEDBACK ON VERIFY ON
```

Here is a sample listing.

```
          Dimension  Level      Column                     Key
Owner     Name       Name       Name                  Position
--------  ---------- ---------- -------------------- ---------

TELE_DBA  TEST_DIM   CHILD_ID   ID                           1
          TEST_DIM   PARENT_ID  PARENT_ID                    1
```

The database dimension-level report should be reviewed to ensure that the levels are assigned to the proper columns.

Reports showing the relationship of dimension to hierarchy and dimension and attribute are shown below. The output is similar to previous reports.

🖫 **dim_hierarchies.sql**

```
--*********************************************
--
--    Copyright © 2003 by Rampant TechPress Inc.
--
--    Free for non-commercial use.
--    For commercial licensing, e-mail info@rampant.cc
--
--    *********************************************

rem
rem NAME: dim_hierarchies.sql
rem FUNCTION: Generate a lit of all dimensions and hierarchies
in the
rem database for a specific user or all users
rem HISTORY: MRA 5/12/98 Created
rem

COLUMN owner              FORMAT a8   HEADING 'Owner'
COLUMN dimension_name     FORMAT a10  HEADING 'Dimension|Name'
COLUMN column_name        FORMAT a10  HEADING 'Column|Name'
COLUMN hierarchy_name     FORMAT a10  HEADING 'Hierarchy|Name'
COLUMN parent_level_name  FORMAT a10  HEADING 'Parent|Level'
COLUMN child_level_name   FORMAT a10  HEADING 'Child|Level'
COLUMN join_key_id        FORMAT a20  HEADING 'Join Key|ID'

BREAK ON owner ON dimension_name
SET PAGES 58 LINES 78 FEEDBACK OFF VERIFY OFF
ttitle 'Database Dimension Hierarchy Report'
SPOOL dim_hierarchies.lis

SELECT
    a.owner,
    a.dimension_name,
    b.hierarchy_name,
    c.parent_level_name,
    c.child_level_name,
    c.join_key_id
FROM
    dba_dimensions       a,
    dba_dim_hierarchies  b,
    dba_dim_child_of     c
```

```
WHERE
    a.Owner LIKE '%&owner%'
AND
    a.owner=b.owner
AND
    a.dimension_name=b.dimension_name
AND
    a.owner=c.owner
AND
    a.dimension_name=c.dimension_name
AND
    b.hierarchy_name=c.hierarchy_name
ORDER BY
    a.owner,
    a.dimension_name,
    b.hierarchy_name;

SPOOL OFF
CLEAR BREAKS
CLEAR COLUMNS
TTITLE OFF
SET FEEDBACK ON VERIFY ON
```

Example of output from database dimension hierarchy

```
                        ORTEST1 database

          Dimension  Hierarchy  Parent      Child       Join Key
Owner     Name       Name       Level       Level       ID
--------  ---------- ---------- ----------- ----------- --------------
TELE_DBA  TEST_DIM   PLAN       PARENT_ID   CHILD_ID
```

The database dimension hierarchy report should be
reviewed to ensure that the hierarchies are using the
proper level assignments and that the parent-child
relationships make sense (that is, they aren't inverted).

dim_attribute.sql

```
--***********************************************
--
--     Copyright © 2003 by Rampant TechPress Inc.
--
--     Free for non-commercial use.
--     For commercial licensing, e-mail info@rampant.cc
--
--     ***********************************************
```

```
COLUMN owner            FORMAT a8    HEADING 'Owner'
COLUMN dimension_name   FORMAT a10   HEADING 'Dimension|Name'
COLUMN column_name      FORMAT a20   HEADING 'Column|Name'
```

```
COLUMN level_name           FORMAT a20  HEADING 'Level|Name'
COLUMN inferred             FORMAT a10  HEADING 'Inferred'

BREAK ON owner ON level_name
SET PAGES 58 LINES 78 FEEDBACK OFF VERIFY OFF
ttitle 'Database OPERATOR Report'
SPOOL dim_attribute.lis

SELECT
    a.owner,
    a.dimension_name,
    b.level_name,
    c.column_name,
    c.inferred
FROM
    dba_dimensions a,
    dba_dim_levels b,
    dba_dim_attributes c
WHERE
    a.owner LIKE '%&owner%'
    AND
    a.owner=b.owner
    AND
    a.dimension_name=b.dimension_name
    AND
    a.owner=c.owner
    AND
    a.dimension_name=c.dimension_name
    AND
    b.level_name=c.level_name
ORDER BY
    a.owner,
    a.dimension_name,
    b.level_name;

SPOOL OFF
CLEAR BREAKS
CLEAR COLUMNS
TTITLE OFF
SET FEEDBACK ON VERIFY ON
```

Here is a sample listing.

```
          Dimension  Level                         Column
Owner     Name       Name                          Name                  Inferred
--------  ---------- ----------------------------- --------------------- -----
TELE_DBA  TEST_DIM   PARENT_ID                     STATEMENT_ID          N
```

The database dimension attribute report should be
reviewed to ensure that the proper attributes are ascribed
to the proper levels.

Monitoring Stored Outlines

Outlines provide a method for forcing the cost-based optimizer to consistently use the same optimization for a specific SQL statement. The DBA needs to be aware of which outlines are currently stored in the database and whether it has been used. The views used to monitor the outlines are *dba_outlines* and *dba_outline_hints*. Note that to create an outline, the *plan_table* must be located in either a publicly available schema or in your own schema. In Oracle9*i*, the OEM tool has been extended to allow for outline editing.

There are also new DBMS packages provided for this purpose. The views relationship is shown in Figure 7.7. An example report using the *dba_outlines* and *dba_outline_hints* views is shown below, with example output from the script following.

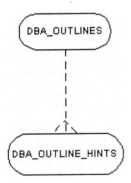

Figure 7.7 *Outline View Cluster*

💾 **outline.sql**

```
--*********************************************
--
--   Copyright © 2003 by Rampant TechPress Inc.
--
```

```
--    Free for non-commercial use.
--    For commercial licensing, e-mail info@rampant.cc
--
-- ***********************************************

COLUMN owner        FORMAT a8    HEADING 'Owner'
COLUMN name         FORMAT a13   HEADING 'Outline|Name'
COLUMN category     FORMAT a8    HEADING 'Category|Name'
COLUMN used         FORMAT a7    HEADING 'Used?'
COLUMN timestamp    FORMAT a16   HEADING 'Date Last|Used'
COLUMN version      FORMAT a9    HEADING 'Version'
COLUMN sql_text     FORMAT a40   HEADING 'SQL Outlined'
WORD_WRAPPED

BREAK ON owner ON category
SET PAGES 58 LINES 130 FEEDBACK OFF VERIFY OFF
ttitle 'Database OUTLINE Report'
SPOOL outline.lis

SELECT
   owner,
   name,
   category,
   used,
   to_char(timestamp,'dd/mm/yyyy hh24:mi') timestamp ,
   version,
   sql_text
FROM
   dba_outlines
WHERE
    owner LIKE '%&owner%'
ORDER BY
    owner,
   category;

SPOOL OFF
CLEAR BREAKS
TTITLE OFF
SET FEEDBACK ON VERIFY ON
```

Here is a sample listing.

```
         Outline      Category       Date Last
Owner    Name         Name    Used?  Used             Version   SQL Outlined
-------- ------------ -------- ------ ---------------- --------- ----------------
TELE_DBA PROD_OUTLINE1 PROD    UNUSED 13/05/1999 23:39 8.1.5.0.0 select
owner,table_name from
                                                                 dba_tables
         PROD_OUTLINE2         UNUSED 13/05/1999 23:39 8.1.5.0.0 select * from
dba_data_files
         TEST_OUTLINE1 TEST    UNUSED 13/05/1999 23:39 8.1.5.0.0 select
a.table_name,
                                                                 b.tablespace_name,
                                                                 c.file_name from
                                                                 dba_tables a,
dba_table
         TEST_OUTLINE2         UNUSED 13/05/1999 23:39 8.1.5.0.0 select * from
dba_data_files
```

In the outline report, monitor for outlines that either haven't been used or haven't been used recently, and review whether they are still pertinent to the database application. The *outln_utl* package is used to maintain outlines.

Monitoring Outline Hints

Outlines generate and use outline hints. The outline hints are viewed in the *dba_outline_hints* view. The report below demonstrates how to monitor the outline hints. A sample output from that report is shown below.

🖫 Outline_hint.sql

```
--*************************************************
--
--    Copyright © 2003 by Rampant TechPress Inc.
--
--    Free for non-commercial use.
--    For commercial licensing, e-mail info@rampant.cc
--
--    *************************************************

rem
rem NAME: outline_hint.sql
rem FUNCTION: Generate a lit of all outlines in the
rem database for a specific user and outline or all users
rem and outlines
rem HISTORY: MRA 5/13/98 Created
rem
COLUMN owner        FORMAT a8    HEADING 'Owner'
COLUMN name         FORMAT a13   HEADING 'Outline|Name'
COLUMN category     FORMAT a10   HEADING 'Category|Name'
COLUMN node         FORMAT 9999  HEADING 'Node'
COLUMN join_pos     FORMAT 9999  HEADING 'Join|Pos'
COLUMN hint         FORMAT A27   HEADING 'Hint Text' WORD_WRAPPED
BREAK ON owner ON category ON name
SET PAGES 58 LINES 78 FEEDBACK OFF VERIFY OFF
ttitle 'Database OUTLINE Report'
SPOOL outline_hint.lis
SELECT
    a.owner, a.name,
    a.category, b.node,
    b.join_pos, b.hint
FROM
    Dba_outlines a, dba_outline_hints b
WHERE
```

```
        a.Owner LIKE UPPER('%&owner%')
        AND a.name LIKE UPPER('%&outline%')
        AND a.owner=b.owner
        AND a.name=b.name
ORDER BY
        owner,category,name,b.node;
SPOOL OFF
CLEAR BREAKS
TTITLE OFF
SET FEEDBACK ON VERIFY ON
```

Here is a sample listing.

```
          Outline       Category        Join
Owner     Name          Name      Node  Pos  Hint Text
-------   ------------  ---------- ----- ---- ---- ----------------------
TELE_DBA  TEST_OUTLINE2 TEST         1     0  NO_EXPAND
                                     1     0  ORDERED
                                     1     1  NO_ACCESS(DBA_DATA_FILES)
                                     1     0  NOREWRITE
                                     1     0  NO_FACT(DBA_DATA_FILES)
                                     1     0  NOREWRITE
                                     2     0  NO_EXPAND
                                     2     0  ORDERED
                                     2     0  NOREWRITE
                                     2     0  NOREWRITE
                                     3     0  NO_EXPAND
                                     3     0  PQ_DISTRIBUTE(TS NONE NONE)
                                     3     0  PQ_DISTRIBUTE(HC NONE NONE)
                                     3     0  PQ_DISTRIBUTE(F NONE NONE)
                                     3     0  ORDERED
                                     3     0  NO_FACT(HC)
                                     3     0  NO_FACT(X$KCCFN)
                                     3     3  FULL(HC)
                                     3     1  FULL(X$KCCFN)
                                     3     0  NOREWRITE
                                     3     0  NOREWRITE
                                     3     2  INDEX(F I_FILE1)
                                     3     4  INDEX(TS)
                                     3     0  NO_FACT(F)
                                     3     0  NO_FACT(TS)
                                     3     0  USE_NL(F)
                                     3     0  USE_NL(HC)
                                     3     0  USE_NL(TS)
                                     4     0  NO_EXPAND
                                     4     0  NOREWRITE
                                     4     0  PQ_DISTRIBUTE(TS NONE NONE)
                                     4     0  PQ_DISTRIBUTE(F NONE NONE)
                                     4     0  USE_NL(TS)
                                     4     0  USE_NL(F)
                                     4     0  ORDERED
                                     4     0  NO_FACT(TS)
                                     4     0  NO_FACT(F)
                                     4     0  NO_FACT(X$KCCFN)
                                     4     3  INDEX(TS)
                                     4     2  INDEX(F I_FILE1)
                                     4     1  FULL(X$KCCFN)
                                     4     0  NOREWRITE
                                     5     0  NOREWRITE
                                     6     0  NOREWRITE
                                     7     0  NOREWRITE
                                     8     0  NOREWRITE
```

The output from the database outline hints report should be reviewed to verify that the proper hints are being used for the specific SQL outline.

Monitoring of Materialized Views and Materialized View Logs Using DBA_ and V Type Views

Oracle7 and Oracle8 provided the snapshot and snapshot log features. Under Oracle8*i*, the localized snapshot (materialized views) also became available. Snapshots make it possible to maintain read-only copies of a table or columns from multiple tables in several locations. The refresh rate of the materialized views can be varied and accomplished automatically.

The DBA needs tools to monitor materialized views and materialized view logs. The OEM in Oracle8, Oracle8*i*, and Oracle9*i* provide screens that allow the DBA see the status of the database's materialized views. The Replication Manager application also provides monitoring and control functionality. At times, however, it is more convenient to have hard-copy documentation of materialized views and materialized view logs. The two scripts below, along with the output report, document a database's materialized views and materialized view logs.

🖫 **mv_rep.sql**

```
--**********************************************
--
--   Copyright © 2003 by Rampant TechPress Inc.
--
--   Free for non-commercial use.
--   For commercial licensing, e-mail info@rampant.cc
--
--   **********************************************

rem
rem Name:     mv_rep.sql
rem Purpose:Report on database Materialized views
rem Use:     From an account that accesses DBA_MVIEWS
rem
rem   When      Who        What
```

```
rem   -------        ---------      ----------------
rem   5/27/93    Mike Ault   Initial Creation
rem   10/10/01   Mike Ault   Update to 9i
rem
SET PAGES 56 LINES 130 FEEDBACK OFF VERIFY OFF
rem
COLUMN mv         FORMAT a30        HEADING "Materialized|View"
COLUMN source         FORMAT a30     HEADING "Source Table"
COLUMN log                           HEADING "Use|Log?"
COLUMN type           FORMAT a10     HEADING "Ref|Type"
COLUMN refreshed                     HEADING "Last Refresh"
COLUMN start          FORMAT a13     HEADING "Start Refresh"
COLUMN error                         HEADING "Error"
COLUMN next           FORMAT a13     HEADING "Next Refresh"
rem
PROMPT Percent signs are wild card
ACCEPT mv_owner PROMPT Enter the materialized view owner
ttitle "Materialized View Report for &mv_owner"
SPOOL mv_rep&db
rem
SELECT
    Owner||'.'||mview_name mv, master_view,
    master_link Source,
    substr(query,1,query_len) query,
    updatable,
    update_log Log, last_refresh_date Refreshed,
DECODE(refresh_mode,'FAST','F','COMPLETE','C','FORCE','FR','COMM
IT','CM'),
    query,
    master_rollback_segment rbk
FROM dba_mviews
WHERE owner LIKE UPPER('%&mv_owner%')
ORDER BY owner,mview_name;
rem
SPOOL OFF
```

Here is a sample listing.

Snapshot	View	Source	Use Log	Last Ref	Ref Typ	Next Ref	Started	Query
TEST.SNAP$_TEST CHECK_DATE	MVIEW$_	DEV7_DBA.	YES	10-JUN-93	F	SYSDATE+7	10-JUN-93	SELECT
	TEST	HIT_RATIO						FROM HIT_RATIOS

🖫 **mv_log_rep.sql**

```
--*********************************************
--
--    Copyright © 2003 by Rampant TechPress Inc.
--
--    Free for non-commercial use.
--    For commercial licensing, e-mail info@rampant.cc
--
-- *********************************************
```

```
rem
rem Name:      mv_log_rep.sql
rem Purpose:      Report on database materialized view Logs
rem Use:      From an account that accesses DBA_ views
rem
rem    When        Who         What
rem    -------     ---------   -----------------
rem    5/27/93     Mike Ault   Initial Creation
rem    10/10/01    Mike Ault    Updated to oracle9i
rem
SET PAGES 56 LINES 130 FEEDBACK OFF
ttitle "Materialized View Log Report"
SPOOL mv_log_rep
rem
COLUMN log_owner       FORMAT a10 HEADING "Owner"
COLUMN master          FORMAT a20 HEADING "Master"
COLUMN log_table       FORMAT a20 HEADING "Materialized View"
COLUMN trigger         FORMAT a20 HEADING "Trigger Text"
COLUMN current                    HEADING "Last Refresh"
rem
SELECT
     log_owner, master, log_table table,
     log_trigger trigger, rowids, filter_columns filtered,
     object_id id, sequence seq,Include_new_values new
FROM
     dba_mview_logs
ORDER BY 1;
rem
SPOOL OFF
CLEAR COLUMNS
SET FEEDBACK ON
TTITLE OFF
```

These reports provide the DBA with hard-copy documentation of all materialized views and materialized view logs in the database. Each can be made more restrictive by using WHERE clauses, by selecting a specific set of values such as owner or *log_owner,* type, or date since last refresh (last_refresh > &date or current_snapshots > &date).

Conclusion

The later versions of Oracle have offered an array of new object features. This chapter has sought to familiarize the DBA with these features, as well as the various methods of monitoring them.

Index functionality has also evolved in the later Oracle versions. In the next chapter, we will look at some new index features and how to monitor them.

Index Internals Scripting

CHAPTER

Monitoring Indexes

The bitmapped index was added in Oracle7.3.2. Indexes were expanded to include partitions in Oracle8, in addition to the old monitoring requirements. In Oracle8*i*, partitioning was further expanded to include sub-partitions and the additional functionality of function-based indexes, as well as indextypes. Oracle8*i* also added support for descending indexes. To those capabilities, Oracle9*i* added the bitmap join index and the skip scan index.

The DBA still needs to monitor table indexes to verify uniqueness, determine if the appropriate columns have been indexed, and determine proper ownership of indexes for a given application in Oracle9*i*. The DBA also needs a convenient reference to show which tables have indexes, as well as what is indexed, in case of the loss of a table or for use during table maintenance. The diagram in Figure 8.1 shows the cluster of *dba_* views that are needed for monitoring indexes.

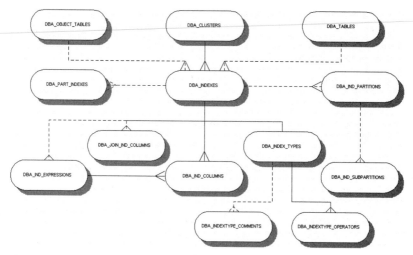

Figure 8.1 *dba_view cluster for monitoring indexes*

The report below provides a convenient format for the DBA to review indexed tables and columns; it is selective down to the single-table, single-owner level. The report should be run after database maintenance involving table rebuilds, exports and imports, or database rebuilds. An example of the output from the script follows.

🖫 ind_rep.sql

```
--*************************************************
--
--   Copyright © 2003 by Rampant TechPress Inc.
--
--   Free for non-commercial use.
--   For commercial licensing, e-mail info@rampant.cc
--
-- *************************************************
rem
rem NAME: ind_rep.sql
rem FUNCTION: Report on indexes
rem HISTORY: MRA 6/14/97 Creation
rem
COLUMN owner              FORMAT a8     HEADING 'Index|Owner'
COLUMN index_name         FORMAT a27    HEADING 'Index'
COLUMN index_type         FORMAT a6     HEADING 'Type|Index'
COLUMN table_owner        FORMAT a8     HEADING 'Table|Owner'
```

```
COLUMN table_name          FORMAT a24    HEADING 'Table Name'
COLUMN table_type          FORMAT a10    HEADING 'Table|Type'
COLUMN uniqueness          FORMAT a1     HEADING 'U|n|i|q|u|e'
COLUMN tablespace_name     FORMAT a13    HEADING 'Tablespace'
COLUMN column_name         FORMAT a25    HEADING 'Col. Name'
SET PAGES 58 LINES 130 FEEDBACK OFF VERIFY OFF
BREAK ON owner
ttitle 'Expandeded Index Report'
SPOOL ind_exp.lis
SELECT
      a.owner,
      a.index_name,
      a.index_type,
      a.table_owner,
      a.table_name,
      a.table_type,
      DECODE
      (a.uniqueness, 'UNIQUE', 'U','NONUNIQUE','N') uniqueness,
      a.tablespace_name,
      b.column_name
FROM
      dba_indexes a, dba_ind_columns b
WHERE
      owner LIKE UPPER('%&owner%')
      AND a.owner=b.index_owner(+)
      AND a.index_name=b.index_name(+)
ORDER BY
      owner, index_type;
SPOOL OFF
```

Here is a sample listing.

```
Index                        Type   Table                      Table u
Owner  Index                 Index  Owner  Table Name          Type  e Tablespace Col
Name
------ --------------------- ------ ------ ------------- ----- - ---------- -------
--
SYSTEM PK_TEST_IOT           IOT -  SYSTEM TEST_IOT            TABLE U RAW_DATA   TEST1
                             TOP

       SYS_IL0000001562C00035$ LOB    SYSTEM DEF$_AQCALL    TABLE U SYSTEM
       SYS_IL0000001571C00035$ LOB    SYSTEM DEF$_AQERROR   TABLE U SYSTEM
       SYS_IL0000001588C00005$ LOB    SYSTEM DEF$_LOB       TABLE U SYSTEM
       SYS_IL0000001597C00002$ LOB    SYSTEM DEF$_TEMP$LOB  TABLE U SYSTEM
       SYS_IL0000001597C00001$ LOB    SYSTEM DEF$_TEMP$LOB  TABLE U SYSTEM
       SYS_IL0000001588C00006$ LOB    SYSTEM DEF$_LOB       TABLE U SYSTEM
       SYS_IL0000001588C00004$ LOB    SYSTEM DEF$_LOB       TABLE U SYSTEM
       SYS_IL0000001597C00003$ LOB    SYSTEM DEF$_TEMP$LOB  TABLE U SYSTEM
       AQ$_QUEUES_CHECK        NORMAL SYSTEM AQ$_QUEUES     TABLE U SYSTEM    NAME
       AQ$_QUEUES_PRIMARY      NORMAL SYSTEM AQ$_QUEUES     TABLE U SYSTEM    OID
       BM_TEST_BITMAP          BITMAP SYSTEM TEST_BITMAP    TABLE N SYSTEM
TEST_COL1
```

Monitoring Index Statistics

Under Oracle7, the *dba_indexes* view was extended to include B-tree level, number of leaf blocks, number of

---

distinct keys, average number of leaf blocks per key, average number of data blocks per key, and the index clustering factor. Under Oracle8 and Oracle8*i,* columns covering partitions, domain indexes, and function-based indexes where added. Under Oracle9*i,* columns for index types and join indexes where added, along with a column to show the index status, either DIRECT LOAD or VALID. The TYPE column specifies whether the index is NORMAL, an IOT, an LOB, or a BITMAP index. This is essentially the only indicator for BITMAP-type indexes.

Index statistics generated from the ANALYZE command are stored in the *index_stats* view. The major limitation of the *index_stats* view is that it shows only the index analyzed most recently.

Run the script below if results from all the indexes in a particular schema are needed. An example of a report follows the script.

🖫 **brown.sql**

```
--*************************************************
--
--    Copyright © 2003 by Rampant TechPress Inc.
--
--    Free for non-commercial use.
--    For commercial licensing, e-mail info@rampant.cc
--
-- *************************************************
rem
rem NAME: brown.sql
rem FUNCTION: Analyze indexes and produce stat report
rem FUNCTION: Including browning indicator
rem
rem HISTORY: MRA 6/15/97 Created
rem
COL del_lf_rows_len FORMAT 999,999,999 HEADING 'Deleted Bytes'
COL lf_rows_len     FORMAT 999,999,999 HEADING 'Filled Bytes'
COL browning        FORMAT 999.90      HEADING 'Percent|Browned'
COL height          FORMAT 999,999     HEADING 'Height'
```

Oracle Internals Monitoring & Tuning Scripts

```
COL blocks           FORMAT 999,999       HEADING 'Blocks'
COL disti
nct_keys    FORMAT 999,999,999 HEADING '#|Keys'
COL most_repeated_key FORMAT 999999999 HEADING
'Most|Repeated|Key'
COL used_space       FORMAT 999999999     HEADING 'Used|Space'
COL rows_per_key     FORMAT 999999        HEADING 'Rows|Per|Key'
ACCEPT owner PROMPT 'Enter table owner name: '
SET HEADING OFF FEEDBACK OFF VERIFY OFF ECHO OFF RECSEP OFF
SET PAGES 0
TTITLE OFF
DEFINE cr='CHR(10)'
SPOOL index_sz.sql
SELECT
  'CREATE TABLE stat_temp AS SELECT * FROM index_stats;'||&&cr||
  'TRUNCATE TABLE stat_temp;'
FROM dual;
SELECT
'ANALYZE INDEX '||owner||'.'||index_name||
' VALIDATE STRUCTURE;'||&&cr||
    'INSERT INTO stat_temp SELECT * FROM index_stats;'||&&cr||
    'COMMIT;'
FROM
    dba_indexes
WHERE
    owner=UPPER('&owner');
SPOOL OFF
PROMPT 'Analyzing Indexes'
SET FEEDBACK OFF TERMOUT OFF LINES 132 VERIFY OFF
START index_sz.sql
SET TERMOUT ON FEEDBACK ON VERIFY ON LINES 132 PAGES 58
ttitle "Index Statistics Report"
SPOOL browning.lst
SELECT
    name,
    del_lf_rows_len,
    lf_rows_len,
(del_lf_rows_len/
DECODE((lf_rows_len+del_lf_rows_len),0,1,lf_rows_len+
del_lf_rows_len))*100 browning,
    height,
    blocks,
    distinct_keys,
    most_repeated_key,
    used_space,
    rows_per_key
FROM
    stat_temp
WHERE rows_per_key>0;
SPOOL OFF
SET FEEDBACK ON TERMOUT ON LINES 80 VERIFY ON
HOST del stat_temp
```

Here is a sample listing.

Most

NAME	Rows Deleted	Filled	Percent Browned	Height	Blocks	# Keys	Repeat Key	Used Space	Per Key
FK_ADDRESSES_2	0	10,126,346	.00	3	12800	583996	2	10159315	1
FK_ADDRESSES_3	0	12,115,956	.00	3	12800	758357	1	12153926	1
FK_FRANC_CDS_1	0	1,880,298	.00	3	2560	19619	6	1888613	6
FK_SIC_CODES_1	0	15,896,017	.00	3	12800	875966	3	15948812	1
LI_LOAD_TEST	0	22,568,301	.00	3	10240	875966	8461	22676759	1
PK_ADDRESSES	0	21,249,760	.00	3	25600	1392036	1	21312498	1
PK_CLIENTS	0	13,121,655	.00	3	25600	875966	1	13159342	1
PK_EARNINGS	0	11,357,779	.00	3	25600	758369	1	11390423	1
PK_FRANC_CDS	0	2,340,249	.00	3	12800	117714	1	2349540	1
PK_SIC_CODES	0	19,856,433	.00	3	12800	994826	1	19921338	1
PK_USERS	0	13	.00	1	25600	1	1	13	1
SYS_C00800	0	27	.00	1	25600	1	1	27	1
TEST_INDEX	0	17	.00	1	5	1	1	17	1
UI_EARNINGS_1	0	18,200,856	.00	3	12800	758369	1	18295755	1
UK_CLIENTS	0	17,519,320	.00	3	12800	875966	1	17584123	1

16 rows selected

If the rows-per-key column in the report above exceeds 100, consider making the index a bitmap index (post-7.3.2). If the index shows excessive "browning" (30 percent maximum), then a rebuild is in order.

The clustering factor column shows how well the index is ordered in comparison to the base table. If the value for the clustering factor is near the number of table blocks, it means the index is well ordered; conversely, if the value is near the number of rows in the table, the index is not well ordered (unless the row size is close to blocksize). For indexes with high clustering factors, consider rebuilding, as a high clustering factor indicates that under index scan conditions, the same blocks will be read numerous times.

A script for reporting some of the statistics stored in the *dba_indexes* view is shown below. Note that these statistics are not dynamic; they are 100 percent valid only at the time the ANALYZE command is run. Oracle conveniently includes the last-date-analyzed field in Oracle8. Corresponding sample output is shown following the script.

🖫 **in_stat.sql**

```
--*************************************************
--
--     Copyright © 2003 by Rampant TechPress Inc.
--
--     Free for non-commercial use.
--     For commercial licensing, e-mail info@rampant.cc
--
-- *************************************************
rem   NAME: IN_STAT.sql
rem
rem   FUNCTION: Report on index statistics
rem   INPUTS:    1 = Index owner    2 = Index name
rem
```

```
DEF iowner = '&OWNER'
DEF iname  = '&INDEX'
SET PAGES 56 LINES 130 VERIFY OFF FEEDBACK OFF
COLUMN owner                     FORMAT a8          HEADING
"Owner"
COLUMN index_name                FORMAT a25         HEADING
"Index"
COLUMN status                    FORMAT a7          HEADING
"Status"
COLUMN blevel                    FORMAT 9,999       HEADING
"Tree|Level"
COLUMN leaf_blocks               FORMAT 999,999,999 HEADING "Leaf
Blk"
COLUMN distinct_keys             FORMAT 999,999,999 HEADING "#
Keys"
COLUMN avg_leaf_blocks_per_key FORMAT 9,999         HEADING
"Avg.|LB/Key"
COLUMN avg_data_blocks_per_key FORMAT 9,999         HEADING
"Avg.|DB/Key"
COLUMN clustering_factor         FORMAT 999,999     HEADING
"Clstr|Factor"
COLUMN num_rows                  FORMAT 999,999,999 HEADING
"Number|Rows"
COLUMN sample_size               FORMAT 99,999      HEADING
"Sample|Size"
COLUMN last_analyzed             HEADING 'Analysis|Date'
rem
BREAK ON owner
ttitle "Index Statistics Report"
SPOOL ind_stat
rem
SELECT
    owner, index_name, status, blevel, leaf_blocks,
    distinct_keys, avg_leaf_blocks_per_key,
    avg_data_blocks_per_key, clustering_factor,
    num_rows, sample_size, last_analyzed
FROM
    dba_indexes
WHERE
    owner LIKE UPPER('&&iowner')
    AND index_name LIKE UPPER('&&iname')
    AND num_rows>0
ORDER BY
    1,2;
rem
SPOOL OFF
SET PAGES 22 LINES 80 VERIFY ON FEEDBACK ON
CLEAR COLUMNS
UNDEF iowner
UNDEF iname
UNDEF owner
UNDEF name
TTITLE OFF
```

Here is a sample listing.

Owner	Index	Status	Tr. Lev	Lf. Blk	# Keys	Avg. LB/Key	Avg. DB/Key	Clstr Factor	Number Rows	Sam. Size	Anl. Date
TELE_DBA	FK_ADDRESS_2	VALID	2	2650	583996	1	1	14191	633679	0	14-JUN-97
TELE_DBA	FK_ADDRESS_3	VALID	2	3171	758357	1	1	18637	758357	0	14-JUN-97
TELE_DBA	FK_FRAN_CD_1	VALID	2	492	19619	1	1	803	117714	0	14-JUN-97
TELE_DBA	FK_SIC_CDS_1	VALID	2	4160	875966	1	1	16765	994826	0	14-JUN-97
TELE_DBA	LI_LOAD_TEST	VALID	2	6474	875966	1	1	140442	1074681	0	14-JUN-97
TELE_DBA	PK_ADDRESSES	VALID	2	5560	1392036	1	1	32827	1392036	0	14-JUN-97
TELE_DBA	PK_CLIENTS	VALID	2	3433	875966	1	1	61587	875966	0	14-JUN-97
TELE_DBA	PK_EARNINGS	VALID	2	2972	758369	1	1	28485	758369	0	14-JUN-97
TELE_DBA	PK_FRAN_CDS	VALID	2	613	117714	1	1	803	117714	0	14-JUN-97
TELE_DBA	PK_SIC_CODES	VALID	2	5204	994826	1	1	16765	994826	0	14-JUN-97
TELE_DBA	PK_USERS	VALID	0	1	1	1	1	1	1	0	14-JUN-97
TELE_DBA	SYS_C00800	VALID	0	1	1	1	1	1	1	0	14-JUN-97
TELE_DBA	TEST_INDEX	VALID	0	1	1	1	1	1	1	0	14-JUN-97
TELE_DBA	UI_EARNINGs_1	VALID	2	6738	758369	1	1	727251	758369	0	14-JUN-97
TELE_DBA	UK_CLIENTS	VALID	2	4493	875966	1	1	61587	875966	0	14-JUN-97
TELE_DBA	UK_LOAD_TEST	VALID	2	5456	758369	1	1	733393	758369	0	14-JUN-97

The various values in the report above are interpreted as follows:

- **Tr. Lev.** The depth, or number of levels, from the root block of the index to its leaf blocks. A depth of 1 indicates that they are all on the same level.

- **LFBLK.** The number of leaf blocks in the index.

- **AVG_LB/KEY.** Indicates a non-unique index if its value is greater than 1.

- **BLOCKS_PER_KEY.** If greater than 1, indicates the key has duplicate values.

- **AVG DB/Key-.** Indicates the average number of data blocks in the *blocks_per_key* indexed table that are pointed to by a distinct value in the index.

- **CLSTR FACTOR.** Indicates the orderliness of the table being indexed. If it is near the number of blocks in table, it indicates a well-ordered table; if it is near the number of rows, it indicates a disorganized table.

- **SAM. SIZE.** Tells the sample size specified if the index was analyzed using the estimate clause.

- **ANL. DATE.** The last date on which the index was analyzed.

Monitoring for Clustering Factor Ratio

Looking at the index clustering factor without comparison to the number of dirty blocks and number of rows in the index source table is useless. The clustering factor will range from the number of dirty (used) blocks, to the number of rows. Generally, the closer to the number of dirty blocks the better the index will be for range scans and will result in lower overall cost for use. The following script is to be run against analyzed tables and indexes to generate the comparison between clustering factor and the number of dirty blocks and number of rows. The ratio is clustering factor against number of dirty blocks.

💾 Cfb_ratio.sql

```
--***********************************************
--
--    Copyright © 2003 by Rampant TechPress Inc.
--
--    Free for non-commercial use.
--    For commercial licensing, e-mail info@rampant.cc
--
-- ***********************************************
REM
REM Clustering factor ratio report
REM Use with analyzed tables and indexes.
REM M.R. Ault 2003 initial creation
REM
column table_name format a20 heading 'Table|Name'
column index_name format a20 heading 'Index|Name'
column dirty_blocks heading 'Dirty|Blocks'
column clustering_factor heading 'Clustering|Factor'
column cfb_ratio heading 'Clustering Factor|To Blocks Ratio'
format 99,999.99
column owner format a15 heading 'Owner'
ttitle 'Clustering Factor to Block Ratio Report'
set lines 132 verify off pages 55 feedback off
break on owner on table_name
spool cfb_ratio
select t.owner,t.table_name,i.index_name, t.num_rows, t.blocks
dirty_blocks,i.clustering_factor,
i.clustering_factor/decode(t.blocks,0,decode(i.clustering_factor
,0,1,i.clustering_factor),t.blocks) cfb_ratio, i.blevel
from dba_tables t, dba_indexes i
where t.owner=i.table_owner and t.table_name=i.table_name
and t.owner not in
('SYS','SYSTEM','DBAUTIL','OUTLN','DBSNMP','SPOTLIGHT','PERFSTAT
','RMAN','IWATCH') and
i.clustering_factor/decode(t.blocks,0,decode(i.clustering_factor
,0,1,i.clustering_factor),t.blocks)>&&min_ratio
order by
t.owner,i.clustering_factor/decode(t.blocks,0,decode(i.clusterin
g_factor,0,1,i.clustering_factor),t.blocks)
desc,t.table_name,i.index_name
/
spool off
set lines 80 pages 22 feedback on verify on
clear columns
ttitle off
```

The above report generates an output similar to the following example.

Owner	Table Name	Index Name	NUM_ROWS	Dirty Blocks	Clustering Factor	Clustering Factor To Blocks Ratio	BLEVEL
APP	APP_ALL_USER_ROLES	PK_APP_ALL_USER_ROLES	1630	7	282	40.29	1
CUS	DAC_FILTER_LIST	PK_DAC_FILTER_LIST	13423	35	9457	270.20	1
	DAC_ISSUEFILES	DAIF_IXA	1166503	8129	921093	113.31	2
	ART_DESELECT_MAP	SYS_C0015133	381	2	183	91.50	2
	DAC_ISSUEFILES	PK_DAC_ISSUEFILES	1166503	8129	737788	90.76	2
	DAC_FILTER	PK_DAC_FILTER	2047	15	1338	89.20	1
	DAC_OVERRIDE_MCODE	PK_OVERRIDE_MCODE	637	4	231	57.75	1
	DAC_X_ISSUEFILES	PK_DAC_X_ISSUEFILES	85714	649	37129	57.21	2
	PRD_USER_MAN_INDEX_PERM	PK_PRD_USER_MAN_INDEX_PERM	747	4	172	43.00	1
	ART_GSEC_MAP	SYS_C0015134	8703	50	2051	41.02	1
	ASEC_GSEC_MAPPING	PK_ASEC_GSEC_MAPPING	4683	46	1831	39.80	1
	DAC_ID	IND_DAC_ID	334505900	386259	13006188	33.67	3
	PRD_USER	PK_PRD_USER	165	2	59	29.50	0
	DAC_FILTER_COMMAND	PK_DAC_FILTER_COMMAND	651	10	275	27.50	1
	DAC_ISSUES	PK_DAC_ISSUES	11980020	32024	832638	26.00	2
	DAC_ID	PK_DAC_ID	334505900	386259	9204321	23.83	3
	DAC_X_ISSUES	PK_DAC_X_ISSUES	85679	2254	50395	22.36	2
	DAC_FILTER_DETAIL	PK_DAC_FILTER_DETAIL	818	4	87	21.75	1
	DAC_ID	IND_DAC_ID_ACCESSION	334505900	386259	7985587	20.67	2
	ART_REPLACEMENT_MAP	SYS_C0015138	2133	10	188	18.80	1
	PRD_USER_MAN_QC_PERM	PK_PRD_USER_MAN_QC_PERM	251	2	36	18.00	0
DDEWITT	DAC_ITEM_DETAIL	SYS_C0015157	7832113	81209	1336689	16.46	2
	ASEC_MAPPING_FILE	FILTER_NAME	105	2	31	15.50	0
	BT_LOCKED_ISSUES	SYS_C0015142	509	3	36	12.00	0
	DAC_ITEMS	PK_DAC_ITEMS	392800994	15362669	16924557	11.02	3
	DELETES	SYS_C0015162	131160	330	3434	10.41	1
	MYISSUE	PEIS_IXB	145876	3839	539212	140.46	2
	MYISSUE	XIF83PER_ISSUE	145876	3839	285078	74.26	1
	MYARTICLEWORKFLOW_P	XPKPER_ARTICLE_WORKFLOW_P	4278283	72318	3652002	50.50	2
MERCURY	MYISSUE	PEIS_IXD	145876	3839	181442	47.26	2
	MYISSUE_P	PEIS_IXC_P	145876	2534	98892	39.03	2
	MYISSUE_P	XPKPER_ISSUE_P	145876	2534	98882	39.02	2
	MYISSUE_P	PEIS_IXD_P	145876	2534	98757	38.97	2
	MYISSUE	PEIS_IXC	145876	3839	146667	38.20	2
	MYISSUE_P	PEIS_IXB_P	145876	2534	91468	36.10	2
	MYISSUE	XPKPER_ISSUE	145876	3839	99662	25.96	2
	MYISSUE_P	XIF83PER_ISSUE_P	145876	2534	64011	25.26	1
	PER_ARTICLE_EXTRACT_	XPKPER_ARTICLE_EXTRA	9011837	72704	24329544	334.64	2

Indexes with high clustering factor to blocks ratios should be investigated for possible rebuild. One thing to remember is that character based indexes will generally have a high clustering factor to blocks ratio while those indexes based on key values will have low ratios. Sometimes re-ordering the columns in a concatenated key will dramatically reduce clustering factor, however, any SQL that uses the index must also be modified to reflect any changes in column order.

Index and Table Co-Location

Even with RAID, co-location of index and table segments can result in contention. While for a single process, index and table scanning may be fairly linear, when you multiple that by 50, 100 or 1000 users the chance for contention increases dramatically. Therefore the co-location of table and index segments should be avoided or minimized. A script to monitor for index and table co-location follows.

🖫 **Co_lo_index.sql**

```
--*************************************************
--
--    Copyright © 2003 by Rampant TechPress Inc.
--
--    Free for non-commercial use.
--    For commercial licensing, e-mail info@rampant.cc
--
--  *************************************************
REM
REM Script for determiniation of co-location
REM of indexes and tables
REM M.R. Ault 2003 Initial creation
REM
col owner format a10
col tablespace_name format a10
col table_name format a30
```

```
set lines 132 pages 47
ttitle 'Indexes Co-Located With Data'
spool co_lo_ind
select i.owner, i.index_name, i.tablespace_name,
      i.table_name,i.index_type
from
   dba_indexes i, dba_tables t
where
   i.owner not in
('SYS','SYSTEM','SCOTT','SYSMAN','ORDSYS','CTXSYS','ODM',

'XDB','RMAN','ODSYS','CTXSYS','MDSYS','WKSYS','WMSYS','OUTLN')
and (i.table_name=t.table_name
      and i.owner=t.owner
      and i.tablespace_name=t.tablespace_name)
order by owner,index_name
/
spool off
ttitle off
set lines 80
```

An example of the output from the abover script is shown below.

```
OWNER    INDEX_NAME                            TABLESPACE TABLE_NAME
INDEX_TYPE
-------  ------------------------------------- ---------- ---------------------------- ------
----
DDEWITT ACTI_PK                                USER_DATA  ACTIVITY                     NORMAL
DDEWITT FIELDS_PK                              USER_DATA  FIELDS                       NORMAL
DDEWITT MERCURY_STATS                          USER_DATA  MERCURY_STATS                NORMAL
DDEWITT PEAR_IXA                               DDEWITT    MYARTICLE                    NORMAL
DDEWITT PEAW_IXC                               DDEWITT    MYARTICLEWORKFLOW            NORMAL
DDEWITT PEIS_IXA                               DDEWITT    MYISSUE                      NORMAL
DDEWITT PEIS_IXB                               DDEWITT    MYISSUE                      NORMAL
DDEWITT PEIS_IXC                               DDEWITT    MYISSUE                      NORMAL
DDEWITT PEIS_IXD                               DDEWITT    MYISSUE                      NORMAL
DDEWITT PEWI_IXA                               DDEWITT    MYWORKITEM                   NORMAL
DDEWITT PEWI_UXA                               DDEWITT    MYWORKITEM                   NORMAL
DDEWITT SYS_IL0000042775C00004$$               DDEWITT    MYARTICLE                    LOB
DDEWITT SYS_IL0000042781C00004$$               DDEWITT    MYARTICLETMP                 LOB
DDEWITT XIF111PER_ARTICLE                      DDEWITT    MYARTICLE                    NORMAL
DDEWITT XIF14PER_ARTICLE_WORKFLOW              DDEWITT    MYARTICLEWORKFLOW            NORMAL
DDEWITT XIF1PER_ARTICLE                        DDEWITT    MYARTICLE                    NORMAL
DDEWITT XIF1PER_ISSUE                          DDEWITT    MYISSUE                      NORMAL
DDEWITT XIF2PER_ARTICLE_WORKFLOW               DDEWITT    MYARTICLEWORKFLOW            NORMAL
DDEWITT XIF2PER_ISSUE                          DDEWITT    MYISSUE                      NORMAL
DDEWITT XIF2PPER_ARTICLE_WORKFLOW              DDEWITT    MYARTICLEWORKFLOW            NORMAL
DDEWITT XIF2PPER_WORK_ITEM                     DDEWITT    MYWORKITEM                   NORMAL
DDEWITT XIF71PER_WORK_ITEM                     DDEWITT    MYWORKITEM                   NORMAL
DDEWITT XIF7PER_ARTICLE_WORKFLOW               DDEWITT    MYARTICLEWORKFLOW            NORMAL
DDEWITT XIF80PER_WORK_ITEM                     DDEWITT    MYWORKITEM                   NORMAL
DDEWITT XIF83PER_ISSUE                         DDEWITT    MYISSUE                      NORMAL
DDEWITT XIF97PER_ARTICLE_WORKFLOW              DDEWITT    MYARTICLEWORKFLOW            NORMAL
DDEWITT XPKPER_ARTICLE                         DDEWITT    MYARTICLE                    NORMAL
DDEWITT XPKPER_ARTICLE_WORKFLOW                DDEWITT    MYARTICLEWORKFLOW            NORMAL
DDEWITT XPKPER_ISSUE                           DDEWITT    MYISSUE                      NORMAL
DDEWITT XPKPER_WORK_ITEM                       DDEWITT    MYWORKITEM                   NORMAL
MERCURY PAAS_IXA                               MERCURY_DA PER_ACTIVE_ARTICLE_STYLE     NORMAL
                                               TA_LG
MERCURY SYS_IL0000042516C00006$$               MERCURY_DA PER_BROWSE_BLOB_CACHE        LOB
                                               TA
MPD     MPIS_IXA                               MPD_DATA_L MPD_ISSUE                    NORMAL
                                               G
MPD     PK_MPD_H_CONTRACT_COMPONENT            MPD_DATA_L MPD_H_CONTRACT_COMPONENT     NORMAL
                                               G
VAL     PK_VAL_ANNOTATION_TYPE                 VAL_INDEX_ VAL_ANNOTATION_TYPE          NORMAL
```

		SM		
VAL	PK_VAL_BROWSE_DATA_ELEMENT	VAL_INDEX_ VAL_BROWSE_DATA_ELEMENT		NORMAL
VAL	PK_VAL_BROWSE_ELEMENT_LINK_ID	SM VAL_INDEX_ VAL_BROWSE_ELEMENT_LINK_ID		NORMAL
VAL	PK_VAL_BROWSE_ELEMENT_NOTE_TYP	SM VAL_INDEX_ VAL_BROWSE_ELEMENT_NOTE_TYPE		NORMAL
VAL	PK_VAL_BROWSE_FILTER_CATEGORY	SM VAL_INDEX_ VAL_BROWSE_FILTER_CATEGORY		NORMAL
VAL	PK_VAL_DATA_ELEMENT	SM VAL_INDEX_ VAL_DATA_ELEMENT		NORMAL

One thing that you should know is that the index segments for LOB data is always co-located with the lob segment.

Monitoring Partitioned Indexes

Partitioned indexes in Oracle8, Oracle8*i,* and Oracle9*i* also require monitoring by the DBA. The *dba_ind_partitions* view is almost identical to the *dba_tab_partitions* view, with the exception of the index / table-specific statistics. The scripts shown here are examples that can be modified for your own needs. The first script, *ind_part.sql,* shows partition file parameters. The output from this script is shown following.

🖫 ind_part.sql

```
--*************************************************
--
--   Copyright © 2003 by Rampant TechPress Inc.
--
--   Free for non-commercial use.
--   For commercial licensing, e-mail info@rampant.cc
--
--   *************************************************

rem
rem Name: ind_part.sql
rem Function : Report on partitioned index structure
rem History: MRA 6/14/97 Created
rem MRA 5/10/99 Updated for Sub-partitions
rem
COLUMN index_owner          FORMAT a10 HEADING 'Owner'
COLUMN index_name           FORMAT a15 HEADING 'Index'
COLUMN partition_name       FORMAT a15 HEADING 'Partition'
COLUMN sub-partition_name    FORMAT a15 HEADING 'Sub|Partition'
```

```
COLUMN tablespace_name        FORMAT a15 HEADING 'Tablespace'
COLUMN high_value             FORMAT a10 HEADING 'Partition|Value'
COLUMN status                 FORMAT a10 Heading 'Status'
SET LINES 130
START title132 'Index Partition Files'
BREAK ON index_owner ON index_name
SPOOL rep_out/&&db/ind_part.lis
SELECT
     a.index_owner,
     a.index_name,
     a.partition_name,
     a.high_value,
     b.sub-partition_name,
     b.tablespace_name,
     b.logging,
     b.status
FROM sys.dba_ind_partitions a, sys.dba_ind_sub-partitions b
WHERE a.owner=b.owner
   AND a.index_name=b.index_name
   And a.partition_name=b.partition_name
ORDER BY a.index_owner,a.index_name,a.partition_name,
        b.sub-partition_position
/
SPOOL OFF
```

Here is a sample listing.

```
                                Partition
Owner   Index         Partition Value   Tablespace      LOG Status
------- ------------- --------- -------- --------------- --- ------
SYSTEM  PART_IND_TEST TEST_P1        10 RAW_DATA        YES VALID
                      TEST_P2        20 RAW_DATA        YES VALID
                      TEST_P3        30 RAW_DATA        YES VALID

3 rows selected.
```

The *dba_ind_partitions* view also provides the statistics and storage characteristics for partitioned indexes. The example below shows a script to use for monitoring some of these statistics. The output from this script resembles the report above.

🖫 ind_pstor.sql

```
--*************************************************
--
--    Copyright © 2003 by Rampant TechPress Inc.
--
--    Free for non-commercial use.
--    For commercial licensing, e-mail info@rampant.cc
--
```

```
--  **********************************************

rem
rem NAME:        ind_pstor.sql
rem FUNCTION: Provide data on partitioned index storage
charcacteristics
rem HISTORY: MRA 6/13/97 Created
rem
COLUMN owner              FORMAT a6        HEADING 'Owner'
COLUMN index_name         FORMAT a14       HEADING 'Index'
COLUMN partition_name     FORMAT a9        HEADING 'Partition'
COLUMN tablespace_name    FORMAT a11       HEADING 'Tablespace'
COLUMN pct_free           FORMAT 9999      HEADING '%|Free'
COLUMN ini_trans          FORMAT 9999      HEADING 'Init|Tran'
COLUMN max_trans          FORMAT 9999      HEADING 'Max|Tran'
COLUMN initial_extent     FORMAT 9999999   HEADING 'Init|Extent'
COLUMN next_extent        FORMAT 9999999   HEADING 'Next|Extent'
COLUMN max_extent                          HEADING 'Max|Extents'
COLUMN pct_increase       FORMAT 999       HEADING '%|Inc'
COLUMN distinct_keys      FORMAT 9999999   HEADING '#Keys'
COLUMN clustering_factor  FORMAT 999999    HEADING 'Clus|Fact'
SET LINES 130
START title132 'Index Partition File Storage'
BREAK ON index_owner on index_name
SPOOL rep_out/&&db/ind_pstor.lis
SELECT
     index_owner,
     index_name,
     tablespace_name,
     partition_name,
     pct_free,
     ini_trans,
     max_trans,
     initial_extent,
     next_extent,
     max_extent,
     pct_increase,
     distinct_keys,
     clustering_factor
FROM sys.dba_ind_partitions
ORDER BY index_owner,index_name
/
SPOOL OFF
```

Here is a sample listing.

Owner	Index	Tablespace	Partition	% Free	Init Tran	Max Tran	Init Extent	Next Extent	Max Extents	% Inc	#Keys	Clus Fac
SYSTEM	P_IND_TEST	RAW_DATA	TEST_P1	10	2	255	20480	20480	249	50	0	0
		RAW_DATA	TEST_P2	10	2	255	20480	20480	249	50	0	0
		RAW_DATA	TEST_P3	10	2	255	20480	20480	249	50	0	0

3 rows selected.

The index sub-partitions also have statistics collected against them and they are found in the *dba_ind_subpartitions* view. The report below will generate a listing of some of these statistics. Feel free to modify as needed to monitor the statistics you feel are important. The output from the script resembles previous reports.

ind_subpstor.sql

```
--******************************************
--
--     Copyright © 2003 by Rampant TechPress Inc.
--
--     Free for non-commercial use.
--     For commercial licensing, e-mail info@rampant.cc
--
-- ******************************************

rem
rem NAME:      ind_subpstor.sql
rem FUNCTION: Get data on sub-partitioned index charcacteristics
rem HISTORY: MRA 5/10/99 Created
rem
COLUMN owner              FORMAT a6        HEADING 'Owner'
COLUMN index_name         FORMAT a14       HEADING 'Index'
COLUMN partition_name     FORMAT a9        HEADING 'Partition'
COLUMN sub-partition_name FORMAT a9        HEADING
'Sub|Partition'
COLUMN tablespace_name    FORMAT a11       HEADING 'Tablespace'
COLUMN pct_free           FORMAT 9999      HEADING '%|Free'
COLUMN ini_trans          FORMAT 9999      HEADING 'Init|Tran'
COLUMN max_trans          FORMAT 9999      HEADING 'Max|Tran'
COLUMN initial_extent     FORMAT 9999999   HEADING 'Init|Extent'
COLUMN next_extent        FORMAT 9999999   HEADING 'Next|Extent'
COLUMN max_extent                          HEADING 'Max|Extents'
COLUMN pct_increase       FORMAT 999       HEADING '%|Inc'
COLUMN distinct_keys      FORMAT 9999999   HEADING '#Keys'
COLUMN clustering_factor  FORMAT 999999    HEADING 'Clus|Fact'
COLUMN num_rows           FORMAT 9999999   HEADING 'Number|Rows'
SET LINES 130
START title132 'Index Sub-partition File Storage'
BREAK ON index_owner on index_name
SPOOL rep_out/&&db/ind_pstor.lis
SELECT
     index_owner,
     index_name,
     partition_name,
     sub_partition_name,
     tablespace_name,
     pct_free,
     ini_trans,
     max_trans,
     initial_extent,
     next_extent,
     max_extent,
     pct_increase,
```

```
      distinct_keys,
      clustering_factor,
      num_rows
FROM sys.dba_ind_sub-partitions
ORDER BY index_owner,index_name,partition_name,sub-
partition_position
/
SPOOL OFF
```

Here is a sample listing.

Owner	Index	Tablespace	Partition	% Free	Init Tran	Max Tran	Init Extent	Next Extent	Max Extents	% Inc	#Keys	Clus Fac
SYSTEM	P_IND	RAW_DATA	TEST_P1	10	2	255	20480	20480	249	50	0	0
		RAW_DATA	TEST_P2	10	2	255	20480	20480	249	50	0	0
		RAW_DATA	TEST_P3	10	2	255	20480	20480	249	50	0	0

Function-based Index (FBI) Internals

The concept of a *function-based index* was added in Oracle8*i*. A functional index uses a function or collection of functions to operate on its column, thus allowing the same function or collection of functions to be applied in the WHERE clause of a SELECT that uses the index. A simple example would be a functional index using UPPER on a name field. This would allow selects of the form:

```
SELECT * FROM emp WHERE UPPER(last_name)='AULT';
```

The new functionality will simplify table and application design tremendously in applications that retrieve data based on UPPER, LOWER, SOUNDEX, and other function-based queries.

The DBA will want to know about, and track, the use of function-based indexes in his or her database. The *dba_indexes* view has a new column that makes this easier, the *funcidx_status* column. The *funcidx_status* column contains NULL if the index is not a function-based index, ENABLED if it is a function-based index and is ready for use, and DISABLED if it is a function-based index that is disabled and can't be used. If the value in *funcidx_status* is not NULL, a join to the *dba_ind_expressions* view will provide the information on the expression used to create the function-based column in the index. The script below demonstrates this type of report; an example of the output from this script follows.

🖫 ind_func.sql

```
--*************************************************
--
--    Copyright © 2003 by Rampant TechPress Inc.
--
--    Free for non-commercial use.
--    For commercial licensing, e-mail info@rampant.cc
--
-- *************************************************
rem
rem NAME:       ind_func.sql
rem FUNCTION: Get data on functional index charcacteristics
rem HISTORY: MRA 5/12/99 Created
rem
COLUMN owner              FORMAT a6      HEADING 'Owner'
COLUMN index_name    .    FORMAT a14     HEADING 'Index'
COLUMN table_name         FORMAT a20     HEADING 'Table'
COLUMN column_expression FORMAT a80 WORD_WRAPPED HEADING
'Expression'
SET LINES 130
ttitle 'Functional Index Report'
BREAK ON index_owner on index_name
SPOOL ind_func.lis

SELECT
     Index_owner,
     index_name,
     table_name,
     column_expression
FROM
     Dba_ind_expressions
WHERE
     Index_owner LIKE '%&&owner%'
     And index_name like '%&&index%'
ORDER BY
     Index_owner,index_name,column_position;
SPOOL OFF
TTITLE OFF
```

Here is a sample listing.

```
Owner       Index            Table            Expression
----------  ---------------- ---------------- ----------------------
TELE_DBA    DEC_CLIENTSV8i   CLIENTSV8i       DECODE ("CREATION_SY_USER",1,'B
                                              OSS',2,'Manager',3,'Clerk','Ev
                                              eryone else')
```

Domain Index Internals

Oracle8*i* also introduced *extensible indexing*, sometimes known as *domain indexing*. A domain index is usually used in cartridge development. In fact, it is called a domain index because it is used only within the domain of its parent cartridge. A domain index extends the basic types of hash, bitmapped, and B-tree indexes by allowing the developer to create his or her own index methods and apply them to a specific type of data set.

An example of the use of domain indexing would be the use of R-tree indexes for spatial data. A domain index is based on the concept of an INDEXTYPE, which, like a User Defined Type (UDT), is created and maintained by the user. In order to use a domain index, a data cartridge that implements its structures, methods, and types must be created.

Note that the domain indexes in Oracle8*i* are indicated by a non-NULL value in the *domidx_status* and *domidx_opstatus* columns in the *dba_indexes* view. Cartridge development is beyond the scope of this book. However, it is assumed that a join can be based on either the *index_name* and *indextype_name* in the *dba_indexes* and *dba_indextypes* table, supplemented by the OWNER columns in each, or the *index_type* and *indextype_name* columns (even though they don't match in size). It is left to the DBA who is involved in a cartridge development effort to actually create the reports required, based on the supplied join data.

Bitmap Join Index Internals

As noted earlier, bitmap join indexes were introduced in Oracle9*i*. If the *join_index* column in the *dba_indexes* is set to YES, then the index is a bitmap join index, meaning that a join to the *dba_join_ind_columns* view will produce the data on the tables and columns that are linked through the bitmap join index. You will need to join against the *index_owner* and *index_name* columns.

The script below shows a report against the *dba_join_ind_columns* view to show the bitmap join indexes in the database. An example output from the script follows.

🖫   **bmj_index.sql**

```
--***********************************************
--
--     Copyright © 2003 by Rampant TechPress Inc.
--
--     Free for non-commercial use.
--     For commercial licensing, e-mail info@rampant.cc
--
--  ***********************************************
REM bmj_index.sql
REM M.R. Ault 5/7/2003
REM
col index_owner format a11 heading 'Index|Owner'
col index_name format a10 heading 'Index|Owner'
col inner_table_owner format a11 heading 'Inner|Table Owner'
col inner_table_name format a11 heading 'Inner|Table Name'
col inner_table_column format a13 heading 'Inner|Table Column'
col outer_table_owner format a12 heading 'Outer|Table Owner'
col outer_table_name format a11 heading 'Outer|Table Name'
col outer_table_column format a13 heading 'Outer|Table Column'
set lines 132
ttitle 'Bitmap Join Indexes'
spool bmj_indexes
select
```

```
        index_owner, index_name,
        inner_table_owner, inner_table_name,inner_table_column,
        outer_table_owner,outer_table_name,outer_table_column
from
        dba_join_ind_columns
where
        index_owner = UPPER('&owner');
spool off
clear columns
ttitle off
set lines 80
```

Here is a sample listing.

Index Owner	Index Owner	Inner Table Owner	Inner Table Name	Inner Table Column	Outer Table Owner	Outer Table Name	Outer Table Column
DBAUTIL	OBJTAB_IDX	DBAUTIL	TABLES	OBJECT_ID	DBAUTIL	OBJECTS	OBJECT_ID

Conclusion

This chapter discussed the monitoring of all non-table and non-index items in an Oracle database. The numerous scripts provided here are designed to make monitoring and documenting these other Oracle structures easier for both the novice and the experienced DBA.

Next, lets take a look at how to monitor the remaining database objects.

Security Internals Scripts

CHAPTER

9

Chapter 8 covered the monitoring of table-related objects in Oracle; this chapter continues to discuss monitoring, but as it applies to virtually all other database objects. Note that because information about users is stored in the database, and because a DBA creates users, users are included in the "other" database object category. Like tables, clusters, snapshots, types, and indexes, all other database objects are monitored using the data dictionary tables and views.

Refer to the reference manual on the documentation website, http://technet.oracle.com, as you review the scripts provided here. The data dictionary is a powerful tool in the hands of someone who knows how to use it.

Table security Internals

The DBA needs to monitor grants on tables. It is good to know who is granting which privileges to whom. The script to determine this is shown below. A sample output follows.

🖫 **db_tgnts.sql**

```
--*************************************************
--
--    Copyright © 2003 by Rampant TechPress Inc.
--
--    Free for non-commercial use.
--    For commercial licensing, e-mail info@rampant.cc
--
--  *************************************************
```

```
rem***********************************************************
******
rem  NAME: db_tgnts.sql
rem
rem  FUNCTION: Produce report of table or procedure grants
showing
rem  GRANTOR, GRANTEE or ROLE and specific GRANTS.
rem
rem  INPUTS: Owner name
rem
*************************************************************
****
rem
COLUMN grantee         FORMAT A18      HEADING "Grantee|or Role"
COLUMN owner           FORMAT A18      HEADING "Owner"
COLUMN table_name      FORMAT A30      HEADING "Table|or Proc"
COLUMN grantor         FORMAT A18      HEADING "Grantor"
COLUMN privilege       FORMAT A10      HEADING "Privilege"
COLUMN grantable       FORMAT A19      HEADING "Grant|Option?"
rem
BREAK ON owner SKIP 4 ON table_name SKIP 1 ON grantee ON grantor
ON REPORT
rem
SET LINESIZE 130 PAGES 56 VERIFY OFF FEEDBACK OFF
ttitle "TABLE GRANTS BY OWNER AND TABLE"
DEFINE OUTPUT = db_tgnts
SPOOL &output
REM
SELECT
     owner,
     table_name,
     grantee,
     grantor,
     privilege,
     grantable
FROM
     dba_tab_privs
WHERE
     owner NOT IN ('SYS','SYSTEM')
ORDER BY
     owner,
     table_name,
     grantor,
     grantee;
REM
SPOOL OFF
PAUSE Press enter to continue
```

Here is a sample listing.

Owner	Table or Proc	Grantee or Role	Grantor	Privilege	Grant Option?
DSPTDBA	ACCCAR	DSPT_DEV	DSPTDBA	DELETE	NO
				INSERT	NO
				SELECT	NO

Table security Internals   **333**

			UPDATE	NO
			ALTER	NO
	DSPT_USER	DSPTDBA	DELETE	NO
			UPDATE	NO
			SELECT	NO
			INSERT	NO
ACT	DSPT_DEV	DSPTDBA	DELETE	NO
			SELECT	NO
			UPDATE	NO
			ALTER	NO
			INSERT	NO
	DSPT_USER	DSPTDBA	DELETE	NO
			UPDATE	NO
			SELECT	NO
			INSERT	NO
ADD_REC	DSPT_USER	DSPTDBA	EXECUTE	NO

Using the above report makes it is easy to monitor the grants on specific objects. A close look at the generation script shows that this report may be as selective as the individual object level, or as general as the entire database. Using this script, the DBA can find the level of protection for any and all database objects.

Using the V$ and *dba_* Views for Monitoring Users

What exactly do DBAs need to know about the users of their databases? The DBA needs to keep track of many important facts about each user, including privileges, quotas, tables owned, filespace used, and database default locations, just to name a few.

The *dba_users* view is the root of a tree of related *dba_* views that give a full picture of the privileges, resources, and roles granted to users.

How can the DBA keep track of this information for hundreds or possibly thousands of users? Scribble it down as it displays on the SVRMGR or OEM screen?

Use some sort of screen capture or screen print facility? Hardly. To keep track of this information, the DBA needs reports. Whether a DBA stores these reports online or uses a three-ring binder, good reports detail exactly what a DBA needs to know. Let's address the relevant topics.

Monitoring User Setup

The first report uses the *dba_users* view to provide information on users, user default, temporary tablespace assignments, and user database-level privileges. The script for this report is shown below.

🖫   **db_users.sql**

```
--*************************************************
--
--    Copyright © 2003 by Rampant TechPress Inc.
--
--    Free for non-commercial use.
--    For commercial licensing, e-mail info@rampant.cc
--
--    *************************************************

SET PAGESIZE 58  LINESIZE 131 FEEDBACK OFF
rem
COLUMN username                  FORMAT a12 HEADING User
COLUMN account_status            FORMAT a6  HEADING Status
COLUMN default_tablespace        FORMAT a14 HEADING Default
COLUMN temporary_tablespace      FORMAT a10 HEADING Temporary
COLUMN granted_role              FORMAT a22 HEADING Roles
COLUMN default_role              FORMAT a8  HEADING Default?
COLUMN admin_option              FORMAT a6  HEADING Admin?
COLUMN profile                   FORMAT a10 HEADING Profile
COLUMN initial_rsrc_consumer_group FORMAT a22 HEADING
'Resource|Group'
rem
ttitle 'ORACLE USER REPORT'
DEFINE output = db_user
BREAK ON username SKIP 1 ON default_tablespace ON
temporary_tablespace ON profile ON account_status ON
initial_rsrc_consumer_group
SPOOL &output
rem

SELECT
    a.username,
```

```
      a.default_tablespace,
      a.temporary_tablespace,
      a.profile,a.account_status,
      a.initial_rsrc_consumer_group,
      b.granted_role,b.admin_option,
      b.default_role
FROM
      sys.dba_users a,
      sys.dba_role_privs b
WHERE
      a.username = b.grantee
ORDER BY
      username,
      default_tablespace,
      temporary_tablespace,
      profile,
      granted_role;

SPOOL OFF
SET TERMOUT ON FLUSH ON FEEDBACK ON VERIFY ON
CLEAR COLUMNS
CLEAR BREAKS
```

Several items about this report script bear mentioning. First, notice the header format. Each report should contain a header section similar to this one. It tells what the report script does, who wrote it, and, most importantly, what changes have been made to it. Next, notice the START command. This command is calling a script that generates a standard 132-column header for use in reports.

The report header programs also return the database name so that it may be included in the filename. This report was written for use on the UNIX platform. To use it on other platforms, only the file specification format would have to be modified; no other changes would have to be made. Notice also that *lock_date* and *expiry_date* have been moved from this report to another script.

The report below is useful if you invoke the password control options available in Oracle8, Oracle8*i*, and

Oracle9*i*. The resource group has been added to the report below, so if resource groups are implemented, you will have a record of who is assigned to each resource group. The output is shown following the script.

🖫 db_user.sql

```
--*********************************************
--
--    Copyright © 2003 by Rampant TechPress Inc.
--
--    Free for non-commercial use.
--    For commercial licensing, e-mail info@rampant.cc
--
--  *******************************************

REM
REM NAME        : DB_USER.SQL
REM
REM FUNCTION    : GENERATE USER_REPORT
REM Limitations : None
REM
REM Updates     : MRA 6/10/97 added Oracle8 account status
REM               MRA 5/14/99 Added Oracle8i Resource Group
REM
SET PAGESIZE 58  LINESIZE 131 FEEDBACK OFF
rem
COLUMN username                     FORMAT a10 HEADING User
COLUMN account_status               FORMAT a10 HEADING Status
COLUMN default_tablespace           FORMAT a15 HEADING Default
COLUMN temporary_tablespace         FORMAT a15 HEADING Temporary
COLUMN granted_role                 FORMAT a21 HEADING Roles
COLUMN default_role                 FORMAT a9  HEADING Default?
COLUMN admin_option                 FORMAT a7  HEADING Admin?
COLUMN profile                      FORMAT a15 HEADING Profile
COLUMN initial_rsrc_consumer_group FORMAT a10 HEADING
'Resource|Group'
COLUMN lock_date                    HEADING 'Date|Locked'
COLUMN expiry_date                  HEADING 'Expiry_date'

rem
ttitle 'ORACLE USER REPORT'
DEFINE output = db_user
BREAK ON username SKIP 1 ON account_status ON default_tablespace
ON temporary_tablespace ON profile
SPOOL &output
rem

SELECT a.username,
       a.account_status,
       TO_CHAR(a.lock_date,'dd-mon-yyyy hh24:mi') lock_date,
       TO_CHAR(a.expiry_date,'dd-mon-yyyy hh24:mi') expiry_date,
```

```
              a.default_tablespace,a.temporary_tablespace,
              a.profile,b.granted_role,
              b.admin_option,b.default_role,
              a.initial_rsrc_consumer_group
FROM sys.dba_users a,
     sys.dba_role_privs b
WHERE a.username = b.grantee
ORDER BY username,
         default_tablespace,temporary_tablespace,
         profile, granted_role;
rem
SPOOL OFF
SET TERMOUT ON FLUSH ON FEEDBACK ON VERIFY ON
CLEAR COLUMNS
CLEAR BREAKS
PAUSE Press Enter to continue
```

Here is a sample listing.

Resource Default	Temp	Profile	Status	Group	User Roles	Admin?	Def?
DBSNMP	SYSTEM	TEMP	DEFAULT	OPEN	DEFAULT_CONSUMER_GROUP CONNECT	NO	YES
					RESOURCE	NO	YES
					SNMPAGENT	NO	YES
MIGRATE	SYSTEM	TEMP	DEFAULT	OPEN	DEFAULT_CONSUMER_GROUP DBA	NO	YES
					RESOURCE	NO	YES
ORDSYS	SYSTEM	TEMP	DEFAULT	OPEN	DEFAULT_CONSUMER_GROUP CONNECT	NO	YES
					RESOURCE	NO	YES
OUTLN	SYSTEM	TEMP	DEFAULT	OPEN	DEFAULT_CONSUMER_GROUP CONNECT	NO	YES
					RESOURCE	NO	YES
SYS	SYSTEM	TEMP	DEFAULT	OPEN	SYS_GROUP	AQ_ADMINISTLE	YES	YES
						AQ_USER_ROLE	YES	YES
						CONNECT	YES	YES
						DBA	YES	YES
						DELETE_CATAL	YES	YES
						EXECUTE_CATA	YES	YES
						EXP_FULL_DAT	YES	YES
						IMP_FULL_DAT	YES	YES
						RECOVERY_CATER	YES	YES
						RESOURCE	YES	YES
						SELECT_CATAL	YES	YES
						SNMPAGENT	YES	YES
SYSTEM	TOOLS	TEMP	DEFAULT	OPEN	SYS_GROUP	AQ_ADMINISTRE	YES	YES
						DBA	YES	YES
						TEST	YES	YES
TEL_DBA	TELE_DATA	TEMP	DEFAULT	OPEN	DEFAULT_CONSUMER_GROUP CONNECT	NO	YES
					RESOURCE	NO	YES

As you can see, this report takes care of several requirements: user names, default tablespace assignments, temporary tablespace assignments, and database roles. The report is currently sorted, using the ORDER BY command, by user name, tablespace assignments, profile, resource group assignment, and status. If you prefer, it could be sorted by default or temporary tablespace or by individual role. In this script, there will be one row for each role granted to the user.

The script below shows user expiration information. The report columns will be populated only with date information if you are using the password expiration features in Oracle8 and Oracle8*i* in profiles. The expiry date in a profile will be set based on the last password change. If a user has just been assigned to a profile, use the ALTER USER command to expire the user's password, forcing him or her to reset it, and set the expiry date. The output follows the script.

🖫 user_expire.sql

```
--***********************************************
--
--   Copyright © 2003 by Rampant TechPress Inc.
--
--   Free for non-commercial use.
--   For commercial licensing, e-mail info@rampant.cc
--
--   ***********************************************
COLUMN account_status          FORMAT a15 HEADING Status
COLUMN default_tablespace      FORMAT a14 HEADING Default
COLUMN temporary_tablespace    FORMAT a10 HEADING Temporary
COLUMN username                FORMAT a12 HEADING User
COLUMN lock_date               FORMAT a11 HEADING 'Date|Locked'
COLUMN expiry_date             FORMAT a11 HEADING 'Expiry|Date'
COLUMN profile                 FORMAT a15 HEADING Profile

SET PAGESIZE 58  LINESIZE 131 FEEDBACK OFF
ttitle 'ORACLE USER EXPIRATION REPORT'
BREAK ON username SKIP 1 ON default_tablespace ON
temporary_tablespace ON profile ON account_status
SPOOL user_expire
rem

SELECT
   username,
   default_tablespace,
   temporary_tablespace,
   profile,account_status,
   TO_CHAR(lock_date,'dd-mon-yyyy') lock_date,
   TO_CHAR(expiry_date,'dd-mon-yyyy') expiry_date
```

```
FROM
    sys.dba_users
ORDER BY
    username,
    default_tablespace,
    temporary_tablespace,
    profile,
    account_status;

SPOOL OFF
SET TERMOUT ON FLUSH ON FEEDBACK ON VERIFY ON
CLEAR COLUMNS
CLEAR BREAKS
PAUSE Press Enter to continue
```

Here is a sample listing.

Date User	Expiry Default	Temporary	Profile	Status	Locked	Date
DBSNMP	SYSTEM	TEMP	DEFAULT	OPEN		
GRAPHICS_DBA	GRAPHICS_DATA	TEMP	DEFAULT	OPEN		
MIGRATE	SYSTEM	TEMP	DEFAULT	OPEN		
ORDSYS	SYSTEM	TEMP	DEFAULT	OPEN		
OUTLN	SYSTEM	TEMP	DEFAULT	OPEN		
SYS	SYSTEM	TEMP	DEFAULT	OPEN		
SYSTEM	TOOLS	TEMP	DEFAULT	OPEN		
TELE_DBA 1999	TELE_DATA	TEMP	TELE_PROFILE	OPEN		09-aug-
TEST1 1999	USER_DATA	TEMP	TELE_PROFILE	OPEN		20-aug-
TEST_IT	USER_DATA	TEMP	TELE_PROFILE	LOCKED(TIMED)	22-may-1999	

Monitoring User Roles

Monitoring user setup is important, but it is only the
beginning of user monitoring. A companion script to
show roles and administration options is also required.
This is shown in the script below. As you can see, it is
very important under Oracle to assign roles to users, due
to the large number of required grants for the modern
environment.

If you assign each privilege to each user as it is required, you will soon find it impossible to manage your user base. Start by assigning only the default roles, and then expand those roles as required. For example, for a user who needs to create tables and indexes, a role called CREATOR could be constructed that has the role CONNECT, plus the *create_table* and *create_index* privileges. It should also be obvious that the DBA will need to track the roles and have a hard copy immediately available to be referenced as users are assigned to the system. See the listing below for an Oracle roles report.

sys_role.sql

```
--*********************************************
--
--   Copyright © 2003 by Rampant TechPress Inc.
--
--   Free for non-commercial use.
--   For commercial licensing, e-mail info@rampant.cc
--
-- *********************************************
REM PURPOSE     : GENERATE SYSTEM GRANTS and ROLES REPORT
REM USE         : CALLED BY SQLPLUS
REM Limitations : None
REM Revisions   :
REM Date          Modified by   Reason for change
REM 08-Apr-1993   MIKE AULT     INITIAL CREATE
REM 10-Jun-1997   Mike Ault     Update to Oracle8
REM 15-May-1999   Mike Ault     No changes for Oracle8i
REM
SET FLUSH OFF TERM OFF PAGESIZE 58  LINESIZE 78
COLUMN grantee          HEADING 'User or Role'
COLUMN admin_option     HEADING Admin?
ttitle 'SYSTEM GRANTS AND ROLES REPORT'
DEFINE output = role_report
SPOOL &output

SELECT
    grantee,
    privilege,
    admin_option
FROM
    sys.dba_sys_privs
GROUP BY
    grantee;
SPOOL OFF
```

```
SET FLUSH ON TERM ON
CLEAR COLUMNS
TTITLE OFF
```

Here is a sample listing.

```
User or Role            PRIVILEGE                                Adm
--------------------    ------------------------------------     ---
CONNECT                 ALTER SESSION                            NO
                        CREATE CLUSTER                           NO
                        CREATE DATABASE LINK                     NO
                        CREATE SEQUENCE                          NO
                        CREATE SESSION                           NO
                        CREATE SYNONYM                           NO
                        CREATE TABLE                             NO
                        CREATE VIEW                              NO


DBA                     ALTER ANY CLUSTER                        YES
                        ALTER ANY INDEX                          YES
                        ALTER ANY PROCEDURE                      YES
                        ALTER ANY ROLE                           YES
                        CREATE SEQUENCE                          YES
                        CREATE SESSION                           YES
                        CREATE SNAPSHOT                          YES

DEV8_DBA                UNLIMITED TABLESPACE                     NO
```

Monitoring User Table and Column Grants

Keeping track of which users and roles have access to which objects in the database is a vital part of the process of monitoring users. Two reports, one on table-level grants and one on column-level grants, are required to monitor the users' permissions and grants profile. A script is shown below to generate information on a user's table-level grants. The output is similar to previous reports.

🖫 **tab_grant.sql**

```
--*************************************************
--
--     Copyright © 2003 by Rampant TechPress Inc.
--
--     Free for non-commercial use.
--     For commercial licensing, e-mail info@rampant.cc
```

```
--
-- *************************************************
COLUMN GRANTEE           FORMAT A19    HEADING "Grantee"
COLUMN OWNER             FORMAT A10    HEADING "Owner"
COLUMN TABLE_NAME        FORMAT A26    HEADING "Table"
COLUMN GRANTOR           FORMAT A10    HEADING "Grantor"
COLUMN PRIVILEGE         FORMAT A10    HEADING "Privilege"
COLUMN GRANTABLE         FORMAT A6     HEADING "With|Grant|Option?"
COLUMN HIERARCHY         FORMAT A3     HEADING 'HRY'
REM
BREAK ON owner SKIP 2 ON table_name ON grantee ON grantor ON
REPORT
REM
SET LINESIZE 100 PAGES 56 VERIFY OFF FEEDBACK OFF
ttitle "TABLE GRANTS BY OWNER AND TABLE"
SPOOL tab_grants
REM

SELECT
   owner,
   table_name,
   grantee,
   grantor,
   privilege,
   grantable,
   hierarchy
FROM
   dba_tab_privs
WHERE
   owner LIKE UPPER('%&owner&')
   AND
   privilege !='EXECUTE'
 ORDER BY
   owner,
   table_name,
   grantor,
   grantee;

SPOOL OFF
PAUSE Press Enter to continue
SET LINESIZE 80 PAGES 22 VERIFY ON FEEDBACK ON
CLEAR BREAKS
CLEAR COLUMNS
TTITLE OFF
```

Notice that the report above excludes grants of
EXECUTE. The EXECUTE grant is given only on
stored objects, such as packages, functions, and
procedures (also Java stored objects). They are excluded
because this is a table grant report. Also, you will have to
remove the call for the hierarchy column if you want to

run this report on earlier versions of Oracle. Below is a sample output from the script above.

```
With
                                                                   Grant
Owner   Table                       Grantee               Grantor   Privilege   Option  HRY
------  --------------------------  --------------------  --------  ----------  ------  ---
OE      CUSTOMERS                   PM                    OE        SELECT      NO      NO
                                    QS_ADM                OE        SELECT      NO      NO
                                                                    REFERENCES  NO      NO
        INVENTORIES                 PM                    OE        SELECT      NO      NO
        ORDERS                      PM                    OE        SELECT      NO      NO
        ORDER_ITEMS                 PM                    OE        SELECT      NO      NO
        PRODUCT_DESCRIPTIONS        PM                    OE        SELECT      NO      NO
        PRODUCT_INFORMATION         PM                    OE        SELECT      NO      NO
                                                                    REFERENCES  NO      NO
                                    QS_ADM                OE        SELECT      NO      NO
                                                                    REFERENCES  NO      NO
        WAREHOUSES                  PM                    OE        SELECT      NO      NO


ORDSYS  DBA_CARTRIDGES              SELECT_CATALOG_ROLE   ORDSYS    SELECT      NO      NO
        DBA_CARTRIDGE_COMPONENTS    SELECT_CATALOG_ROLE   ORDSYS    SELECT      NO      NO


OUTLN   OL$                         SELECT_CATALOG_ROLE   OUTLN     SELECT      NO      NO
        OL$HINTS                    SELECT_CATALOG_ROLE   OUTLN     SELECT      NO      NO
        OL$NODES                    SELECT_CATALOG_ROLE   OUTLN     SELECT      NO      NO
```

Another bit of data to be gathered on user (or role) table grants is whether they have column-level grants. Column-level grants don't seem to be used much in Oracle. Perhaps this is because SELECT and DELETE privileges cannot be granted in this manner (they are considered table-level grants). A script to re-create table column-level grants is shown below. Of course, since Oracle8*i*, there are row-level grants and security options. These row-level security options are known as *policies* and are maintained through the use of the *dbms_context* and *dbms_rls* package procedures.

🖫 grt_cols.sql

```
--*********************************************
--
--    Copyright © 2003 by Rampant TechPress Inc.
--
--    Free for non-commercial use.
--    For commercial licensing, e-mail info@rampant.cc
--
-- *********************************************
SET VERIFY OFF FEEDBACK OFF TERMOUT OFF ECHO OFF PAGESIZE 0
```

```
SET EMBEDDED ON HEADING OFF
SET TERMOUT ON
PROMPT Creating table grant script...
SET TERMOUT OFF
DEFINE cr=CHR(10);
BREAK ON line1
COLUMN dbname NEW_VALUE db NOPRINT
SELECT name dbname FROM v$database;
SPOOL cols_grants.sql
rem
SELECT
  'CONNECT '||grantor||'/'||grantor line1,
  'GRANT '||&&cr||lower(privilege)||'('||column_name||
  ') ON '||owner||'.'||table_name||&&cr||
  ' TO '|| lower(grantee) ||&&cr||
  decode(grantable,'YES',' WITH ADMIN OPTION;',';')
FROM
  sys.dba_col_privs
WHERE
  grantee NOT IN ('SYS','CONNECT','RESOURCE','DBA',
'EXP_FULL_DATABASE','IMP_FULL_DATABASE')
ORDER BY grantor, grantee
/
SPOOL OFF
SET VERIFY ON FEEDBACK ON TERMOUT ON PAGESIZE 22 EMBEDDED OFF
CLEAR COLUMNS
CLEAR COMPUTES
CLEAR BREAKS
```

The output from the table column grant-capture script is
shown below.

```
CONNECT TELE_DBA/TELE_DBA
GRANT
insert(DELETE_STATUS) ON TELE_DBA.CLIENTS
 TO system
;

GRANT
update(DELETE_STATUS) ON TELE_DBA.CLIENTS
 TO system
;
```

In most environments, weekly monitoring of users is
sufficient. In some high-use, rapidly changing
environments, where several DBAs or other types of
administrative personnel are adding users, the reports
may have to be run more frequently. Below is an
example of a script to monitor row-level security
policies. The output follows.

```
--*************************************************
--
--     Copyright © 2003 by Rampant TechPress Inc.
--
--     Free for non-commercial use.
--     For commercial licensing, e-mail info@rampant.cc
--
--*************************************************
COLUMN object_owner     FORMAT A10    HEADING 'Object|Owner'
COLUMN object_name      FORMAT A19    HEADING 'Object|Name'
COLUMN policy_group     FORMAT A12    HEADING 'Policy|Group'
COLUMN policy_name      FORMAT A16    HEADING 'Policy|Name'
COLUMN pf_owner         FORMAT A10    HEADING
'Policy|Function|Owner'
COLUMN function         FORMAT A15    HEADING 'Function|Name'
COLUMN sel              FORMAT A3    HEADING 'Sel|?'
COLUMN ins              FORMAT A3    HEADING 'Ins|?'
COLUMN upd              FORMAT A3    HEADING 'Upd|?'
COLUMN del              FORMAT A3    HEADING 'Del|?'
COLUMN chk_option       FORMAT A3    HEADING 'Check|Option'
COLUMN enable           FORMAT A3    HEADING 'Enabled?'
COLUMN static_policy    FORMAT A7    HEADING 'Static?'

SET LINES 132 VERIFY OFF FEEDBACK OFF PAGES 47
ttitle 'DB Policies Report'
BREAK ON object_owner
SPOOL db_policies

SELECT
  object_owner,
  object_name,
  policy_group,
  policy_name,
  pf_owner,function,
  sel,ins,
  upd,
  del,
  chk_option,
  enable,static_policy
FROM
 dba_policies
ORDER BY
 1,2,3;

SPOOL OFF
SET LINES 80 VERIFY ON FEEDBACK ON PAGES 22
CLEAR BREAKS
CLEAR COLUMNS
TTITLE OFF
```

Here is a sample listing.

Object Owner	Object Name	Policy Group	Policy Name	Policy Function Owner	Function Name	Sel ?	Ins ?	Upd ?	Del ?	Che Opt	Ena	Static?
WKSYS	WK$ATTRIBUTE	SYS_DEFAULT	WK$INSTADMIN_POL	WKSYS	WK$INSTADMIN_PF	YES	YES	YES	YES	YES	YES	NO
	WK$ATTR_MAPPING	SYS_DEFAULT	WK$INSTADMIN_POL	WKSYS	WK$INSTADMIN_PF	YES	YES	YES	YES	YES	YES	NO
	WK$CRAWLER_CONFIG	SYS_DEFAULT	WK$INSTADMIN_POL	WKSYS	WK$INSTADMIN_PF	YES	YES	YES	YES	YES	YES	NO
	WK$CRAWLER_SCHED	SYS_DEFAULT	WK$INSTADMIN_POL	WKSYS	WK$INSTADMIN_PF	YES	YES	YES	YES	YES	YES	NO
	WK$CRAWLER_STAT	SYS_DEFAULT	WK$INSTADMIN_POL	WKSYS	WK$INSTADMIN_PF	YES	YES	YES	YES	YES	YES	NO
	WK$DATA_SOURCE	SYS_DEFAULT	WK$INSTADMIN_POL	WKSYS	WK$INSTADMIN_PF	YES	YES	YES	YES	YES	YES	NO
	WK$GROUP_DS_MAPPING	SYS_DEFAULT	WK$INSTADMIN_POL	WKSYS	WK$INSTADMIN_PF	YES	YES	YES	YES	YES	YES	NO
	WK$JOB_INFO	SYS_DEFAULT	WK$INSTADMIN_POL	WKSYS	WK$INSTADMIN_PF	YES	YES	YES	YES	YES	YES	NO
	WK$MAILLIST	SYS_DEFAULT	WK$INSTADMIN_POL	WKSYS	WK$INSTADMIN_PF	YES	YES	YES	YES	YES	YES	NO
	WK$SCHED_MAPPING	SYS_DEFAULT	WK$INSTADMIN_POL	WKSYS	WK$INSTADMIN_PF	YES	YES	YES	YES	YES	YES	NO
	WK$SOURCE_GROUP	SYS_DEFAULT	WK$INSTADMIN_POL	WKSYS	WK$INSTADMIN_PF	YES	YES	YES	YES	YES	YES	NO
	WK$SYSINFO	SYS_DEFAULT	WK$SYSINFO_POL	WKSYS	WK$SYSINFO_PF	YES	YES	YES	YES	YES	YES	NO
	WK$SYS_ADMIN	SYS_DEFAULT	WK$INSTADMIN_POL	WKSYS	WK$INSTADMIN_PF	YES	YES	YES	YES	YES	YES	NO
	WK$TDS_LOG	SYS_DEFAULT	WK$INSTADMIN_POL	WKSYS	WK$INSTADMIN_PF	YES	YES	YES	YES	YES	YES	NO
	WK$TRACE	SYS_DEFAULT	WK$INSTADMIN_POL	WKSYS	WK$INSTADMIN_PF	YES	YES	YES	YES	YES	YES	NO

Monitoring Currently Logged-in User Processes

A final useful report lists currently logged-in processes, their user IDs, and operating system IDs, as well as any programs they are currently running. Of course, the Q product on the Precise web site does a better job, but there is not always time to start it up just to check on users. The script, called *pid.sql*, is shown below, and an example of its output follows.

🖬 pid.sql

```
--*********************************************
--
--    Copyright © 2003 by Rampant TechPress Inc.
--
--    Free for non-commercial use.
--    For commercial licensing, e-mail info@rampant.cc
--
-- *********************************************

COLUMN terminal FORMAT a10    HEADING 'Terminal'
COLUMN program FORMAT  a30    HEADING 'Program'
COLUMN pid      FORMAT  9999   HEADING 'Process|ID'
COLUMN sid      FORMAT  9999   HEADING 'Session|ID'
COLUMN osuser   FORMAT  A15    HEADING 'Operating|System|User'
COLUMN spid     FORMAT  A7     HEADING 'OS|Process|ID'
COLUMN serial#  FORMAT  99999  HEADING 'Serial|Number'

SET LINES 132 PAGES 58
BREAK ON username
COMPUTE COUNT OF pid ON username
ttitle "Oracle Processes"
SPOOL cur_proc

SELECT
   NVL(a.username,'Null') username,
   b.pid,
   a.sid,
   ECODE(a.terminal,'?','Detached',a.terminal) terminal,
   b.program,
   b.spid,
   a.osuser,
   a.serial#
 FROM
   v$session a,
   v$process b
WHERE
   a.PADDR = b.ADDR
ORDER by
```

```
      a.username,
      b.pid
;

SPOOL OFF
CLEAR BREAKS
CLEAR COLUMNS
SET PAGES 22
TTITLE OFF
PAUSE Press Enter to continue
```

Here is a sample listing.

OS Operating USERNAME	Process ID	Session ID	Terminal	Program	Process System ID	System User	Serial Number
DBAUTIL	12	7	pts/1	oracle (TNS V1-V3)	1182	oracle	46
count							1
SYSTEM	13	8	pts/3	oracle@diogenes (TNS V1-V3)	15885	oracle	3146
	14	10	MRAMOBILE	oracle@diogenes (TNS V1-V3)	19156	Administrator	191
count							2
Null	2	1	UNKNOWN	oracle@diogenes (PMON)	147	oracle	1
	3	2	UNKNOWN	oracle@diogenes (DBW0)	149	oracle	1
	4	3	UNKNOWN	oracle@diogenes (LGWR)	151	oracle	1
	5	4	UNKNOWN	oracle@diogenes (CKPT)	153	oracle	1
	6	5	UNKNOWN	oracle@diogenes (SMON)	155	oracle	1
	7	6	UNKNOWN	oracle@diogenes (RECO)	157	oracle	1
count							6

Monitoring Profiles

Oracle uses profiles to determine process limits and password expiry, aging and complexity rules. The data dictionary view *dba_profiles* is the main source for profile monitoring as the next script shows.

🖫 Profile.sql.sql

```
-- **************************************************
--
--   Copyright © 2003 by Rampant TechPress Inc.
--
--   Free for non-commercial use.
--   For commercial licensing, e-mail info@rampant.cc
--
-- **************************************************

REM NAME        : PROFILE.SQL
REM
REM FUNCTION    : GENERATE USER PROFILES REPORT
REM
REM USE         : CALLED BY PROFILE_REPORT.COM
REM
set flush off term off pagesize 58 linesize 78
column profile              format A20     heading Profile
column resource_name                       heading 'Resource:'
column limit                format A15     heading Limit
break on profile
start ttitle 'ORACLE PROFILES REPORT'
define output = profiles_rep
spool &output
select profile, resource_name, limit  from sys.dba_profiles
order by profile;
spool off
set flush on term on pagesize 22 linesize 80
clear columns
clear breaks
pause Press enter to continue
```

The output from this report for the default profile specification would be:

```
Profile              Resource:                          Limit
-------------------- ---------------------------------- ---------
DEFAULT              COMPOSITE_LIMIT                    UNLIMITED
                     FAILED_LOGIN_ATTEMPTS             UNLIMITED
                     SESSIONS_PER_USER                 UNLIMITED
                     PASSWORD_LIFE_TIME                UNLIMITED
```

```
            CPU_PER_SESSION                     UNLIMITED
            PASSWORD_REUSE_TIME                 UNLIMITED
            CPU_PER_CALL                        UNLIMITED
            PASSWORD_REUSE_MAX                  UNLIMITED
            LOGICAL_READS_PER_SESSION           UNLIMITED
            PASSWORD_VERIFY_FUNCTION            NULL
            LOGICAL_READS_PER_CALL              UNLIMITED
            PASSWORD_LOCK_TIME                  UNLIMITED
            IDLE_TIME                           UNLIMITED
            PASSWORD_GRACE_TIME                 UNLIMITED
            CONNECT_TIME                        UNLIMITED
            PRIVATE_SGA                         UNLIMITED
```

If you need to restrict resource usage the profile is the first line of defense, then use the resource groups. The profiles act immediately when ever a violation of a limit occurs, the resource group limits only kick in once the CPU saturates. The only way to restrict passwords is through a profile unless you want to write the login triggers yourself.

Audit Table Monitoring

Essentially there is one audit table in Oracle, *aud$,* and it is by default owned by the *sys* user and is located in the *system* tablespace. All of the other audit trail views are based on this master table. The *aud$* table has the action# entry which is defined in the *audit_actions* view. By joining the *aud$* table and the *audit_actions* view the DBA can see what users are doing in the database, providing the DBA has turned on auditing for the actions they wish to monitor. An example SELECT to monitor for logon and logoff activities is shown below.

```
SELECT
     a.sessionid, a.entryid, a.statement,
     to_char(a.timestamp#,'dd-mon-yyyy hh24:mi:ss) timestamp,
     c.username, a.userhost,a.terminal, b.name, a.returnvalue
FROM
     Aud$ a, audit_actions b, dba_users c
WHERE
     a.action# in (100,101,102)
and  a.action#=b.action#
```

```
and   a.userid=c.userid
ORDER BY
        c.username;
```

By monitoring for unsuccessful logon attempts you can find when someone is attempting to crack passwords on the Oracle system. By watching the userhost and terminal values you can watch for unauthorized access on restricted accounts.

Conclusion

Security monitoring is a complex topic (indeed, we are pulling together an entire reference on Oracle and security) and we can cover only the beginnings in a single chapter. I hope that with the various scripts provided here as a start you can implement your own security monitoring methods.

Index